BOOKS AND READERS
IN THE PREMODERN WORLD

WRITINGS FROM THE GRECO-ROMAN WORLD SUPPLEMENT SERIES

Clare K. Rothschild, General Editor

Number 12

BOOKS AND READERS IN THE PREMODERN WORLD

Essays in Honor of Harry Gamble

Edited by
Karl Shuve

Atlanta

Copyright © 2018 by SBL Press

All rights reserved. No part of this work may be reproduced or transmitted in any form or by any means, electronic or mechanical, including photocopying and recording, or by means of any information storage or retrieval system, except as may be expressly permitted by the 1976 Copyright Act or in writing from the publisher. Requests for permission should be addressed in writing to the Rights and Permissions Office, SBL Press, 825 Houston Mill Road, Atlanta, GA 30329 USA.

Library of Congress Cataloging-in-Publication Data

Names: Gamble, Harry Y., 1941– honouree. | Shuve, Karl, editor.
Title: Books and readers in the premodern world : essays in honor of Harry Gamble / edited by Karl Shuve.
Description: Atlanta : SBL Press, 2018. | Series: Writings from the Greco-Roman world Supplement series ; Number 12 | Includes bibliographical references and index.
Identifiers: LCCN 2018033037 (print) | LCCN 2018044868 (ebook) | ISBN 9780884143314 (ebk.) | ISBN 9781628372236 (pbk. : alk. paper) | ISBN 9780884143291 (hbk. : alk. paper)
Subjects: LCSH: Sacred books—History and criticism. | Judaism. | Christianity. | Islam. | Books and reading—Religious aspects. | Material culture—Religious aspects
Classification: LCC BL71 (ebook) | LCC BL71 .B66 2018 (print) | DDC 208—dc23
LC record available at https://lccn.loc.gov/2018033037

Printed on acid-free paper.

Contents

Acknowledgments vii
Abbreviations ix

Introduction
    Karl Shuve 1

Part 1: The Materiality of Books

Papyrus beyond Writing: Early Christian Texts and Ancient Natural History
    C. M. Chin 15

The Transformative Role of Paper in the Literary Culture of the Islamic Lands
    Jonathan M. Bloom 33

From the Oral to the Written: Qur'an Manuscripts from the Early Centuries of Islam
    Sheila Blair 47

From Ancient to Medieval Books: On Reading and Illuminating Manuscripts in the Seventh Century
    Lawrence Nees 69

Part 2: Literary Cultures

Books and Private Readers in Early Christian Oxyrhynchus: "A Spiritual Meadow and a Garden of Delight"
    AnneMarie Luijendijk 101

The Bible in the Qur'an; the Qur'an in the Bible: Scriptural
Intertextuality in the Language of Islam
    Sidney H. Griffith 137

Unreliable Books: Debates over Falsified Scriptures at the
Frontier between Judaism and Christianity
    Karl Shuve 171

Contributors..207
Primary Sources Index 211
Modern Authors Index..215

Acknowledgments

This volume has been over three years in the making, and I have accrued many debts along the way. I must begin by expressing my deepest gratitude to my colleague, mentor, and friend, Martien Halvorson-Taylor, with whom I co-organized the conference at which these essays were first presented. "Books and Readers in the Premodern World: A Conference in Honor of Harry Gamble" took place at the University of Virginia on April 16 and 17, 2015, sponsored in large part by the Page-Barbour Fund. It was a truly energizing time of intellectual exchange. I am grateful to the many colleagues who lent their support to that event, especially Ahmed al-Rahim, Elizabeth Meyer, and Janet Spittler, who graciously chaired sessions. Marc Michael Epstein, Bruce Holsinger, Andrew Quintman, Kurtis Schaeffer, and Megan Hale Williams all delivered brilliant papers, although for various reasons decided not to put them forth for publication in this volume. Also, I cannot fail to single out Ashley Tate, one of our talented PhD students, whose work behind the scenes was instrumental for the conference's success.

Many thanks go to SBL Press for taking a chance on a rather unconventional volume. I was fortunate to have had the opportunity to begin the process with Ron Hock, who was deeply supportive of this project from the start, and to see it come to fruition under the careful editorial eye of Clare Rothschild. I am also grateful to Nicole Tilford and her colleagues at SBL Press for their skillful and patient work bringing this volume to print. Finally, I sincerely thank another of our gifted PhD students, Jeannie Sellick, for her many hours of bibliographic work.

It seems entirely appropriate to finish by thanking Harry Gamble, whose work and career we celebrate in this volume. Harry was the first person with whom I spoke during my interview process at the University of Virginia, and from that time on it was a consistent pleasure having the opportunity to work and teach alongside him until his well-deserved retirement in 2014. For a young scholar of early Christianity, it is difficult to imagine a more ideal pair of senior colleagues than Harry and Judith Kovacs. In addition to being a scholar of great accomplishment and influence, Harry was a tireless advocate for the Department of Religious Studies at the University of Virginia, which he joined in its infancy in 1970. He devoted his forty-four-year career to this institution, founding the graduate program in Judaism and Christianity in Antiquity and serving for a staggering fourteen-year period as chair of Religious Studies, from 1992 to 2006. We present this volume to him in recognition and celebration of his long, rich, and productive years of service to the profession and to the wider scholarly community.

Karl Shuve
Charlottesville, 2018

Abbreviations

< >	conjecture inserted by editor of a critical edition
2 Apol.	Justin, *Apologia ii*
Ab. Urbe Cond.	Livy, *Ab Urbe Condita*
AH	*anno Hegirae*
AHR	*American Historical Review*
AJP	*American Journal of Philology*
Alph. Gal.	Alphabetum Galieni
ANF	Ante-Nicene Fathers
ANTF	Arbeiten zur neutestamentlichen Textforschung
Arabica	*Arabica: Journal of Arabic and Islamic Studies/Revue d'études arabes et islamiques*
ArsOr	*Ars Orientalis*
ASE	Anglo-Saxon England
Att.	Cicero, *Epistulae ad Atticum*
BARIS	BAR (British Archaeological Reports) International Series
Biotr	*Biotropica*
BJS	Brown Judaic Studies
BKT	Berliner Klassikertexte
BSOAS	*Bulletin of the School of Oriental and African Studies*
C. Ap.	Josephus, *Contra Apionem*
ca.	circa
cat. no.	catalog number
CBQ	*Catholic Biblical Quarterly*
CCSL	Corpus Christianorum: Series Latina. Turnhout: Brepols, 1953–
Cels.	Origen, *Contra Celsum*
Civ.	Augustine, *De civtate Dei*
CLA	Elias Avery Lowe, ed. *Codices Latini Antiquiores*. 12 vols. Oxford: Clarendon, 1934–1971.

cm	centimeters
CMR	History of Christian-Muslim Relations
CP	*Classical Philology*
CQ	*Classical Quarterly*
CRBR	*Critical Review of Books in Religion*
CSCO	Corpus Scriptorum Christianorum Orientalium. Edited by Jean Baptiste Chabot et al. Paris, 1903.
Cult. fem.	Tertullian, *De cultu feminarum*
d.	died
De alim. fac.	Galen, *De alimentorum facultatibus*
De an.	Aristotle, *De anima*
Deit.	Gregory of Nyssa, *De deitate filii et spiritus sancti*
Der Islam	*Der Islam: Journal of the History and Culture of the Middle East*
EC	*Early Christianity*
EI²	Bosworth, Clifford E., et al., eds. *Encyclopedia of Islam*. 2nd ed. 12 vols. Leiden: Brill, 1954–2005.
EIr	Yarshater, Ehsan, ed. *Encyclopedia Iranica*. London: Routledge & Kegan Paul, 1982–.
EJIW	Stillman, Norman A., ed. *Encyclopedia of Jews in the Islamic World*. 5 vols. Leiden: Brill, 2010.
Ep.	*Epistula*
Epit.	Vergilius Maro Grammaticus, *Epitomae*
EQ	McAuliffe, Jane Dammen, ed. *Encyclopaedia of the Qurʾan*. 6 vols. Leiden: Brill, 2001–2006.
ETL	*Ephemerides Theologicae Lovanienses*
Eutrop.	John Chrysostom, *In Eutropium*
FC	Fathers of the Church
FJTC	Flavius Josephus: Translation and Commentary
fol(s).	folio(s)
GCS	Die griechischen christlichen Schriftsteller der ersten [drei] Jahrhunderte
Gen. Rab.	Genesis Rabbah
GR	*Greece and Rome*
Haer.	Irenaeus, *Adversus Haereses*
Hist.	Herodotus, *Historiae*
Hist. eccl.	Eusebius, *Historia ecclesiastica*
Hist. plant.	Theophrastus, *Historia plantarum*
Hom. Act.	John Chrysostom, *Homiliae in Acta apostolorum*

Hom. Ezek.	Gregory the Great, *Homilies on the Book of the Prophet Ezekiel*
Hom. Jo.	John Chrysostom, *Homiliae in Joannem*
Hom. Matt. 9:37	John Chrysostom, *In illud: Messis quidem multa*
Hom. princ. act.	John Chrysostom, *In principium Actorum*
HTR	*Harvard Theological Review*
HUCA	*Hebrew Union College Annual*
Hug	*Hugoye: Journal of Syriac Studies*
ICMR	*Islam and Christian Muslim Relations*
Il.	Homer, *Iliad*
Is. Os.	Plutarch, *De Iside et Osiride*
JA	*Journal Asiatique*
JAC	*Jahrbuch für Antike und Christentum*
JBL	*Journal of Biblical Literature*
JECS	*Journal of Early Christian Studies*
JJP	*Journal of Juristic Papyrology*
JNES	*Journal of Near Eastern Studies*
JQR	*Jewish Quarterly Review*
JQS	*Journal of Qur'anic Studies*
JSNT	*Journal for the Study of the New Testament*
JTS	*Journal of Theological Studies*
JudChr	Judaica et Christiana
KJV	King James Version
LCL	Loeb Classical Library
LSJ	Liddell, Henry George, Robert Scott, and Henry Stuart Jones. *A Greek-English Lexicon*. 9th ed. with revised supplement. Oxford: Clarendon, 1996.
LXX	Septuagint
MH	*Museum Helveticum*
mm	millimeters
MS	manuscript
Muq	*Muqarnas*
MW	*Muslim World*
Nat.	Pliny, *Naturalis Historia*
NHS	Nag Hammadi Studies
NovT	*Novum Testamentum*
NovTSup	Supplements to Novum Testamentum
NPNF	*Nicene and Post-Nicene Fathers*
NRSV	New Revised Standard Version

NTS	New Testament Studies
Onir.	Artemidorus, *Onirocritica*
OrChr	*Oriens Christianus*
Orig. Princ.	Rufinus, *Origenis Libri Peri archon seu De principiis libri IV*
OTP	Charlesworth, James H., ed. *Old Testament Pseudepigrapha*. 2 vols. New York: Doubleday, 1983, 1985.
P.Amh.	Grenfell, B. P., and A. S. Hunt, eds. *The Amherst Papyri, Being an Account of the Greek Papyri in the Collection of the Right Hon. Lord Amherst of Hackney, F.S.A. at Didlington Hall, Norfolk*. London: Oxford University Press, 1900–1901.
P.Bodl. I	Salomons, R. P., ed. *Papyri Bodleianae* I. Amsterdam: Gieben, 1996.
Paed.	Clement, *Paedagogus*
Pan.	Epiphanius, *Panarion*
ParOr	*Parole de l'Orient*
PERF	Archduke Rainer Collection
PG	Patrologia Graeca [= Patrologiae Cursus Completus: Series Graeca]. Edited by Jacques-Paul Migne. 162 vols. Paris, 1857–1886.
Phaedr.	Plato, *Phaedrus*
Phil.	Cicero, *Orationes philippicae*
Philoc.	Origen, *Philocalia*
PL	Patrologia Latina [= Patrologiae Cursus Completus: Series Latina]. Edited by Jacques-Paul Migne. 217 vols. Paris, 1844–1864.
pl(s).	plate(s)
P.Lips.	Mitteis, L., ed. *Griechische Urkunden der Papyrussammlung zu Leipzig*. Leipzig: Teubner, 1906–2002.
P.Lond.	*Greek Papyri in the British Museum*. London: British Museum, 1893–1917.
P.Mich. I	*Michigan Papyri*. Ann Arbor: University of Michigan Press, 1931–.
P.Oxy.	Grenfell, Bernard P., et al., eds. *The Oxyrhynchus Papyri*. London: Egypt Exploration Fund, 1898–.
Ps.-Clem. Hom.	Pseudo-Clementine Homilies
Ps.-Clem. Rec.	Pseudo-Clementine Recognitions

PSI	Vitelli, G., and M. Norsa, eds. *Papiri greci e latini*. Florence: Tipografia E. Ariani, 1912–.
r.	reigned
Radioc	*Radiocarbon*
RBén	*Revue bénédictine*
Resp.	Plato, *Respublica*
RSQ	Routledge Studies in the Qur'an
Ruf.	Jerome, *Adversus Rufinum libri III*
SC	Sources chrétiennes
SD	Studies and Documents
SecCent	*Second Century*
SHR	Studies in the History of Religions (supplements to *Numen*)
Spec	*Speculum*
StSin	Studia Sinaitica
Stud. praes.	John Chrysostom, *De studio praesentium*
Tanh.	Midrash Tanhuma
Theaet.	Plato, *Theaetetus*
TSAJ	Texte und Studien zum antiken Judentum
TynBul	*Tyndale Bulletin*
VC	*Vigiliae Christianae*
Vit. soph.	Philostratus, *Vitae sophistarum*
WUNT	Wissenschaftliche Untersuchungen zum Neuen Testament
y.	Jerusalem Talmud
ZPE	*Zeitschrift für Papyrologie und Epigraphik*

Introduction

Karl Shuve

On the afternoon of April 16, 2015, a group gathered in the Harrison Small Auditorium at the University of Virginia for a small conference marking the twentieth anniversary of the publication of Harry Gamble's *Books and Readers in the Early Church: A History of Early Christian Texts*.[1] Over the course of that evening and the following day, esteemed scholars of Judaism, Christianity, Islam, and Buddhism gave illuminating lectures on subjects that ranged from Roman reflections on the edibility of papyrus to the intertextual resonances between the Bible and the Qur'an. Each speaker, in his or her own way, paid homage to and grappled with questions raised by Gamble's pioneering work. Since we did not record any of the sessions, the events of the conference exist, if they can be said to exist at all, only in the memories of those who were present.

But the legacy of the conference does live on in another, although rather different, form: this book that you are holding in your hands (or reading on your screen). Academic conferences are, as many readers well know, often followed by the publication of what we term conference proceedings, although usually at some distance of years from the conference itself. Papers and lectures are revised and submitted, edited and typeset, and finally made available to a broader academic readership than was initially reached by the conference itself. We usually accept without much further thought that the published essays reflect a distillation of the events of the conference—indeed, we would likely say that they reflect a far more refined, *final* version of papers that had been composed (perhaps hastily on the flight to the conference or late at night in one's hotel room). But, since this volume explicitly concerns itself with books, it seems worth

---

1. Harry Y. Gamble, *Books and Readers in the Early Church: A History of Early Christian Texts* (New Haven: Yale University Press, 1995).

spending a moment considering in more depth what it actually represents. After all, several of the conference participants declined to submit their lectures as essays, while others drastically rewrote their communications into lengthy contributions. What might it mean to treat this particular book as an object in and of itself, rather than as a mere extension of an academic conference?

To begin, this book is a form of academic currency that bestows concrete value on the ideas and arguments that were articulated at the conference, allowing them to circulate in the scholarly world. Indeed, had we recorded the lectures and made them available for wider consumption, there would still be a specific need for this book, even if the essays that it contains agreed verbatim with the oral versions. Although it does occasionally happen that unpublished conference papers and informal conversations are cited in academic work, this is the exception, not the rule; for ideas to *gain currency* in academic circles, they must first be expressed in a very specific essay form and published by an appropriate press, as either a journal article, an essay in an edited volume, or a chapter in a monograph. A work's value is reliant on it having been vetted by multiple authorities—colleagues, anonymous reviewers, editors at a press—and this process ensures not only that the judgments of multiple individuals have been sought but also that the work is not rushed to the light of day and has thus been considered and reconsidered many times by the author. The published essay thus has a particular gravity to it, which is shored up by the imprimatur of a (hopefully prestigious) press, and this gravity is coded *visually* (we might also say *materially*), both by the formality of the typeset page and by the presence of footnotes. Footnotes, of course, provide valuable information to the reader, but of equal importance, they signal the author's depth of erudition; there is a temptation to marvel as the tiny superscript numbers creep into the triple digits or to wonder at the sight of a page that has only a few lines of text, with long lists of book titles and learned digressions crowding underneath.[2] In their oral performances, scholars are not so clearly able to signal their debts to scholarship.

Moreover, not only does this book *give currency* to the ideas expressed therein, but also it can be used *as currency* by its editors and authors. Numbers of academic publications are one of the most significant factors

---

2. On the history of the scholarly footnote, see Anthony Grafton, *The Footnote* (Cambridge: Harvard University Press, 1999).

used in determining whether a candidate will be hired to an academic position or whether a faculty member receives tenure, promotion, or even a yearly merit raise. Even beyond these explicitly monetized incentives, status in the academic world is in large part dependent on the contributions one has made to scholarship (that is, on the essays and chapters one has published), and, much like the lengthy footnote, the crowded curriculum vitae sends an immediate message to its readers. And as nearly every scholar in the humanities quickly learns, the *academic monograph*—not, notably, the *book*, broadly conceived—is the gold standard of scholarship, being of considerably greater value than a collection of articles or essays of the same length (or, indeed, the popular book, published by either a trade press or the trade arm of a university press and meant for a nonacademic readership). Indeed, volumes of collected essays, such as this book, are treated entirely differently from monographs; editors are seen to be performing more of a service to the profession than a robust scholarly task deserving of the same level of recognition as an *author*.

Finally, this book is a very particular species of edited volume: a Festschrift. It is, in a fundamental sense, a *gift*. Martien Halvorson-Taylor and I—along with the help of many colleagues—organized the conference on Books and Readers in the Premodern World both to mark the anniversary of the publication of a field-changing book and to celebrate the career of our esteemed and cherished colleague Harry, who had retired the previous year after an astounding forty-four years of service to the University of Virginia as professor of New Testament and early Christianity. The publication of this volume of essays, based on the presentations delivered at that conference, participates in a long tradition of honoring scholars of exceptional accomplishment and merit with a book that traces their legacy into the next generation(s). And how especially fitting it is it to honor with a book a scholar of books!

But this is also a very unusual Festschrift. It is typically the case that contributors to Festschriften are close colleagues and former students who work in the honoree's immediate field of study. In this volume, however, only one contributor could properly be called a New Testament scholar, and indeed none of the essays deal with the books of the New Testament canon. Over half of the contributors are scholars of early Islamic or medieval European culture. But this seems only fitting for a book of such unusually broad influence. *Books and Readers in the Early Church* was published at a moment when the history of the book was still in its infancy, and it served as a model and an inspiration not only for scholars in New

Testament Studies but also for those working in fields as geographically and historically remote as early modern Tibet.³

In the years preceding the publication of *Books and Readers in the Early Church*, questions of orality were dominating the field, as indeed they long had been. The form critics of the early twentieth century assumed the oral nature of early Christian culture, and they concerned themselves with establishing the original (oral) forms of later (written) traditions about Jesus. Influential studies by Albert Lord, Ruth Finnegan, and Walter Ong, however, compelled scholars to rethink how they conceptualized the relationship between oral and written traditions.⁴ This led to the publication in 1983 of Werner Kelber's monograph *The Oral and the Written Gospel*, in which he takes to task not only Bultmann and the form critics but also Birger Gerhardsson and his memory approach, for chirographic bias and for downplaying the radical differences between oral and literary cultures. Kelber agrees with the form critics that early Christian culture was fundamentally oral in nature, but he postulates that this means that the writing of gospel traditions represented a transformative break, not an inevitable development. He concludes his book by forcefully arguing, "The decisive break in the synoptic tradition did thus not come, as Bultmann thought, with Easter, but when the written medium took full control, transforming Jesus the speaker of kingdom parables into the parable of the kingdom of God."⁵

Books and Readers in the Early Church thus represents a profound reorientation of the field of New Testament studies itself. Gamble calls into question Kelber's argument that there is a deep disjuncture—perhaps even a mutual exclusivity—between oral and written cultures, although he does so not to posit a smoother transition from an oral stage to a textual

---

3. This was made especially clear in a short communication at the conference by Kurtis Schaeffer, chair of the Department of Religious Studies at the University of Virginia, who reflected on the influence that *Books and Readers* had on his composition of *The Culture of the Book in Tibet* (New York: Columbia University Press, 2009).

4. Ruth Finnegan, "Literacy vs. Non-Literacy: The Great Divide?," in *Modes of Thought: Essays on Thinking in Western and Non-Western Societies*, ed. Robin Horton and Ruth Finnegan (London: Faber & Faber, 1973), 112–44; Albert Lord, *The Singer of Tales* (Cambridge: Harvard University Press, 1960); Walter J. Ong, SJ, *Orality and Literacy: The Technologizing of the Word* (New York: Methuen, 1982).

5. Werner Kelber, *The Oral and the Written Gospel: The Hermeneutics of Speaking and Writing in the Synoptic Tradition, Mark, Paul, and Q* (Minneapolis: Fortress, 1983), 220.

one but to argue that Christianity had been a deeply literate culture from its inception, even as "an oral tradition was both current and influential in the first century of Christianity's existence."[6] For Gamble, if one wants to understand Christianity, even in its earliest stages, one must understand the material dimensions of texts. In 2018, with the history of the book rapidly growing as a field of inquiry, it may be difficult to imagine that only two decades ago this was such a novel approach in New Testament studies. Yet in a 1997 review of *Books and Readers in the Early Church* in the *American Historical Review*, Bart Ehrman succinctly and powerfully states in praise of the book, "There is nothing like the study available; it completely dwarfs its closest relation."[7] Perhaps the only true precursor to Gamble's monograph was C. H. Roberts and T. C. Skeat's *The Birth of the Codex*—published in the same year as Kelber's *Oral and Written Gospel*—which traces the seismic technological shift from scroll to codex and makes several tentative hypotheses regarding why Christians adopted the codex form for their texts.[8]

Gamble's trajectory of research made the writing of such a book a logical development. His first monograph, *The Textual History of the Letter to the Romans*, published in 1977, weds textual criticism and literary criticism to argue for the literary unity of Paul's letter to the Romans.[9] He followed this seven years later with a small but rich volume, *The New Testament Canon: Its Making and Meaning*, in which he seeks to provide an analysis of "the form of the NT *as a whole*."[10] Although this work was an important contribution to the field and is still widely read, it also sowed the seeds for what would become *Books and Readers in the Early Church*. In the preface to the latter work, Gamble notes explicitly, "The idea of this book arose several years ago in the course of research on the history of

---

6. Gamble, *Books and Readers*, 32. Harry generously gave me his personal copy of Kelber's book, and the heavy underlinings and countless annotations throughout reveal the depth of his engagement with this work, even though he only references it briefly in the first chapter (28–29).

7. Bart D. Ehrman, review of *Books and Readers in the Early Church*, by Harry Y. Gamble, *AHR* 102 (1997): 794–95.

8. C. H. Roberts and T. C. Skeat, *The Birth of the Codex* (Oxford: Oxford University Press, 1983).

9. Harry Y. Gamble, *The Textual History of the Letter to the Romans: A Study in Textual and Literary Criticism*, SD 42 (Grand Rapids: Eerdmans, 1977).

10. Harry Y. Gamble, *The New Testament Canon: Its Making and Meaning* (Philadelphia: Fortress, 1985), 11, emphasis original.

the New Testament canon."[11] He notes that while an analysis of how the twenty-seven books of the New Testament came to be circulated, collated, and rendered authoritative, he argues that a major part of the story has gone largely unexamined:

> Yet there are prior questions, questions about the production, circulation, and use of books in the ancient church, that are almost never raised by historians of the canon even though the whole process of the formation of the canon depends on them. What physical forms did early Christian writings take ...? How and by whom were they transcribed? By what means was a text published and made known to a readership? Once published, how were these books duplicated and disseminated? How rapidly and extensively did they become available to Christian communities? Who were the sponsors and custodians of such texts? How were they transported, stored, collected, and used? Who, in fact, read them, and in what circumstances and to what purpose?[12]

Gamble thoroughly and persuasively answers these questions over the course of the book's meticulously researched 337 pages.

Books and Readers in the Early Church has stood the test of time. No scholar has found it necessary to produce a similarly comprehensive work. But it played a crucial role in the flowering of scholarship on the book in early Christianity. Important works such as Kim Haines-Eitzen's *Guardians of Letters: Literacy, Power, and the Transmission of Early Christian Literature* and Larry Hurtado's *The Earliest Christian Artifacts: Manuscripts and Christian Origins* engage directly with Gamble's work and reveal the extent to which the materiality of Christian books is no longer being neglected.[13] Further, beyond the bounds of the world of Christianity are such influential and masterful works as Anthony Grafton's *The Footnote*, Jonathan Bloom's *Paper before Print: The History and Impact of Paper in the Islamic World*, Kurtis Schaeffer's *The Culture of the Book in Tibet*, and Konrad Hirschler's *The Written Word in the Medieval Arabic Lands*.[14]

---

11. Gamble, *Books and Readers*, ix.
12. Gamble, *Books and Readers*, ix.
13. Kim Haines-Eitzen, *Guardians of Letters: Literacy, Power, and the Transmission of Early Christian Literature* (New York: Oxford University Press, 2000); Larry Hurtado, *The Earliest Christian Artifacts: Manuscripts and Christian Origins* (Grand Rapids: Eerdmans, 2006).
14. Jonathan Bloom, *Paper and Print: The History and Impact of Paper in the*

The present volume of essays seeks to emulate the breadth of Gamble's pioneering monograph by attending to a number of the questions that he posed, but it also seeks to push beyond the (relatively) narrow confines of the early Christian world and to consider the relevance of Gamble's research in other fields of study. Thus *Books and Readers in the Premodern World* does not seek to be in any way comprehensive but aims to put into conversation scholars of different epochs, regions, and religious traditions in order to open up new avenues of inquiry and to raise new questions. Thus it is our goal that readers will have the opportunity to engage not only with arguments and information about material in their direct area of expertise but also with materials that lie well beyond it. In order to promote comparative inquiry, the essays have been organized thematically into two main sections: "The Materiality of Books" and "Literary Cultures." But the essays range widely within these broad (and overlapping) categories, considering the nature of the materials used to make writing surfaces; how the use of a particular material—whether papyrus, paper, or parchment—could drastically shape the availability and function of books; what the visual layout of a page can reveal about the practice of reading; who owned books and what they did with them; and how ancient readers themselves reflected on their position within a bookish culture.

"The Materiality of Books" begins with an essay by C. M. Chin on the natural history of papyrus books, in which the papyrus plant is allowed to become the central agent in its own history. What Chin thus offers readers is an examination of a world of intellection that is "neither strictly Christian nor entirely human." In his telling, intellectual history need not only be an analysis of the human. Although when scholars think of papyrus, it is usually as a dead and treated writing surface, in Chin's evocative prose we encounter *living* papyrus, thriving within a vibrant ecosystem. He also reminds us that for Roman Egyptians—not to mention for the creatures of the Nile Delta—papyrus was, first and foremost, *food*. Chin directs us to the vitality of parchment even it its death, when it collaborates with humans in what he terms a "botanical colonization process." In his compelling account, the pervasive ancient metaphor of eating books no longer

---

Islamic World (New Haven: Yale University Press, 2001); Grafton, *Footnote*; Konrad Hirschler, *The Written Word in the Medieval Arabic Lands: A Social and Cultural History of Reading Practices* (Edinburgh: Edinburgh University Press, 2011); Schaeffer, *Book in Tibet*.

appears to be quite so metaphorical, with the book itself becoming an "extended papyrus colony."

Papyrus, of course, was not the only vegetal substance used in the premodern world as a writing surface, and Jonathan M. Bloom explores the emergence of the use of paper in the Islamic lands in the ninth and tenth centuries. Prior to that time, Islamic texts were written on parchment, that is, on the skins of calves, sheep, and goats. But, as Bloom demonstrates, parchment was expensive business; hundreds of sheep would need to be slaughtered for the production of an ornate Qur'an. Paper, by contrast, can be made "virtually anywhere that plants and water are available," and it was thus a far less costly medium, even if considerable labor went into its production. As a result of the adoption of paper, the production of books exploded, allowing for the proliferation of the libraries for which the medieval Islamic lands were so famous. Indeed, Bloom concludes that it was not only literary production that was affected but literacy itself. It was precisely because of the use and availability of paper that medieval Islam became "a culture of books and writing."

If, as Bloom reminds us, Islam became a religion of the book, it was also a religion of the Book. Sheila Blair's essay on the history of early manuscripts of the Qur'an is thus a fitting complement to this analysis of the material dimensions of Islamic book culture. The earliest qur'anic manuscripts, as she demonstrates through careful analysis of the surviving evidence, were meant to serve in the capacity of aide-mémoire during public recitation; the script would not have permitted an ease of reading, even for those fluent in Arabic. In the Umayyad period, however, there was a move toward uniformity in script and layout, and the script became eminently easier to read. She also charts the emergence of elaborate decoration in these Umayyad manuscripts—although the decoration is always geometric. She concludes with a detailed comparison of these Umayyad Qur'an manuscripts with the eighth-century Christian Codex Amiatinus, convincingly demonstrating their shared reliance on late antique models. She thus helps the reader to appreciate the intertwined histories of Islamic and Christian books.

Lawrence Nees turns our attention to a different way in which the material dimension of texts—in this case, the decoration of the page—affected literary practices. Although it is commonplace to use the terms *illustration* and *illumination* synonymously when referring to the decoration of manuscripts, Nees offers a convincing basis for differentiating between the two, and he argues that the illuminated book is an invention of the early

Middle Ages, first appearing in Europe at the turn of the eighth century. Fundamental to Nees's definition of the illuminated manuscript is that it integrates text and decoration on multiple levels; such manuscripts, he contends, were meant for readers and not for gazers. Nees offers us characteristically thick descriptions of two manuscripts that were associated with the monastery of Luxeuil in Burgundy, which are in places so evocative that the reader may feel as though she has engaged with the manuscript herself. For Nees, the novel form of decoration in these manuscripts demonstrates a culture that is moving away from the oral consumption of books to a decidedly more visual one, in which vocalization of the text is no longer expected or even desired. Through his careful codicological analysis, Nees helps us to appreciate the profound transformation from the noisy reading culture of antiquity to the silence of the medieval scriptorium.

The book's second part, "Literary Cultures," opens with another essay that focuses on readers, although in a much earlier period. AnneMarie Luijendijk takes us back to late antique Egypt and asks what papyri can tell us about private owners and readers of Scripture in Oxyrhynchus. Luijendijk demonstrates that there were a wide range of Christian texts that were being read in the city, including texts that later obtained canonical status, such as the Gospel of Matthew and Revelation, and those that did not, such as Hermas and the Gospel of Thomas. She offers us a fine-grained analysis of four different readers in Oxyrhynchus, and through this up-close examination she reveals wider trends and patterns about the ownership and consumption of books in late antiquity. Luijendijk convincingly demonstrates that when elite theologians and churchmen recommended the reading of sacred and edifying Christian texts in the home, there were many who put this advice into practice.

Sidney Griffith returns our attention to the Qur'an, but rather than focus on its material dimensions, he draws us to what he terms its "scriptural diction." Arabic is, of course, the language of the Qur'an, but it equally became the language of the Hebrew Bible and of the New Testament for the people of the book living in the Islamic lands. Since translation is never a neutral endeavor, it is worth asking and exploring what factors shaped the ways Jews and Christians proclaimed their scriptures in Arabic. This is precisely the task that Griffith undertakes in this essay. Through a learned and rigorous philological analysis, Griffith concludes that a qur'anic diction decisively shaped the translations of other holy books into the Arabic language. The reader is able to appreciate the Qur'an's pivotal role in shaping scriptural transmission in the interreligious world, where Arabic was spoken in synagogues, churches, and mosques collectively.

In the concluding essay of the volume, I consider the negative light in which writing and book production were often viewed in antiquity and what the implications of this were for such thoroughly bookish traditions as Judaism and Christianity. More to the point, I consider how such polemics surrounding book culture could be used and exploited by competing religious groups in their attempts to claim authoritative status for themselves and to disinherit others. My essay focuses specifically on a fourth-century apocryphal narrative text, the Pseudo-Clementine Homilies, and its remarkable claim that the Torah has been falsified and interpolated over the centuries. Rather than attempt to discern a coherent hermeneutic in this claim, I argue instead that it is an ideological construct meant to displace the centrality of the public archive of Scripture and to elevate its own private archive of teachings. Far from being a unique or eccentric claim, I demonstrate how this claim that Scripture has been falsified shares fundamental ideological similarities with the Christian concept of the rule of faith/truth and the rabbinic concept of torah in the mouth.

Taken together, these essays demonstrate the vibrant, ongoing legacy of Gamble's seminal text and point toward new and interdisciplinary lines of inquiry and investigation.

Bibliography

Bloom, Jonathan. *Paper and Print: The History and Impact of Paper in the Islamic World*. New Haven: Yale University Press, 2001.

Ehrman, Bart D. Review of *Books and Readers in the Early Church*, by Harry Y. Gamble. *AHR* 102 (1997): 794–95.

Finnegan, Ruth. "Literacy vs. Non-literacy: The Great Divide?" Pages 112–44 in *Modes of Thought: Essays on Thinking in Western and Non-Western Societies*. Edited by Robin Horton and Ruth Finnegan. London: Faber & Faber, 1973.

Gamble, Harry. *Books and Readers in the Early Church: A History of Early Christian Texts*. New Haven: Yale University Press, 1995.

———. *The New Testament Canon: Its Making and Meaning*. Philadelphia: Fortress, 1985.

———. *The Textual History of the Letter to the Romans: A Study in Textual and Literary Criticism*. SD 42. Grand Rapids: Eerdmans, 1977.

Grafton, Anthony. *The Footnote*. Cambridge: Harvard University Press, 1999.

Haines-Eitzen, Kim. *Guardians of Letters: Literacy, Power, and the Transmission of Early Christian Literature*. New York: Oxford University Press, 2000.

Hirschler, Konrad. *The Written Word in the Medieval Arabic Lands: A Social and Cultural History of Reading Practices*. Edinburgh: Edinburgh University Press, 2011.

Hurtado, Larry. *The Earliest Christian Artifacts: Manuscripts and Christian Origins*. Grand Rapids: Eerdmans, 2006.

Kelber, Werner. *The Oral and the Written Gospel: The Hermeneutics of Speaking and Writing in the Synoptic Tradition, Mark, Paul, and Q*. Minneapolis: Fortress, 1983.

Lord, Albert. *The Singer of Tales*. Cambridge: Harvard University Press, 1960.

Ong, Walter J., SJ. *Orality and Literacy: The Technologizing of the Word*. New York: Methuen, 1982.

Roberts, C. H., and T. C. Skeat. *The Birth of the Codex*. Oxford: Oxford University Press, 1983.

Schaeffer, Kurtis. *The Culture of the Book in Tibet*. New York: Columbia University Press, 2009.

Part 1
The Materiality of Books

Papyrus beyond Writing:
Early Christian Texts and Ancient Natural History

C. M. Chin

> The gardeners gazing through their open shears
> Or staring sightless from their wooden ladders
> Stand helpless by and dream they cannot lower
> Their upraised sickles poised a hundred years
> Above the labyrinth of stems, as briars,
> Even while dreaming of their destinies
> As smoke and ashes in the gardeners' fires
> Fasten themselves around the spellbound blades
> And steal the dreamers' hats in mockery
> —"Imaginary Prisons," a version of Sleeping Beauty, by
> Gjertrud Schnackenberg

The world in which early Christians lived and wrote was, like our own world, full of natural wonders. Terrestrial and celestial cycles spun into being an environment in which abundant living things encountered, surprised, and transformed one another. The ancient accounts of what papyrus is and how papyrus books were made that have been most influential in modern understandings of the ancient papyrus book—the accounts of Theophrastus and Pliny the Elder—both place papyrus firmly into this rich natural and botanical context. The study of early Christian papyrus texts owes a great deal to Harry Y. Gamble's foundational *Books and Readers in the Early Church*, which uses Pliny's description of the manufacture of papyrus books as one of the starting points for his wide-ranging discussion of how the materiality of scriptural texts shaped the intellectual world of early Christianity.[1] This notable shift in perspective, from dematerialized "text"

---

1. Harry Y. Gamble, *Books and Readers in the Early Church: A History of Early*

to "book," enabled scholars to reconsider the tangled relationship between the content of early Christian texts and the media in which those texts were encountered; intellectual history and book history became productive symbionts in Gamble's description of the early Christian intellectual ecosystem. In this essay, I use Pliny and Theophrastus to examine a world of intellection that is neither strictly Christian nor entirely human. This is an imagined world, a potential, if not a demonstrably actual, ancient thought-world, in which papyrus books themselves have a natural history, one that follows the logic of Theophrastus and Pliny's accounts. I take my cues loosely from contemporary environmental history, in its commitment to bringing nonhuman actors such as plants, animals, climates and ecosystems into the narratives that we create about the past. Rather than relying strictly on contemporary environmental science to explain ancient phenomena, however, I use the parameters of the ancient natural sciences to sketch out the boundaries of the imagined natural world in which the papyrus book came into being. In this way I hope to suggest an imaginative ancient biology of the papyrus book and to suggest a way of understanding the biological place of books in an environmental description of ancient intellectual history. I begin by describing the papyrus plant, in its Theophrastean form, as a natural collaborator in human activity, and then turn to a brief natural-historical account of two aspects of ancient books that consistently recur in both classical and early Christian writing, first the idea of reading as eating, and second the idea of the book as a vehicle for remembrance.

Such Is the Papyrus and Such Its Uses

In his description of plants that grow in the rivers and wetlands of Egypt, at *Hist. plant.* 4.8, Theophrastus offers us a chance to think about human intellectual history and book history as a very small part of the life and usefulness of the papyrus plant. Famously, he places the production of *biblia* in a simple aside, as a misrecognition of the most important of papyrus's characteristics. His larger interest is the variety and classification of aquatic plants in Egypt, and so perhaps we should begin with the place of papyrus in this larger world, as a way of understanding the environmental setting of the ancient book.

Christian Texts (New Haven: Yale University Press, 1995), 44–46, with notes at 264–66.

Herodotus believed that the sun was the cause of the yearly rise and fall of the Nile. The sun, he wrote, drew off and gave shape to the water that fed the marshes and fields of Egypt (*Hist.* 2.24–26). Further down the solar scale, Theophrastus describes the interactions between the Egyptian water lily and the daily cycles of sunlight:

> The flower is white, resembling in the narrowness of its petals those of the lily, but there are many petals growing close upon one another. When the sun sets, these close and cover up the "head," but with the sunrise they open and appear above the water. This the plant does until the "head" is matured and the flowers have fallen off.... These "heads" the Egyptians heap together and leave to decay, and when the "pod" has decayed, they wash the "head" in the river and take out the "fruit," and having dried and pounded it, they make loaves of it, which they use for food. (*Hist. plant.* 4.8.9)[2]

Sun, response, water, maturation, and consumption are Theophrastus's themes, and this is understandable in any ancient description of Egypt: the necessary elements collaborated on large and small scales to make Egypt an environment that was an agricultural wonder for the ancient world. Papyrus was merely one of the many living beings that thrived in the sun and water of Egypt. This elemental nourishment is, in Aristotelian terms, what sustains the animation of papyrus in the larger animate world. The close association between food and animation is appropriate to the souls of ancient plants, which, as Aristotle after all suggests, are exclusively nutritive: plants do not have rationality or sensation in themselves, according to Aristotle, but they do have growth and can feed themselves (Aristotle, *De an.* 2.2).[3] We may rightly think of the rich physical environment of the Nile Delta as both the food and the animating principle of papyrus's world: it is nourishment directly and soul indirectly. Papyrus lived in this abundant, hungry, and nourishing world.

---

2. Throughout, I use the text and translation found in Theophrastus, *Enquiry into Plants*, trans. Arthur F. Hort, 2 vols., LCL (Cambridge: Harvard University Press, 1916, 1926). For Pliny's *Historia Naturalis* (*Nat.* 13), I have consulted the text of A. Ernout (Paris: Belles Lettres, 1956), but translations are taken from John F. Healy, *Pliny the Elder, Natural History: A Selection* (London: Penguin, 2004).

3. It is possible, but not certain, that Theophrastus differed from Aristotle on the ability of plants to sense their surroundings. See discussion in Matthew Hall, *Plants as Persons: A Philosophical Botany* (Albany: SUNY Press, 2011), 28–35.

It did not live in isolation. As a typical sedge, papyrus is not a singular, easily individuated plant but a network of stalks, roots, rhizomes, and sometimes-flowering umbels, feeding and growing as a community above and below water. It is typical for papyrus, as a rhizomatic aquatic plant, to form stands of varying size and to entangle itself into floating mats that spread to colonize the areas in which they live. These papyrus colonies are necessarily the manifold protagonists of their own history. One modern papyrus island's slow movements and rotations in a lagoon in the Okavango Delta, in northern Botswana, have been observed via aerial photography over the course of more than fifty years.[4] Such floating mats are dense, interconnected entities, sometimes stationary and sometimes moved by wind or water; they shape and constrain the movements of other beings through the area. Although he does not specify which plants make up these floating islands, Theophrastus notes that "in Egypt very large [islands] form, so that even a number of boars are found in them, and men go across to the islands to hunt them" (*Hist. plant.* 4.12.4). The floating mat is a microcosm of animate abundance. It is hard, in this context, to delineate clearly the life of an individual papyrus stalk from the lives of the stalks and other beings around it.[5] A stand of papyrus is an entangled, collective living being inhabited by other forms of life and made mobile by forces, such as wind and water, that are at times external to it but that it also consumes for its own continued growth.[6] The vitality of papyrus is diffuse and circuitous as the physical state of the plant itself is diffuse and circuitous; a great deal lives at the edges and in the midst of papyrus.

---

4. S. C. Child and P. A. Shaw, "A Floating Island in the Okavango: Some Observations Made by Brian Wilson," *Botswana Notes and Records* 22 (1990): 51–55; see also T. S. McCarthy and W. N. Ellery, "The Okavango Delta," *Transactions of the Royal Society of South Africa* 53 (1998): 157–82.

5. Although the use of rhizomes as theoretical models was popularized by Gilles Deleuze and Felix Guattari (*A Thousand Plateaus: Capitalism and Schizophrenia*, trans. Brian Massumi [Minneapolis: University of Minnesota Press, 1987], 3–25), I find Bruno Latour's similar actor-network-theory, as described in *Reassembling the Social: An Introduction to Actor-Network-Theory* (Oxford: Oxford University Press, 2005), more conceptually useful in describing the literal entanglements of rhizomatic plants.

6. M. B. Jones and F. M. Muthuri, "The Canopy Structure and Microclimate of Papyrus (*Cyperus Papyrus*) Swamps," *Journal of Ecology* 73 (1985): 481–91; Rosalind R. Boar, David M. Harper, and Christopher S. Adams, "Biomass Allocation in *Cyperus Papyrus* in a Tropical Wetland, Lake Naivasha, Kenya," *Biotropica* 31 (1999): 411–21.

This vitality continues even when the plant is what we might conventionally call dead. For Theophrastus, the primary human use of papyrus is not as a vehicle for written communication but as food.

> Of those [aquatic plants] that grow in Egypt the list is too long to enumerate separately; however, to speak generally, they are all edible and have sweet flavors. But they differ in sweetness, and we may distinguish also three as the most useful for food, namely, the papyrus, the plant called *sari*, and the plant which they call *mnesion*. (*Hist. plant.* 4.8.3)

He continues, regarding papyrus: "Most familiar to foreigners are the papyrus-rolls made of it, but above all the plant also is of very great use in the way of food. For all the natives chew the papyrus both raw, boiled, and roasted; they swallow the juice and spit out the quid. Such is the papyrus and such its uses" (*Hist. plant.* 4.8.4).[7] Humans, of course, were not the only consumers of papyrus: "All the things that grow in such places may be eaten by oxen and sheep," writes Theophrastus (*Hist. plant.* 4.8.13). Papyrus is a foodstuff for insects, large herbivores, and even, according to one modern study, crocodiles.[8] The nutrients in the detritus that gathers beneath the papyrus mats also become food for aquatic life.[9] The diffusion of vitality that the papyrus colony provides while it is alive extends to the vitality that it grants to other beings upon its own consumption or death. Papyrus continues and extends the work of living in the swamps and rivers it occupies, even as it is itself constantly in the process of living and dying. Papyrus forms a community of the living and the dead. If we view papyrus as the central agent in its own history, papyrus is always a living and dead being, with its dead parts traveling into the life of other beings, as it pursues its own extension and diffusion. It is in this way a great-souled plant, even if its soul in Aristotelian terms is concerned entirely with nourishing.

---

7. See also Naphtali Lewis, *Papyrus in Classical Antiquity* (Oxford: Clarendon, 1974), 22–24.

8. S. L. Sutton and P. J. Hudson, "Arthropod Succession and Diversity in Umbels of *Cyperus Papyrus* L.," *Biotropica* 13 (1981): 117–20; F. M. Muthuri and J. I. Kinyamario, "Nutritive Value of Papyrus (*Cyperus Papyrus*, Cyperaceae), a Tropical Emergent Macrophyte," *Economic Botany* 43 (1989): 23–30; Kevin M. Wallace and Alison J. Leslie, "Diet of the Nile Crocodile (*Crocodylus niloticus*) in the Okavango Delta, Botswana," *Journal of Herpetology* 42 (2008): 361–68.

9. Stuart S. Bamforth, Colin R. Curds, and Bland J. Finlay, "Protozoa of Two Kenya Lakes," *Transactions of the American Microscopical Society* 106 (1987): 354–58.

The tendency of papyrus to extend both its own and others' vitality becomes clearer if we note what Theophrastus tells us about the other forms that papyrus takes in death: "They use the roots instead of wood, not only for burning, but also for making a great variety of articles; for the wood is abundant and good. The 'papyrus' itself is useful for many purposes; for they make boats from it and from the rind they weave sails, mats, a kind of raiment, coverlets, ropes and many other things" (*Hist. plant.* 4.8.4).[10] The dense, interwoven, mobile, enveloping nature of papyrus in life is continued as papyrus takes on the life of its human movers. From the viewpoint of the plant, human motion, fueled in part by papyrus, and using papyrus to enclose and transport the human body with clothing, mats, boats, and ropes is not unlike the enclosure and movement of insects, boars, or other animals in floating, entangled papyrus islands. In death, papyrus acts much as it does in life. Crossing the boundary between the animate and the inanimate does not change the actions that papyrus can undertake. Instead, it broadens the extent to which the vitality of papyrus can act in the world. Humans are collaborators with papyrus in this botanical colonization process.

In this world, papyrus books are not exclusively human products, static or removed from the biological home of the plant that constitutes them. Instead, they are themselves vital, entangled papyrus mats, symbiotic systems made up of the words and the biotic plant matter that form and inhabit them. They function as small botanical and intellectual ecosystems, open to interactions from other biological agents, including those that might consume, destroy, or reproduce them. Reading Theophrastus as a natural historian first of all allows us to see the papyrus book in its plantish and vibrant, even invasive, persona.

Son of Man, Eat This Scroll

All of this might seem at best whimsical did it not connect us immediately to one very persistent trope in both Greek and Roman writing about books, namely, the trope of reading as eating, as physical consumption and bodily nourishment. As Theophrastus makes clear and Pliny affirms, papyrus is most intimately involved in both human and animal life as a food.

---

10. Perhaps unsurprisingly, papyrus rafts appear to be depicted on Egyptian pottery from the third millennium BCE onward: Robert B. Partridge, *Transport in Ancient Egypt* (London: Rubicon, 1996), 16.

The book *is* an extended papyrus colony, but as such it is also liable to both human and animal consumption. As Stephanie Ann Frampton notes, classical Latin literature resorts frequently to the trope of reading as eating, as Cicero describes Cato "pigging-out" in the library of Lucullus or describes himself "grazing" in the library of Faustus.[11] Ovid, at *Tristia* 3.14.37–38, laments the lack of books he has available to him in exile because books are a form of nourishment.[12] We also see this figure in early Jewish and Christian contexts, as Kim Haines-Eitzen points out, when in Ezek 3:3 (NIV), the visionary is told, "Son of man, eat this scroll I am giving you"; the same act is described in the vision of Rev 10:9–10. The image persists in late antiquity, for example, when Gerontius describes Melania the Younger reading saints' lives "as if she were eating dessert" (*Vita Melaniae Iunioris* 23).[13] Alternatively, in a non-Christian visionary context, Artemidorus's dream manual advises: "[A dream about] eating books signifies benefits for teachers, sophists, and for all those who earn a living from words or books. But for other men, it portends sudden death" (Artemidorus, *Onir.* 2.45).[14] In the various uses of this figure, the self-conscious enjoyment of Cicero or Melania gives way to the miserable hunger of Ovid, and finally to the potentially fatal books of Artemidorus.

What gives these passages their force is not only the somatic strangeness of the physical book entering the physical body but the continued power of the book as it acts intimately within the larger being that swallows it. To move to a different mode of ancient scientific writing, this combination of active and invasive roles is common if we place the eaten book into a Galenic understanding of food, which possesses its own powers, both

---

11. Stephanie Ann Frampton, "What to Do with Books in the *De finibus*," *Transactions of the American Philological Association* 146 (2016): 119–50; both quotations of Cicero (*De fin.* 3.7 and *Att.* 4.10.1) translated by Frampton at 130. I am grateful to Professor Frampton for allowing me to read the article manuscript in advance of publication, as well as for many extremely helpful conversations on the subject of eating books, as well as on the books of Numa, discussed below.

12. Discussed in Frampton, "What to Do with Books," 132.

13. Gerontius, *The Life of Melania the Younger: Introduction, Translation and Commentary*, trans. Elizabeth A. Clark (Lewiston, NY: Mellen, 1984). All of these examples are discussed in Kim Haines-Eitzen, *The Gendered Palimpsest: Women, Writing, and Representation in Early Christianity* (Oxford: Oxford University Press, 2012), 39–41.

14. Artemidorus, *The Interpretation of Dreams (Oneirocritica) of Artemidorus*, trans. Robert J. White (Park Ridge, NJ: Noyes, 1975); discussed in Haines-Eitzen, *Gendered Palimpsest*, 40.

for nutrition and for medicine. Some plants are best for cooling, heating, moistening, or drying the person in whom they act, perhaps purging them or perhaps creating blood or bile. These actions of plants inside the body are inherent powers or faculties of the plant, through which it acts on its immediate environment even as it is acted on in the human process of *pepsis*, "concoction," or digestion.[15] So the activity of humans eating plants is not an action but an interaction, the ends of which are attained by the process of aligning the physical positions of humans and plants, inside and outside the human body. Galen writes,

> For if a human body were precisely average in mixture, it would be maintained in its existing conditions by food that is average in mixture. But if it were either warmer or colder, or drier or moister, one would do harm by giving this body food and drink that is average in mixture. For every such body needs to be altered in the opposite direction to the same extent that it has departed from the precisely average condition; and this will occur with foods that are the opposite of the existing ill-mixture. (*De alim. fac.* 1.1.469)

The plants that people eat do not lose their energies once they pass the boundaries of the human body; instead they adjust both themselves and their environment according to the qualities that exist in each.

The activity of adjustment also extends to seasonal and temporal environments, and so food becomes more broadly a means of regulating the relationship between the human and its terrestrial surroundings:

> Regarding every food, you must also keep the same things in mind concerning regions, seasons, and constitutions, in autumn being sparing with foods that produce black bile and are drying, but using them in winter; just as in summer you should use moistening and cooling foods. But in spring, since it is of average mixture, one should consume foods that are average in their properties. (*De alim. fac.* 1.18.528)

The powers of food act within the human body but are also constantly in interaction between the human and its larger surround. The late-antique herbal known as the Alphabet of Galen emphasizes this larger scope by

---

15. For discussion of the translation of *pepsis*, see Owen Powell's introduction to *Galen: On the Properties of Foodstuffs* (Cambridge: Cambridge University Press, 2003), 23. Translations of Galen are taken from this source.

including information on the interactions of plants with other materials that might surround them, or beings in their vicinity: mulberry juice "becomes even stronger when stored in a bronze container" (Alph. Gal. 194), and oregano is "good for those with trouble breathing or coughing, and it puts snakes to flight" (206).[16] Working with the powers of plants, in this system, is not exclusively an act performed by one larger being on a smaller being but is a delicate and sometimes dangerous negotiation between forces that interact according to their various powers. When Artemidorus describes book eating as a portent of either great benefit or great harm, we can see that working with the powers of books also varies in its effects, according to the condition of the person who eats them.

The figure of reading as eating, if pursued according to Galenic notions of plant nutrition, allows us to understand ancient interactions between humans and books as both an interaction between different kinds of beings with different kinds of powers and as a process that transforms those beings according to their own dispositions and environments. What is revealed more profoundly in this image, however, is twofold. First, there is a deep insistence on the somatic nature of intellectual work. Words in the ancient world are in large part distributed and consumed on the body of a being that is also truly a food. They are never disembodied and never perfectly abstract. Their work, like the work of all plant foods, is to transform their consumers from inside the body and to bring that body into a new interaction with its material surroundings. Second, and perhaps more importantly, just as the intellectual world is relentlessly somatized in this figure, the material world is inescapably noeticized and animated. Foodstuffs as beings in an animate world have their own powers and dispositions that lead them to interact with humans in particular ways. Books as second-order foodstuffs act similarly. The beings who in our world are the material vehicles for intellectual work are, in this superabundantly alive natural world, their own acting and desiring agents. This shift in perspective captures something literally vital in the process of thinking in the ancient world: the human reading, or eating, is not the exclusive location in which intellection happens. In the last part of this paper, I turn to the question of papyrus thinking and consider how its acts of remembering might ask us to reconfigure our approaches to ancient intellectual history.

---

16. Nicholas Everett, trans. *The Alphabet of Galen: Pharmacy from Antiquity to the Middle Ages* (Toronto: University of Toronto Press, 2012), 291. Translations of this work are taken from this source.

The Dead King's Books

Papyrus can wait a long time in the dark. Pliny records that

> Cassius Hemina, a historian of many years ago states, in his *Annals*, IV, that Gnaeus Terentius, a clerk, when digging his land on the Janiculum, unearthed a chest that held the body of Numa, king of Rome, and some books of his. This happened 535 years after Numa's reign. Hemina further writes that the books were made of paper [papyrus], which is all the more remarkable because they had remained intact. (*Nat.* 13.84–85)

The books are later destroyed, some deliberately and some by accident. Pliny's account is about how old papyrus can be, but it is about more than that. It is a story about trust and about remembering. In his introduction to this story, Pliny says, "At the house of the poet and most distinguished citizen Pomponius Secundus, I have seen records in the hand of Tiberius and Gaius Gracchus that were written nearly two centuries ago. Indeed, I very often see autographs of Cicero, the late Emperor Augustus, and Virgil" (13.83). The dead are entrusted to papyrus. Pliny reaches them because he trusts papyrus to carry the dead to him, to have enclosed them, and to embody them for the living. Plant bodies last longer than people do. In Livy's version of the story of Numa's books, there are only books and no king: the body of the king has been gone a long time. He writes,

> When, on the advice of his friends, the owner had opened the chests, the one which had carried the inscription about the buried king was found empty, with no trace of a human body or anything else, everything having been destroyed by the wasting action of so many years. In the other were two bundles, tied with waxed rope, containing seven books each, not merely whole, but looking absolutely fresh. (Livy, *Ab Urbe Cond.* 40.29.5–6 [Sage and Schlesinger])

The books are buried beside the king and give him a body when his own is gone. That is an office of trust. In these stories, papyrus is the caretaker of the body, and in this role it merges with the body itself.[17] In this relation-

---

17. Strangely, a great deal of scholarship on this story is dedicated to the question of whether the story itself is true or whether Livy (or anyone in antiquity) believed it was true or believed that the books were really the books of Numa or were really Pythagorean books. See, for example, K. R. Prowse, "Numa and the Pythagoreans:

ship of trust, the plant cares for the human, although its care is unconscious and inhumane. It cares for the human in this way simply because it *is* inhumane, for no human could provide the same long afterlife for another.

Let us return briefly to Theophrastus and the Egyptian water lily. After describing its daily opening and closing, Theophrastus compares it to what he has heard of the behavior of water lilies elsewhere:

> In the Euphrates they say that the "head" and the flowers sink and go under water in the evening till midnight, and sink to a considerable depth; for one can not even reach them by plunging one's hand in; and that after this, when dawn comes round, they rise and go on rising towards day-break, being visible above the water when the sun appears; and that then the plant opens its flower, and after it is open, it still rises; and that it is a considerable part which projects above the water. (*Hist. plant.* 4.8.10-11)

A water lily is not papyrus, but the inexorable recession and emergence of this plant, into darkness and again into light, beyond human reach, is also a story of trust. Plants respond to sunlight, but the water lily's motion is not reducible to response, for it begins its return before the sun appears, and from being beyond reach at midnight, it emerges along with the sunrise. Theophrastus is describing a process in which a plant remembers the sun and disappears anticipating the sun's return.[18] This remembering is another kind of trust. It too is materialized in the body of the plant as the plant gradually matures, storing the cycles of light and dark inside itself as its own substance. A plant is not only long lived; its body is its act of remembering time passing: the passage of time entrusted to the living being. A water lily grows little by little as it returns every night to the dark, knowing that it will see sunlight as it continues to grow in the next day's light. Numa's books, like the water lily, are patient.

A Curious Incident," *GR* 11 (1964): 36–42; A. Willi, "Numa's Dangerous Books: The Exegetic History of a Roman Forgery," *MH* 55 (1998): 139–72. For my purposes, these inquiries only show that the underlying motif of the narrative is the idea of trust between plant and human; whether that trust is at times abused, as it certainly is, is not the primary concern here.

18. On plant memory, see Daniel Chamovitz, *What a Plant Knows: A Field Guide to the Senses* (New York: Scientific American; New York: Farrar, Strauss, & Giroux, 2012), 113–33.

A water lily is not papyrus, but for papyrus, too, trust and memory are materialized in the growing body of the plant. This embodiment is less dramatic than the water lily's daily recession and emergence; it is simply the growth and maturation of papyrus itself. Theophrastus describes the plant's movement from the middle downwards and then upwards:

> The papyrus does not grow in deep water, but only in a depth of about two cubits, and sometimes shallower. The thickness of the root is that of the wrist of a stalwart man, and the length above four cubits; it grows above the ground itself, throwing down slender matted roots into the mud, and producing above the stalks which give it its name "papyrus"; these are three-cornered and about ten cubits long, having a plume which is useless and weak, and no fruit whatever; and these stalks the plant sends up at many points. (*Hist. plant.* 4.8.3–4)

Growth and thickening are a record of feeding and sunlight, for as Theophrastus notes, "the root is that by which the plant draws its nourishment" (1.1.9), and "no root goes down further than the sun reaches, since it is the heat that induces growth" (1.7.1). The plant entrusts itself to the reach of the sun and remembers that reach in its depth and thickness. The body of the plant itself is its memory and its trust: the experience of the plant is recorded in its body, while its structure and movement reveal the plant's unconscious predictions about the light and heat it will encounter. As Eduardo Kohn argues, "This play of remembering and forgetting is both unique and central to life; any lineage of living organism—plant or animal—will exhibit this characteristic.... A self ... is the outcome of a process, unique to life, of maintaining and perpetuating an individual form, a form that, as it is iterated over the generations, grows to fit the world around it."[19] Papyrus is a remembering self in the world, like this.

This is the self from which Pliny says Numa's books were made. The idea that written texts have some form of thought and memory is familiar from many of the tropes of text circulation and writing in antiquity. The best-known point of reference is the discussion in Plato's *Phaedrus* in which Socrates claims that writing takes memory out of the human soul and lodges it, imperfectly, elsewhere: "They will trust to the external written characters

---

19. Eduardo Kohn, *How Forests Think: Toward an Anthropology Beyond the Human* (Berkeley: University of California Press, 2013), 76.

and not remember of themselves" (*Phaedr.* 274c–275a).[20] Yet even Socrates concedes that "in the garden of letters [the philosopher] will sow and plant, but only for the sake of recreation and amusement; he will write them down as memorials to be treasured against the forgetfulness of old age, by himself, or by any other old man who is treading the same path" (276d). Cicero later called letters the "conversation of absent friends" (*Phil.* 2.7);[21] Seneca enjoys the "real signs of an absent friend" (*Ep.* 40.1) in a letter; Ovid's separated lovers routinely see letters as bearers of each other's presences.[22] At the end of the fourth century, Jerome, writing from the Syrian desert to Chromatius, Jovinus, and Eusebius, exclaims, "I converse with your letter, I embrace it, it talks to me; it alone of those here speaks Latin" (*Ep.* 7.2).[23] These spatial extensions of human thought and presence are also temporal extensions: human memory uses written matter to reconfigure itself, to draw out its life, to facilitate encounter between inhabitants inside the alive world and inhabitants outside it. Plant memory is similar: it is a physical reconfiguration and extension; it is a record of past encounter and a facilitation of future encounter. Papyrus remembers the sun, but it also remembers the writers entrusted to it. Elaine Scarry takes the vegetal substance of premodern books and ink as a calque of human thought: "Because the practice of writing is, then, a laying down of flowers upon flowers, it may be regarded as an exteriorization of what the imagining mind does, and of what it was doing long before it invented this external form of itself."[24] In Scarry's account of human imagination, she observes that for millennia flowers have been one of the most persistent objects of internalized human remembrance and image making. But this account also works, as it were, in the other direction, and in this direction human thinking is the interiorization of a process of botanical patterning, memory and extension that exist outside their echo in writing.

Although the soul of papyrus is nutritive, it is enmeshed in the material system of a thinking that extends beyond it. This thinking also leads

---

20. Translations from Phaedrus follow that of Plato, *Phaedrus*, trans. Benjamin Jowett (Oxford: Oxford University Press, 1892).

21. For consideration of Cicero's own shaping of the epistolary genre, see G. O. Hutchinson, *Cicero's Correspondence: A Literary Study* (Oxford: Clarendon, 1998).

22. See discussion of the trope in Philip Hardie, *Ovid's Poetics of Illusion* (Cambridge: Cambridge University Press, 2002), 106–42.

23. Translated by W. H. Fremantle, G. Lewis, and W. G. Martley, *NPNF* 2/6:9.

24. Elaine Scarry, *Dreaming by the Book* (New York: Farrar, Straus, & Giroux, 1999), 162.

upwards, in the direction of divinity. In the middle and later Platonism represented by Origen and Celsus, intermediate divine beings are responsible for the growth of plants and are present when they are consumed. Thus Origen, in *Against Celsus*:

> For we say that the earth bears the things that are said to be under the control of nature because of the appointment of invisible husbandmen, so to speak, and other [powers] who control not only the produce of the earth but also all flowing water and air.... We certainly do not maintain that these invisible beings are daemons.... The truth is rather that [those who consume food, wine, fruits, water or air] are associating with the divine angels appointed in charge of these things. (*Cels.* 8.31–32 [Chadwick])

In this terrestrial household, angels and other powers tend to botanical life both in its growth and in its use. Origen also claims, in turn, that angels eat scriptural words as nourishment: "The powers that cooperate with our soul and mind and our entire being are nourished by the rational food of these holy letters and words" (*Philoc.* 12.1.31–34).[25] Gods and demigods are not foreign to papyrus in its many guises: Plutarch, describing Isis searching for the body of Osiris, writes that she searched the swamps of Egypt in a papyrus raft and that for this reason Egyptians believed that crocodiles would not attack any raft made from the plant (Plutarch, *Is. Os.* 18.1 [358A]). And while plants are not themselves gods, Plutarch says, they come from gods; and so some might mistake them for gods, "even as we speak of the man buying the books of Plato as 'buying Plato,' and of the man who represents the poems of Menander as 'acting Menander'" (70.1 [379B; Babbitt]). Plants are not gods, and books are not people, but all of them hold each other close, and in this way they call each other to mind. Papyrus calls to mind and is called to mind, and these minds do their work in many different living things.

In a world in which the natural environment is suffused with its own energies and powers, and at least some of these energies and powers are rational nonhuman beings, attributing rational, animate agency, even if of a very limited kind, to materially organic books is not merely a literary conceit. Instead, it articulates the experience of being a thinking thing sur-

---

25. Origen, *Origène: Philocalie 1–20 et Lettre à Africanus*, ed. M. Harl and N. de Lange, SC 302 (Paris: Cerf, 1983), 390.

rounded by other thinking and acting things in the natural material world. Just as the figure of humans eating biological books alerts us to the ways that books were perceived as acting inside the human, the idea of the book as the bearer of both plant and human memory alerts us to the ways books were perceived to be acting within a larger, nonhumanly rational environment. The papyrus book is the product of encounters between many different kinds of lives and deaths, distilled, as a small part of their larger existence, into a single persistent object. In the world of the papyrus book, the encounters between these lives are embodied in the book's material thinking as well as in its noetic body.

Conclusion

What I have tried to lay out here, in an admittedly impressionistic way, is a rough picture of what intellectual work might look and feel like in a world that is full of nonhuman forces and nonhuman thinkers. This is a world in which one of the fundamental instruments of human intellectual labor, the papyrus book, is not an instrument but is a collaborator, a colonizer, and an actor, possessing its own natural forces and tendencies, while also remaining tied to the energies of other nonhuman actors, including rational divine beings. In this world, human thinking is entangled with the various terrestrial and celestial beings that think inside, outside, and alongside the human. An intellectual history that accepts the fact of this entanglement must create new ways of bringing together narratives about human thought and narratives about the natural world in which that thought comes into being. What does intellectual history become, when intellection is a natural environmental phenomenon? Is there a way to approach ancient intellectual history and ancient environmental history as the intimately conjoined subjects that they necessarily are? I admit to some trepidation at the prospect of answering this question with a simple yes. And yet in the same way that Harry Gamble's *Books and Readers in the Early Church* brought together the fields of book history and intellectual history, to shed new light on each, it is surely worth the attempt to think about intellection beyond the limits of the human frame, to think of thinking as part of a world that early Christian writers felt to be deeply dependent on the powers and realities of plants and angels. An intellectual history beyond the human limit might begin by examining its roots in papyrus beyond writing.

BIBLIOGRAPHY

Artemidorus. *The Interpretation of Dreams (Oneirocritica) of Artemidorus*. Translated by Robert J. White. Park Ridge, NJ: Noyes, 1975.
Bamforth, Stuart S., Colin R. Curds, and Bland J. Finlay. "Protozoa of Two Kenya Lakes." *Transactions of the American Microscopical Society* 106 (1987): 354–58.
Boar, Rosalind R., David M. Harper, and Christopher S. Adams. "Biomass Allocation in *Cyperus Papyrus* in a Tropical Wetland, Lake Naivasha, Kenya." *Biotropica* 31 (1999): 411–21.
Chadwick, Henry. *Origen: Contra Celsum*. Cambridge: Cambridge University Press, 1953.
Chamovitz, Daniel. *What a Plant Knows: A Field Guide to the Senses*. New York: Scientific American; New York: Farrar, Strauss, & Giroux, 2012.
Child, S. C., and P. A. Shaw. "A Floating Island in the Okavango: Some Observations Made by Brian Wilson." *Botswana Notes and Records* 22 (1990): 51–55.
Deleuze, Gilles, and Felix Guattari. *A Thousand Plateaus: Capitalism and Schizophrenia*. Translated by Brian Massumi. Minneapolis: University of Minnesota Press, 1987.
Everett, Nicholas, trans. *The Alphabet of Galen: Pharmacy from Antiquity to the Middle Ages*. Toronto: University of Toronto Press, 2012.
Frampton, Stephanie Ann. "What to Do with Books in the *De finibus*." *Transactions of the American Philological Association* 146 (2016): 119–50.
Gamble, Harry Y. *Books and Readers in the Early Church: A History of Early Christian Texts*. New Haven: Yale University Press, 1995.
Gerontius. *The Life of Melania the Younger: Introduction, Translation and Commentary*. Translated by Elizabeth A. Clark. Lewiston, NY: Mellen, 1984.
Haines-Eitzen, Kim. *The Gendered Palimpsest: Women, Writing, and Representation in Early Christianity*. Oxford: Oxford University Press, 2012.
Hall, Matthew. *Plants as Persons: A Philosophical Botany*. Albany: SUNY Press, 2011.
Hardie, Philip. *Ovid's Poetics of Illusion*. Cambridge: Cambridge University Press, 2002.
Healy, John F. *Pliny the Elder, Natural History: A Selection*. London: Penguin, 2004.

Hutchinson, G. O. *Cicero's Correspondence: A Literary Study*. Oxford: Clarendon, 1998.
Jones, M. B., and F. M. Muthuri. "The Canopy Structure and Microclimate of Papyrus (*Cyperus Papyrus*) Swamps." *Journal of Ecology* 73 (1985): 481–91.
Kohn, Eduardo. *How Forests Think: Toward an Anthropology Beyond the Human*. Berkeley: University of California Press, 2013.
Latour, Bruno. *Reassembling the Social: An Introduction to Actor-Network-Theory*. Oxford: Oxford University Press, 2005.
Lewis, Naphtali. *Papyrus in Classical Antiquity*. Oxford: Clarendon, 1974.
Livy. *History of Rome, Volume XII: Books 40–42*. Translated by Evan T. Sage and Alfred C. Schlesinger. LCL. Cambridge: Harvard University Press, 1938.
McCarthy, T. S., and W. N. Ellery. "The Okavango Delta." *Transactions of the Royal Society of South Africa* 53 (1998): 157–82.
Muthuri, F. M., and J. I. Kinyamario. "Nutritive Value of Papyrus (*Cyperus Papyrus, Cyperaceae*), a Tropical Emergent Macrophyte." *Economic Botany* 43 (1989): 23–30.
Origen. *Origène: Philocalie 1–20 et Lettre à Africanus*. Edited by M. Harl and N. de Lange. SC 302. Paris: Cerf, 1983.
Partridge, Robert B. *Transport in Ancient Egypt*. London: Rubican, 1996.
Plato. *Phaedrus*. Translated by Benjamin Jowett. Oxford: Oxford University Press, 1892.
Pliny. *Historia Naturalis*. Translated by A. Ernout. Paris: Belles Lettres, 1956.
Plutarch. *Moralia*. Translated by Frank Cole Babbitt. LCL. Cambridge: Harvard University Press, 1936.
Powell, Owen. *Galen: On the Properties of Foodstuffs*. Cambridge: Cambridge University Press, 2003.
Prowse, K. R. "Numa and the Pythagoreans: A Curious Incident." *GR* 11 (1964): 36–42.
Scarry, Elaine. *Dreaming by the Book*. New York: Farrar, Straus, & Giroux, 1999.
Sutton, S. L., and P. J. Hudson. "Arthropod Succession and Diversity in Umbels of *Cyperus Papyrus* L." *Biotropica* 13 (1981): 117–20.
Theophrastus. *Enquiry into Plants*. Translated by Arthur F. Hort. 2 vols. LCL. Cambridge: Harvard University Press, 1916, 1926.
Wallace, Kevin M., and Alison J. Leslie. "Diet of the Nile Crocodile (*Crocodylus niloticus*) in the Okavango Delta, Botswana." *Journal of Herpetology* 42 (2008): 361–68.

Willi, A. "Numa's Dangerous Books: The Exegetic History of a Roman Forgery." *MH* 55 (1998): 139–72.

The Transformative Role of Paper in the Literary Culture of the Islamic Lands

Jonathan M. Bloom

I am a historian of Islamic art and wandered into the history of the book quite by accident. About twenty-five years ago, I became interested in the history of paper because I wondered what people in the Muslim world drew on before they had paper. That led me ask when and where they got paper, how and where it was made, and how it was used. It is somewhat embarrassing to recall that I didn't even know that there was such a field as the history of the book until I started writing on the subject: first several articles and then a book on the history and impact of paper in the Islamic lands.[1] I came to realize that the introduction of paper in the Islamic lands had a profound impact on the emergence of literacy and literary culture, subjects parallel to those that Harry Gamble has investigated over his long career studying books and readers in the early church.[2]

The book for Muslims is, of course, the Qur'an, which Muslims believe is God's revelation to Muhammad, delivered to him aurally/orally by the angel Gibra'il (Gabriel) in both Mecca and Medina (after he emigrated there in 622 CE) and transcribed either during or immediately after Muhammad's death ten years later, in 632. Muslim tradition states that Muhammad, who is said to have been "unlettered," had his followers transcribe the revelations on whatever media were available—potsherds,

---

1. Jonathan M. Bloom, "On the Transmission of Designs in Early Islamic Architecture," *Muq* 10 (1993): 21–28; Bloom, "The Introduction of Paper to the Islamic Lands and the Development of the Illustrated Manuscript," *Muq* 17 (2000): 17–23; Bloom, *Paper before Print: The History and Impact of Paper in the Islamic World* (New Haven: Yale University Press, 2001).

2. Harry Y. Gamble, *Books and Readers in the Early Church: A History of Early Christian Texts* (New Haven: Yale University Press, 1995).

bones, and so on. These notes were later transcribed onto parchment leaves that were bound together in codices. According to the standard accounts, a definitive text of the revelations, arranged with the longest of the 114 chapters (*sura*) first and the shortest last, irrespective of where and when they were revealed, was codified during the caliphate of 'Uthman (r. 644–656), when copies of the standard text were sent out to the major cities of the realm. In recent years some non-Muslim scholars have challenged some of the particulars in this account, but it seems likely that some of the earliest surviving qur'anic fragments date from the second half of the seventh century and that full-blown and sophisticated parchment codices of the sacred scripture were produced by the end of the seventh century or beginning of the eighth. Written in a variety of angular scripts that are collectively, if erroneously, known as kufic, the earliest qur'anic manuscripts were produced, like contemporaneous Christian texts, on parchment folios in a portrait format, but by the eighth century a landscape format came to be preferred and remained standard for the qur'anic text (except in the western Islamic lands, where parchment and a square format remained popular) until the eventual adoption of paper in the tenth century.[3]

In such manuscripts, the Arabic text was rarely if ever supplied with diacritical marks to differentiate different letters sharing the same grapheme, and short vowels were not normally written. Spaces between the unconnected letters of a single word and between the letters of adjacent words were rarely differentiated, and words might just as easily be broken at the end of a line. All of these scriptural devices served not only to slow the reader down but also to indicate that the written text served principally as an aide-mémoire for readers, who had already committed the text to memory.

The production of an early parchment manuscript of the Qur'an, a text approximately the length of the New Testament, intended for public display and reading in a mosque, might involve the slaughter of 185 to 260 sheep, an expensive proposition, quite apart from the labor involved in transforming the skins of animals into parchment writing surfaces and the laborious tasks of copying and binding the text.[4] In contrast, paper is

---

3. For the early history of the text, see now Francois Deroche, *Qur'ans of the Umayyads: A First Overview*, Leiden Studies in Islam and Society 1 (Leiden: Brill, 2014).

4. In contrast to the eighth-century Northumbrian Codex, for which Amiatinus required the skins of 515 calves. See Deroche, *Qur'ans of the Umayyads*, 112; Lawrence Nees, "Problems of Form and Function in Early Medieval Illustrated Bibles from

a mat of cellulose fibers (found in plants) that are beaten in the presence of water, collected on a screen, and dried. Paper can be made virtually anywhere that plants and water are available, and neither the raw materials nor the equipment are particularly expensive. Significant labor, however, is needed to extract from raw plants the cellulose fibers suitable for manufacturing paper, and the ability to produce large numbers of sheets of consistent quality is very much an art in itself.

Muslims first encountered paper, which had been invented in China in the centuries before Christ, when they conquered portions of central Asia in the eighth century CE.[5] In previous centuries, Chinese Buddhist monks and missionaries had brought paper and papermaking to this region as they made their way to India to seek out Buddhist texts. Unlike the humid areas of southeast China where paper was invented, the arid regions of central Asia could not grow the same plants, and it seems that papermakers there learned to use recycled old vegetal fibers from linen and hemp rags, ropes, and nets, as well as whatever plants were available.[6] The use of preprocessed fibers tended to speed up production, as the initial transformation of plants into threads had already been done, although the transformation of dirty old rags into a reasonably light-colored pulp was still a laborious process. Under the aegis of Islam, this flexible and relatively inexpensive medium for writing spread remarkably rapidly, reaching Syria by circa 800 and the Iberian Peninsula by circa 1000, a distance of some eight thousand kilometers in less than three hundred years. As the use of paper and knowledge of papermaking spread, they transformed not only the kinds of scripts used and the formats of books produced but also the content of the books written, the role of writing in the culture at large, and the literacy of its population.[7]

The introduction of paper to the Abbasid bureaucracy is sometimes credited to the Barmakid family, who were originally Buddhist administrators from Balkh (now in Afghanistan) who converted to Islam and served several of the late Umayyad and early Abbasid caliphs as viziers as well as

---

Northwest Europe," in *Imaging the Early Medieval Bible*, ed. John Williams (University Park: Pennsylvania State University Press, 1999), 121–78.

5. Tsuen-Hsuin Tsien, *Paper and Printing*, ed. Joseph Needham, Science and Civilisation in China (Cambridge: Cambridge University Press, 1985).

6. A. F. Rudolf Hoernle, "Who Was the Inventor of Rag-Paper?," *Journal of the Royal Asiatic Society* 43 (1903): 663–84.

7. Bloom, *Paper before Print*.

being great patrons of science and learning, until their dramatic fall from power in 803. Indeed, al-Fadl b. Barmak is said to have founded a paper mill in the Dar al-Qazz quarter of Baghdad in 794, and the caliph Harun al-Rashid (r. 786–809) is said to have ordered the use of paper as a writing material in the government offices.[8] Paper was initially used by the government bureaucracy for documents, which became increasingly important as the Islamic empire expanded from Arabia, Syria, and Iraq to North Africa and Spain in the west, and Iran and central Asia in the east. It was relatively cheap and more secure than parchment, which could be erased by scraping or washing the written surface. The carbon ink used to write on paper inevitably soaked beneath the surface, even though paper in the Islamic lands was normally sized (or coated) with starch and polished after manufacture to reduce blotting and to allow the typical reed pen used for writing to move easily across the surface. Few paper documents from the early centuries of Islam have survived the vicissitudes of time, dynastic change, and wanton destruction, although the texts of such documents have often been preserved in later recensions. Some rare examples of government documents from the twelfth century are preserved in the Monastery of Saint Catherine at Mount Sinai.[9] They grant certain privileges and rights to the monks there by the Fatimid caliphs ruling in Cairo. The prodigious use of paper in these examples—a great deal of blank space is left between each line of writing—shows not that paper was cheap but rather that it was expensive and only the ruler could afford to flaunt it in this way.

While few government documents on paper have survived, some three hundred thousand other documents, of which the vast majority are on paper, were preserved in the Cairo Genizah, a storeroom attached to the Ben Ezra synagogue in Cairo, until they were rediscovered in the nineteenth century. These documents, which were put there for safekeeping before eventual (and respectful) disposal, largely date from the period between 900 and 1250 and document the religious, cultural, and commercial life of Cairo's Jewish community.[10] They show how important paper was for the functioning of the medieval economy in the Muslim Middle East,

---

8. Cl. Huart and A. Grohmann, "Kāghād," *EI*² 4:419–20. The ultimate source of this information is difficult to determine.

9. S. M. Stern, *Fatimid Decrees: Original Documents from the Fatimid Chancery*, All Souls Studies (London: Faber & Faber, 1964).

10. S. D. Goitein, *A Mediterranean Society* (Berkeley: University of California Press, 1967–1994).

an idea recently explored by Maya Shatzmiller.[11] The Genizah documents also show that normal people used much smaller sheets of paper than did chancellery scribes, and they did not leave much space between the lines of writing, giving a better sense of how precious people thought paper was.

Just as medieval Jews in the Muslim world used paper, so did the Christians living there. A Greek manuscript on paper of the Doctrina Patrum in the Vatican has been dated on paleographic grounds to Damascus circa 800 and shows not only that paper was already available in Syria at the beginning of the ninth century but also that paper was available to Christians in the Islamic lands as soon as it was available to Muslims.[12] Oddly enough, although Muslims (or Christians) in Syria or Iraq seem to have introduced knowledge of paper to neighboring Byzantium soon after it was accepted in the Islamic lands, it was never made in Byzantium and seems to have remained something of an exotic oddity until after the fourth Crusade, when the Byzantines began using paper imported from Europe.[13] A paper fragment bearing the text of the earliest known version of the *Thousand* (or "Arabian") *Nights* is also ascribed to early ninth-century Syria, although the book of which it formed part seems to have been taken to Egypt (where the fragment was ultimately discovered) and used as scratch paper in October 879 by a certain Ahmad b. Mahfuz, who practiced writing legal phrases in the blank spaces.[14]

The earliest surviving dated manuscript in Arabic on paper is an incomplete copy of Abu 'Ubayd al-Qasim b. Sallam's book *Gharīb al-Ḥadīth*, a study of unusual terms in the traditions of the Prophet Muhammad, now housed in Leiden University Library.[15] Copied in 866, it is the oldest to

---

11. Maya Schatzmiller, *An Early Knowledge Economy: The Adoption of Paper, Human Capital and Economic Change in the Medieval Islamic Middle Ages: 700–1300 AD*, CGEH Working Paper 64 (Utrecht: Centre for Global Economic History, 2015).

12. L. Perria, "Il *Vat. Gr.* 2200. Note codicologiche e paleografiche," *Revista di Studi Byzantini e neoellenici* NS 20–21 (1983–1984): 25–68.

13. Nicolas Oikonomidès, "Le support matériel des documents Byzantins," in *La Paléographie grecque et byzantine*, ed. Jacques Bompaire and Jean Irigoin (Paris: Éditions du CNRS, 1977), 385–416. But see H. Bresc and I. Heullant-Donat, "Pour un réévaluation de la «révolution du papier» dans l'Occident Médiéval," *Scriptorum* 61 (2007): 354–83.

14. Nabia Abbott, "A Ninth-Century Fragment of the 'Thousand Nights': New Light on the Early History of the *Arabian Nights*," *JNES* 8 (1938): 129–64.

15. Jan Just Witkam, "The Neglect Neglected: To Point or Not to Point, That Is the Question," *Journal of Islamic Manuscripts* 6 (2015): 383.

survive in a European library (or elsewhere). Its 241 folios measure 17 by 28 centimeters (6.7 by 11 inches). Copied on a brownish, rather coarse paper using a black carbon ink in a serviceable and readable script, sometimes known as *warrāq* or "stationer's" script, it shows how different in format ordinary books, even on religious subjects, were from copies of holy scripture. Not only does it have a vertical or portrait format, containing about twenty-seven lines to a page, but it is equipped with various devices, such as diacritical marks, vowels, paragraphs and indentations, all designed to facilitate reading by readers who were not previously familiar with the content of the text.

Many of these conventions appear to have been adopted from the practices first used by government scribes. For example, since some Arabic letters share the same grapheme or form, they are normally distinguished by the application of sub- or superscript dots. Thus a particular shape without a dot represents the letter *ḥā*; the same shape with a subscript dot represents *jīm*; and the same shape with a superscript dot represents *khā'*. In order to make sure that the reader distinguished the thirteen unpointed letters from their pointed counterparts, a variety of signs, known as *iḥmāl*, were sometimes used; in this manuscript a subscript semicircle indicates an unpointed letter.

The pages of the *Gharīb al-ḥadīth* measure about the same size as those of some contemporary manuscripts of the Qur'an, such as the manuscript endowed by Amajur, the governor of Damascus from 870 to 878, to a mosque in Syria.[16] There are, however, many differences: parchment versus paper support; landscape versus portrait format; multivolume versus single volume; metallic salts and tannin ink, known in Arabic as *ḥibr*, versus carbon black ink, known in Arabic as *midād*; angular versus rounded script; number of lines per page; and aids for reading (diacritical marks to distinguish letters sharing a similar form; addition of short vowels, paragraph marks, and spaces between words but not between the unconnected letters of a word). All of these features indicate that the two books were "read" in entirely different contexts and ways.

Many of these same features are found in another paper manuscript (Arab 438) preserved at Harvard University, which also provides confirma-

---

16. François Déroche, "The Qur'ān of Amāǧūr," *MME* 5 (1990–1991): 59–66; Alain Fouad George, "The Geometry of the Qur'an of Amajur: A Preliminary Study of Proportion in Early Arabic Calligraphy," *Muq* 20 (2003): 1–16; Sheila S. Blair, *Islamic Calligraphy* (Edinburgh: Edinburgh University Press, 2006), 105–6.

tion about how manuscripts were transmitted and copied in the medieval period. It consists of several sections of a commentary on the grammar of Abu Bishr ʿAmr b. ʿUthman al-Basri, commonly known as Sibawayh, who wrote in the late eighth century, by the tenth-century polymath Abu Saʿid Hasan ibn ʿAbd Allah Sirafi.[17] The manuscript was copied, presumably in Baghdad, by one Abu Muhammad al-Hasan ibn ʿAli al-Madyani in the presence of Sirafi, the author, who approved and signed the copy. The book must have been copied before 979, the year in which Sirafi died, because the last ten folios (356–365) of the manuscript contain a fragment of a dictionary by Abu ʿAbd Allah Muhammad ibn Jaʿfar al-Tamimi al-Nahwi in the hand of ʿAli ibn al-Hasan ibn Abi Hanifa, who states that he copied it on 4 Rajab 368 AH (February 3, 979 CE).[18] The script of this manuscript, which is dotted and furnished with other punctuation marks, is more fluid than that of the Leiden manuscript, and it appears to be the work not of a trained calligrapher but of someone taking dictation, as the colophon indicates.

The widespread availability of paper resulted in a vast explosion of books and book learning in the ninth and tenth centuries.[19] Ibn al-Nadim (d. 995/6) wrote the *Kitab al-Fihrist*, a list of all books written in Arabic that he had seen himself or that had been reported to him by a trustworthy source. He organized them into ten categories: (1) holy scripture, (2) grammar and philology, (3) history and biography, (4) poetry, (5) dialectical philosophy (*kalam*), (6) law (*fiqh*) and traditions (*hadith*); then secular subjects: (7) philosophy and the secular sciences, (8) legends and fables, (9) doctrines of other religions, and (10) alchemy. The index of the authors cited in the English translation of Ibn al-Nadim's work fills some two hundred closely-set pages with about thirty-seven hundred names.[20] We know that there were also books on many other subjects that Ibn al-Nadim did not include, such as astronomy, medicine, geography, cookery, etiquette, or types of popular literature.

---

17. David Pingree, "Sirāfi, Abu Saʿid Hasanin," *EIr*: https://tinyurl.com/SBL4213a.
18. See https://tinyurl.com/SBLPress4213a.
19. Konrad Hirschler, *The Written Word in the Medieval Arabic Lands: A Social and Cultural History of Reading Practices* (Edinburgh: Edinburgh University Press, 2011), 17.
20. Ibn al-Nadim, *The Fihrist of al-Nadīm: A Tenth-Century Survey of Muslim Culture*, ed. and trans. Bayard Dodge (New York: Columbia University Press, 1970), 1.

Dimitri Gutas has written extensively on the works translated from Greek or Syriac into Arabic at the House of Wisdom, the caliphal library, in Baghdad. By the end of the tenth century, nearly all secular Greek works on science and philosophy that were available in late antiquity—including such topics as astrology, alchemy, mathematics, medicine, optics, and philosophy—had been translated into Arabic.[21] In addition, many Persian and Indian works were also translated into Arabic. The previously discussed fragment of the *Thousand Nights*, presumably copied in early ninth-century Syria, demonstrates that popular literature was also produced on paper. Another paper fragment from Egypt now in Vienna contains an unidentified popular romance and concludes with a crude illustration showing the graves of the two protagonists.[22] Thus paper was used for every kind of writing from the most highbrow to the lowbrow, from the official to the popular.

The one type of writing that Muslims were initially reluctant to commit to paper was scripture, but eventually even they gave way. Unlike Peter the Venerable (d. 1156), the abbot of Cluny, who mocked the Jews of Spain who had books of a material made from "pieces of old clothing or even viler things" instead of from the (pure) skins of sheep, goat or calves (that is, parchment), or rushes that grow in Oriental marshes (that is, papyrus), this reluctance seems not to have been because of concerns about ritual purity.[23] A few centuries later, when faced with the problem of copying the Qur'an on European paper bearing potentially offensive watermarks, a North African jurist ruled that the qur'anic text effectively erased and neutralized anything objectionable it might be written over.[24] More likely it was simply habit, for the Qur'an had always been copied on parchment, presumably because both Christians and Jews had used parchment for their scriptures. But beginning in tenth century, particularly in Iran, calligraphers began to copy the Qur'an on paper, and eventually calligraphers

---

21. Dimitri Goutas, *Greek Thought, Arabic Culture* (London: Routledge, 1998).

22. D. S. Rice, "The Oldest Illustrated Arabic Manuscript," *BSOAS* 22 (1959): 207–20.

23. Oriol Valls i Subirà, *The History of Paper in Spain (X–XIV Centuries)* (Madrid: Empresa Nacional de Celulosas SA, 1978), 100; Leor Halevi, "Christian Impurity versus Economic Necessity: A Fifteenth-Century Fatwa on European Paper," *Spec* 83 (2008): 917.

24. Halevi, "Christian Impurity," 936.

elsewhere followed suit, although North African writers continued to prefer parchment for the qur'anic text for several centuries.

Surviving manuscripts indicate that in the tenth century calligraphers transcribing the Qur'an on paper abandoned the angular Kufic script and adapted the style of writing they had used for secular manuscripts such as the *Gharib al-Hadith*.[25] The new script, as exemplified by the Qur'an manuscript on paper copied by 'Ali b. Shadhan al-Razi al-Bayyi in 972, is often known as "broken cursive."[26] It marks a transitional stage in the emergence of paper manuscripts copied in fully rounded scripts, as exemplified by the Qur'an of Ibn al-Bawwab, produced at Baghdad in 1000–1001 and now in the Chester Beatty Library, Dublin.[27] Quite apart from everything else about it, this manuscript, over a thousand years old, is as perfectly legible today as on the day it was written, testifying to the codification of the Arabic script under Ibn al-Bawwab and his predecessor Ibn Muqla as a result of the increased use of paper. One need only compare this legibility with the difficulty we have today reading European scripts that are two hundred, let alone a thousand, years old. Furthermore, such a manuscript—which is small enough to be carried about—shows that it was meant to be read by someone who might or might not have known the text by heart.

The World Survey of Islamic Manuscripts estimates that about three million Islamic manuscripts have survived from the fourteen centuries before the adoption of printing, and this number must represent only a mere fraction of the quantity originally produced.[28] Many of the great cities of the Islamic lands are known to have had large and extensive libraries, both private and public.[29] The shops in the Suq al-Warraqin (Stationers' Market), the street in Baghdad for paper sellers and book dealers, served somewhat like private research libraries, for the polymath al-Jahiz (776–869) used to rent them by the day in order to read the books the

---

25. Blair, *Islamic Calligraphy*, 143–94.
26. Blair, *Islamic Calligraphy*, 152.
27. D. S. Rice, *The Unique Ibn al-Bawwāb Manuscript in the Chester Beatty Library* (Dublin: Chester Beatty Library, 1955); Blair, *Islamic Calligraphy*, 160ff.
28. Al-Furqāan Islamic Heritage Foundation, "The World Survey of Islamic Manuscripts," http://www.al-furqan.com/project/id/425.
29. Youssef Eche, *Les bibliothèques arabes publiques et semi-publiques en Mésopotamie, en Syrie et en Égypte au moyen age* (Damascus: Institut français de Damas, 1967).

booksellers kept in stock.³⁰ The library of the neo-Umayyad caliph of Cordoba, al-Hakam II (r. 961–976), is said to have contained 400,000 volumes, of which only one volume is known to survive.³¹ The library of the Fatimid caliphs in Cairo was comparably large; for example, the caliph is reported to have asked his librarian about some particular titles; the librarian returned with thirty copies of Khalil ibn Ahmad's lexicon, twenty copies of al-Tabari's history, and a hundred copies of Ibn Durayd's dictionary, including some autographs.³² Only two manuscripts are known to survive from the hundreds of thousands once there.³³ Many of the manuscripts in the palace library were looted in the middle of the eleventh century when hungry troops demanded their salaries, but there were still large collections of books in the palace when the Fatimid dynasty expired in 1171.³⁴

In addition to the material on which they were copied, the other factor that made it possible to assemble such large collections of books was the system by which texts were normally transmitted in the Islamic lands. Although writing was certainly important in Islamic societies, the oral transmission of texts was deemed preferable to direct copying.³⁵ An author would sit, often in the mosque, and in the course of several sessions "read" his work aloud to an assembled company, who took dictation. When the reading was finished, the author checked the copies and gave his seal of approval. As ten or more people could listen and copy simultaneously, it was an extremely effective method of publishing multiple copies. With the original author's attestation, the auditor could then dictate to another group of auditors, geometrically multiplying the number of copies of the original work. One was not permitted to transmit a text unless one had actually heard it read; many children were brought to reading sessions so that later in life they would be able to transmit a text they had heard

---

30. Bloom, *Paper before Print*, 117.

31. David Wasserstein, "The Library of al-Hakam II al-Muṡtanṣir and the Culture of Islamic Spain," *MME* 5 (1990–1991): 99–105; E. Lévi-Provençal, "Un manuscrit de la bibliothèque du calife al-Ḥakam II," *Hespéris* 18 (1934): 198–200.

32. Bloom, *Paper before Print*, 121.

33. Paul E. Walker, "Fatimid Institutions of Learning," *Journal of the American Research Center in Egypt* 34 (1997): 179–200; Ayman Fu'ad Sayyid, "L'art du livre," *Dossiers d'archéologie* 233 (1998): 80–83.

34. Bloom, *Paper before Print*, 122.

35. Gregor Schoeler, *The Oral and the Written in Early Islam*, ed. James Montgomery, trans. Uwe Vagelpohl (New York: Routledge, 2006); Hirschler, *Written Word*.

in their youth.³⁶ The manuscript of Sirafi's commentary on Sibawayh's grammar at Harvard is a good example of the process: it indicates that the text was by al-Hasan ibn 'Abdallah al-Sirafi, who read it (aloud) to Abu Muhammad al-Hassan bin Ali al-Madyani, presumably along with a group of others, who copied down what they heard.

The presence of large numbers of books made possible by the widespread availability of paper had far-reaching consequences for the writerly culture of the Islamic lands. Paper had a profound impact not only on the nature and types of literary production but also on literacy itself. In short, medieval Islam was a culture of books and writing, facilitated by paper. We have little means of judging the portion of the population that was literate in medieval Islamic times, but the proliferation of Arabic inscriptions on buildings, objects of daily use such as ceramics and metalwares, textiles, and coins, quite apart from the proliferation of books, suggests that significant segments of the population could read if not write.³⁷ Early medieval authors rarely describe how people acquired these skills, although increased evidence is available beginning in the thirteenth century, particularly for such cities as Cairo, when elementary schools began to proliferate.³⁸ Narrative sources normally represent the elementary school curriculum as stressing the memorization of the Qur'an but say little about whether and how other skills were acquired.

It seems fitting to conclude this short essay by returning to where I began with a bit of Islamic art. To judge from several images on ceramics and manuscripts, particularly of al-Hariri's *Maqamat* and Nizami's *Khamsa*, produced in Iraq, Iran, Syria, and Egypt from the thirteenth to the sixteenth centuries, children learned their letters in school. Significantly, they usually did not practice their writing on paper, presumably because it remained too expensive to waste, but used inexpensive and easily erasable wooden writing boards (*lawḥ*), of a kind and shape that are still known from West Africa.³⁹ Even famed Mamluk historian al-Maqrizi (d. 1442) used notebooks made from discarded government documents with usable unwritten areas that had been sold as scrap paper.⁴⁰ Art also provides evidence not only that both boys and girls learned to read and write but also

---

36. Hirschler, *Written Word*, 36.
37. Hirschler, *Written Word*, 12–17.
38. Hirschler, *Written Word*, 82–83.
39. See the illustrations in Hirschler, *Written Word*, pls. 2–7.
40. Frédéric Bauden, "Maqriziana I: Discovery of an Autograph Manuscript of

that they were taught in the same classroom, a far cry from the segregated classes throughout the region today. A large luster-painted ceramic dish attributed to early thirteenth-century Iran shows a teacher surrounded by boys and girls holding writing boards. The boards show that children first learned the individual letters of the Arabic alphabet, then how they were combined, often changing shape in the process, and finally how they were formed into complete words.[41] Once students had learned how to write, they could then do so on paper.

The availability of paper in the Islamic lands had, therefore, a profound impact on literacy and the development of literary cultures in the Islamic lands. It also had a profound impact on other aspects of human activity in the region, ranging from the development of various systems of notation for mathematics, accounting, and commerce to the eventual transformation of architecture and the visual arts.[42] Europeans learned from the Arabs how to make paper and began making it in Spain and then Italy from the thirteenth century, a period when there was increasing demand not only for books but also for government and commercial documents, and general European literacy was on the rise. Gutenberg's invention of printing with movable type in the fifteenth century is traditionally thought to have been the decisive factor in the transformation of European written culture, but it might be worth exploring whether, as in the Islamic lands, the increased availability of paper was an important contributing factor.

Bibliography

Abbott, Nabia. "A Ninth-Century Fragment of the 'Thousand Nights': New Light on the Early History of the *Arabian Nights*." *JNES* 8 (1938): 129–64.

Al-Furqāan Islamic Heritage Foundation. "The World Survey of Islamic Manuscripts." http://www.al-furqan.com/project/id/425.

Bauden, Frédéric. "Maqriziana I: Discovery of an Autograph Manuscript of al-Maqrīzī: Towards a Better Understanding of His Working Method: Description: Section 1." *Mamlūk Studies Review* 7 (2003): 21–68.

---

al-Maqrīzī: Towards a Better Understanding of His Working Method: Description: Section 1," *Mamlūk Studies Review* 7 (2003): 28.

    41. Hirschler, *Written Word*, pls. 8a–c.

    42. Bloom, *Paper before Print*, 124–201.

Blair, Sheila S. *Islamic Calligraphy*. Edinburgh: Edinburgh University Press, 2006.
Bloom, Jonathan M. "The Introduction of Paper to the Islamic Lands and the Development of the Illustrated Manuscript." *Muq* 17 (2000): 17–23.
———. "On the Transmission of Designs in Early Islamic Architecture." *Muq* 10 (1993): 21–28.
———. *Paper before Print: The History and Impact of Paper in the Islamic World*. New Haven: Yale University Press, 2001.
Bresc, H., and I. Heullant-Donat. "Pour un réévaluation de la «révolution du papier» dans l'Occident Médiéval." *Scriptorum* 61 (2007): 354–83.
Déroche, François. "The Qur'ān of Amāğūr." *MME* 5 (1990–1991): 59–66.
———. *Qur'ans of the Umayyads: A First Overview*. Leiden Studies in Islam and Society 1. Leiden: Brill, 2014.
Eche, Youssef. *Les bibliothèques arabes publiques et semi-publiques en Mésopotamie, en Syrie et en Égypte au moyen age*. Damascus: Institut français de Damas, 1967.
Gamble, Harry Y. *Books and Readers in the Early Church: A History of Early Christian Texts*. New Haven: Yale University Press, 1995.
George, Alain Fouad. "The Geometry of the Qur'an of Amajur: A Preliminary Study of Proportion in Early Arabic Calligraphy." *Muq* 20 (2003): 1–16.
Goitein, S. D. *A Mediterranean Society*. Berkeley: University of California Press, 1967–1994.
Goutas, Dimitri. *Greek Thought, Arabic Culture*. London: Routledge, 1998.
Halevi, Leor. "Christian Impurity versus Economic Necessity: A Fifteenth-Century Fatwa on European Paper." *Spec* 83 (2008): 917–45.
Hirschler, Konrad. *The Written Word in the Medieval Arabic Lands: A Social and Cultural History of Reading Practices*. Edinburgh: Edinburgh University Press, 2011.
Hoernle, A. F. Rudolf. "Who Was the Inventor of Rag-Paper?" *JRAS* 43 (1903): 663–84.
Huart, Cl., and A. Grohmann. "Kāghad." EI^2 4:419–20.
Lévi-Provençal, E. "Un manuscrit de la bibliothèque du calife al-Ḥakam II." *Hespéris* 18 (1934): 198–200.
Nadim, Ibn al-. *The Fihrist of al-Nadīm: A Tenth-Century Survey of Muslim Culture*. Edited and translated by Bayard Dodge. New York: Columbia University Press, 1970.

Nees, Lawrence. "Problems of Form and Function in Early Medieval Illustrated Bibles from Northwest Europe." Pages 121–78 in *Imaging the Early Medieval Bible*. Edited by John Williams. University Park: Pennsylvania State University Press, 1999.

Oikonomidès, Nicolas. "Le support matériel des documents Byzantins." Pages 385–416 in *La Paléographie grecque et byzantine*. Edited by Jacques Bompaire and Jean Irigoin. Paris: Éditions du CNRS, 1977.

Perria, L. "Il *Vat. Gr.* 2200. Note codicologiche e paleografiche." *Revista di Studi Byzantini e neoellenici* NS 20–21 (1983–1984): 25–68.

Pingree, David. "Sirāfi, Abu Saʿid Hasanin." *EIr*: https://tinyurl.com/SBL4213a.

Rice, D. S. "The Oldest Illustrated Arabic Manuscript." *BSOAS* 22 (1959): 207–20.

———. *The Unique Ibn al-Bawwāb Manuscript in the Chester Beatty Library*. Dublin: Chester Beatty Library, 1955.

Sayyid, Ayman Fuʾad. "L'art du livre." *Dossiers d'archéologie* 233 (1998): 80–83.

Schatzmiller, Maya. *An Early Knowledge Economy: The Adoption of Paper, Human Capital and Economic Change in the Medieval Islamic Middle Ages: 700–1300 AD*. CGEH Working Paper 64. Utrecht: Centre for Global Economic History, 2015.

Schoeler, Gregor. *The Oral and the Written in Early Islam*. Edited by James Montgomery. Translated Uwe Vagelpohl. New York: Routledge, 2006.

Stern, S. M. *Fatimid Decrees: Original Documents from the Fatimid Chancery*. All Souls Studies. London: Faber & Faber, 1964.

Tsien, Tsuen-Hsuin. *Paper and Printing*. Edited by Joseph Needham. Science and Civilisation in China. Cambridge: Cambridge University Press, 1985.

Valls i Subirà, Oriol. *The History of Paper in Spain (X–XIV Centuries)*. Madrid: Empresa Nacional de Celulosas SA, 1978.

Walker, Paul E. "Fatimid Institutions of Learning." *Journal of the American Research Center in Egypt* 34 (1997): 179–200.

Wasserstein, David. "The Library of al-Hakam II al-Muṣtanṣir and the Culture of Islamic Spain." *MME* 5 (1990–1991): 99–105.

Witkam, Jan Just. "The Neglect Neglected: To Point or Not to Point, That Is the Question." *Journal of Islamic Manuscripts* 6 (2015): 383.

From the Oral to the Written: Qur'an Manuscripts from the Early Centuries of Islam

Sheila Blair

Muslim tradition holds that the Prophet Muhammad received God's message in western Arabia over the course of some two decades in the early seventh century CE, from circa 610 until his death in 632 CE.[1] It was sent down piecemeal, although already complete in the realm of eternity and preserved on a heavenly tablet. All sources agree that it was not a written document but an oral revelation, delivered through the intermediary of the angel Gabriel.[2] This tradition carried great weight in the Muslim community and was even depicted some seven centuries later in a painting from a Mongol-period universal history, the *Jamiʿ al-tavarikh*, written by and transcribed for the Persian vizier Rashid al-Din at Tabriz in northwestern Iran in AH 714/1314–15 CE.[3]

To ensure an accurate text that could be disseminated broadly, the Prophet and his followers soon gathered oral reports of this revelation and had them written down in codex format as a book known as the Qur'an (from the Aramaic loanword into Arabic *qurʾān*, "recitation").[4] Textual sources, most of them considerably later, tell us relatively little about this

---

1. The basic source is the *Encyclopaedia of the Qurʾan*.
2. Gisela Webb, "Gabriel," *EQ* 2:278–80; and Daniel A. Madigan, "Revelation," *EQ* 4:437–48.
3. Edinburgh University Library, Oriental Manuscripts 20, fol. 45a; David Talbot Rice, *The Illustrations to the "World History" of Rashīd al-Dīn*, ed. Basil Gray (Edinburgh: Edinburgh University Press, 1976), no. 32. The image is also available on the web at https://tinyurl.com/SBL4213d.
4. ʿAlī Ibrāhīm al-Ghabbān, "The Evolution of the Arabic Script in the Period of the Prophet *Muḥammad* and the Orthodox Caliphs," in *The Development of Arabic as a Written Language*, Supplement to the Seminar for Arabian Studies 40 (London: Archeopress, 2010), 93–94.

process, and the main evidence for it lies in the fragmentary manuscripts themselves. But study of the physical remains is difficult. None of these early manuscripts has survived intact, and none of the fragments is signed or dated. Many are inaccessible, and most are poorly published. Nevertheless, during the last half-century, analysis of these patchy remains has intensified, galvanized in part by the spectacular discovery of some fifteen thousand fragments from more than 950 manuscripts found after the roof in the Great Mosque of San'a in the Yemen collapsed in 1972.[5]

Scholars, following the lead of François Déroche, are gradually coming to a consensus about many, though certainly not all, features about the evolution of the written Qur'an.[6] My purpose here is to summarize this work, making it available to the wider community of scholars from other fields, and to compare the suggested evolution of early Qur'an manuscripts to what Harry Gamble and others have presented so lucidly about the physical form of early Christian books.[7] Here I should like to take up similar kinds of questions to those Gamble posed about the history of the New Testament canon.[8] What physical forms did these early Qur'an codices take? How and by whom were they transcribed? How was the text disseminated? How rapidly did these manuscripts become available to the religious community? Who were the sponsors and custodians? How were the books transported, stored, collected, and used? Who read them, and to what purpose? In other words, I want to put these early Qur'an codices into their material, historical, and social contexts, as Gamble did for the early Christian ones.

---

5. The most convenient introduction to these fragments is Ursula Dreibholz, *Frühe Koranfragmente aus der Grossen Moschee in Sana'a/Early Qur'an Fragments from the Great Mosque in Sana'a*, Hefte zur Kulturgeschichte des Jemen 2 (Sana'a: Deutsches Archäologisches Institut Orient-Abteilung Aussenstelle Sana'a, 2003).

6. The most recent survey is François Déroche, *Qur'ans of the Umayyads: A First Overview* (Leiden: Brill, 2014).

7. Virtually all of the many reviews of Harry Y. Gamble's book *Books and Readers in the Early Church: A History of Early Christian Texts* (New Haven: Yale University Press, 1995) mention its clarity. Timothy Teeter, review of *Books and Readers in the Early Church*, by Harry Gamble, VC 50 (1996): 426–28, is the most forthright: "The book's value does not lie principally in original contributions to scholarship, but in the meticulous gathering of the results of hitherto disparate branches of classical scholarship into one place for students of the New Testament and patristic literature. Gamble has done this extremely well, performing an important service."

8. Gamble, *Books and Readers*, ix.

The topic is particularly relevant to Gamble's work, as early Qur'an manuscripts offer some of the closest comparative material in terms of arrangement of the text as well as place and time of production. As standardized in these early codices, the Qur'an, about the same length as the New Testament, is divided into 114 *sūrahs* or chapters. Except for the first chapter, which is generally taken as a prayer, the others are arranged in descending order of length, the same arrangement used in the seven churches version of the Pauline letters, a source that Gamble suggests might have served as the model for the codex format of early Bibles.[9] All of these codices, both Christian and Muslim, were produced somewhere in the Mediterranean region or Near East. Gamble concentrated on manuscripts made in the first five centuries of the Common Era, mainly up to 300 CE, and I shall deal here with early Qur'an manuscripts made during the first two centuries of Islam (seventh and eighth centuries CE).

The earliest Qur'an manuscripts are codices done in the style known as *hijazi*, a name derived from the Hijaz, the area around Mecca and Medina in western Arabia where Muhammad received the revelation, although such a term should not be taken to mean that all manuscripts in this style were necessarily made there.[10] As an exemplar of such a *hijazi* manuscript, Déroche analyzed the Codex Parisino-petropolitanus, a name he coined because most of it had been taken from the Mosque of ʿAmr in Fustat (Old Cairo) to the Bibliothèque Nationale de France in Paris and the National Library of Russia in Saint Petersburg; in addition, there are a few stray folios in the Bibliotheca Apostolica Vaticana in the Vatican, the Nasser D. Khalili Collection in London (fig. 1), and perhaps elsewhere.[11] Because most of the manuscript is in Western libraries, the Codex Parisino-petropolitanus was far more available for study than many early manuscripts that remain in mosques and are often inaccessible, particularly to outside scholars.

Ninety-eight folios of the Codex Parisino-petropolitanus survive, about 45 percent of the entire text, which would have constituted a quarto

---

9. Gamble, *Books and Readers*, 49–51. This important point is noted, although not always accepted, in many reviews of his work.

10. Alain George, *The Rise of Islamic Calligraphy* (London: Saqi Books, 2010), 21–53; Déroche, *Qurʾans of the Umayyads*, 17–35.

11. François Déroche, *La Transmission écrite du Coran dans les débuts de l'Islam: Le Codex Parisino-petropolitanus* (Leiden: Brill, 2009), 7–19; Déroche, *Qurʾans of the Umayyads*, 17–35.

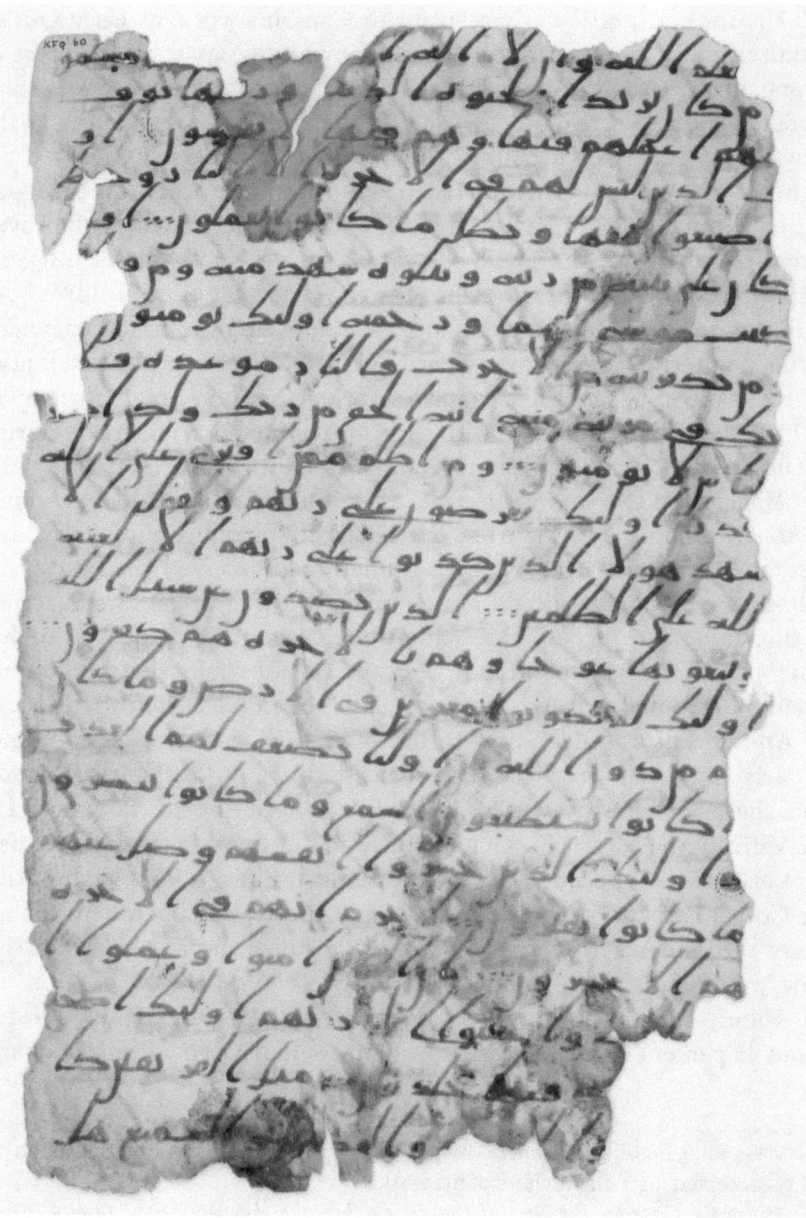

Fig. 1. Recto of a folio from the so-called Codex Parisino-petropolitanus, an early Qur'an manuscript in *hijazi* style. Source: London, The Nasser D. Khalili Collection of Islamic Art, KFQ60.

volume of fair size (33 × 24 cm). Its 220 folios, sheepskin as opposed to the calfskin used in Western manuscripts, were arranged in quaternions, with flesh facing flesh and hair facing hair. Close examination shows that the quires were produced not by folding, the traditional method used in Western manuscripts, but by stacking bifolios equivalent to half a skin. This technique of stacking remains standard in codices made in the Islamic lands, although in later codices the folios were typically arranged in different order, with flesh facing hair, and the number per quire varied. All together, the Codex Parisino-petropolitanus would have consumed seventeen to eighteen square meters of parchment, a useful measurement that allows us to compare the relative costs of different codices.

As in other manuscripts in *hijazi* style, the text in the Codex Parisino-petropolitanus is written in a single column. This layout distinguishes Qur'an codices from the great uncial codices of the Christian tradition, in which the text is written in multiple narrow columns: four in the Codex Sinaiticus (British Library, Add. Ms. 43725; 38 × 34 cm; 330–360 CE), three in the Codex Vaticanus (Vat. gr. 1209; 27 × 27 cm; 325–350 CE), or two in the Codex Alexandrinus (British Library, MS Royal 1. D. V–VIII; 32 × 26 cm; 400–440 CE). All three Christian codices are of the same order of magnitude, but the third (and latest) of them, datable to the early fifth century CE, is particularly close in size and proportion to the Codex Parisino-petropolitanus.

The most notable feature of the Codex Parisino-petropolitanus, like other comparable manuscripts in *hijazi* style, is its inconsistency. Déroche identified at least five hands among the extant folios, and they differ so readily from each other that Déroche had originally catalogued the fifth hand as a separate manuscript.[12] The five scribes made little attempt to ensure uniformity. The shapes of the individual letters differ, as do the number of lines per page, which range from twenty-one to twenty-eight, near the average of twenty-five for this group. The scribes of the Codex Parisino-petropolitanus also differed in their use of diacritical marks to distinguish homographs, in their orthography (e.g., whether or not to write long *alif*, as in *qāla*, an example of *scriptio defectiva*), and in their counting of verses, notably whether to include the basmala or invocation to God as a verse. Although the scribes were careful to indicate individual verses, marked by columns of slashes or dots, these verses do not always

---

12. Déroche, *Qur'ans of the Umayyads*, 113.

correspond with the modern standard systems or with any of the other ones associated with different schools of readings.

The scribes of the Codex Parisino-petropolitanus also felt it incumbent to maximize the amount of text per page without regard to readability or presentation, thereby lending a rough and unpolished aspect to the codex. In many places the scribes wrote to the natural edge of the skin. The lines are uneven, and the scribes regularly divided words between lines, although never from page to page. The scribes also left the same width of space between words as between groups of connected letters. In other words, the scribes used the type of *scriptio continua* known from the late antique world but adapted to the exigencies of Arabic script, in which some letters must always be connected.

The style of script used in these early Qur'an manuscripts is noticeable for its slant to the right, a feature that helps to confirm a seventh-century date for the *hijazi* style on both comparative and textual grounds. The script is comparable to that used in contemporaneous papyrus documents.[13] A tax receipt from Egypt dated AH 57/677 CE, for example, shows a similar slant to the right in the ascenders.[14] As with early Christian books,[15] then, the scripts used for both early Qur'an codices and documents are similar, although the style typical of books tends to be more formal.

The seventh-century dating for the *hijazi* style can also be confirmed by the account of tenth-century Baghdadi bookseller al-Nadim. In his opening passage on the origins of Arab writing, the chronicler writes that the first of the Arab scripts was the script of Mecca, the next that of Madina, then those of Basra and Kufa, adding that to write the *alifs* of the scripts of Mecca and Madina one turned the hand to the right and lengthened the strokes, with one form having a slight slant.[16] This is a rare case where a textual description fits the style found in surviving manuscripts.

---

13. Beatrice Gruendler, *The Development of the Arabic Scripts: From the Nabatean Era to the First Islamic Century according to Dated Texts* (Atlanta: Scholars Press, 1993).

14. PERF 573; Gruendler, *Development of Arabic Scripts*, no. P5, illustrated on p. 157.

15. Gamble, *Books and Readers*, 70–71.

16. Muhammad Ibn Ishāq al-Nadim, *The Fihrist of al-Nadīm*, trans. Bayard Dodge (New York: Columbia University Press, 1970), 10. Dodge notes (n. 15) that al-Nadim's Arabic phrase translated as "the lengthening of the strokes" is literally "the raising of the fingers." It shows the anthropomorphic way in which the Arab chronicler envisioned script.

Déroche dated the Codex Parisino-petropolitanus to the third quarter of the first century AH (670–95 CE), because, despite its inconsistency and rough aspect, the text in it was copied from an older exemplar. This is clear from the visual rather than the verbal mistakes, such as the substitution of *allāh* (God) for the canonical *lillāh* (to God), a mistake that is easy to do when copying from another manuscript but not when writing down oral dictation. In some cases, furthermore, it seemed the individual scribes were trying to improve on defective orthography in the exemplar, making small corrections to the text.

Manuscripts in *hijazi* style such as the Codex Parisino-petropolitanus were meant to be read aloud by those who had already committed the text to memory. Without full pointing, wider spaces to distinguish individual words, and complete words on a single line, it is exceedingly difficult to read the text without already knowing what it says. Modern readers who can read Arabic fluently will still stumble. The clear marking of individual verses fits with the piecemeal style of the revelation, but it may also have helped the reader, because knowing the final word of a verse could jog the memory since many verses rhyme. The large size of these codices (most are quarto, and there is even one folio volume), which required the skins from a flock of animals to produce each complete codex, suggests that these manuscripts were expensive and probably made for recitation in a public setting. They were handled regularly and valued over a long period, for many folios are dog-eared. Someone even updated the Codex Parisino-petropolitanus over several centuries to make the text closer to the canonical version and more recent standard—in other words, to make the book look "more modern."[17]

A major change in Qur'an codices took place at the turn of the eighth century. The new style, which Déroche dubbed O I, meaning Umayyad I and named for the caliphate that ruled from Syria between 661 and 750 CE, has more accurate orthography, more standard diacritical marks and vocalization, more attractive script, and added illumination.[18] We can use a folio from the David Collection in Copenhagen to exemplify

---

17. Changes included the correction of verse endings, the addition of five- and ten-verse markers, the introduction of the alphanumerics to the ten-verse markers, modifications to the text, and reinking of some letters. See Déroche, *Qur'ans of the Umayyads*, 32–33.

18. Déroche, *Qur'ans of the Umayyads*, 75–105. Much of this material is also discussed in George, *Rise of Islamic Calligraphy*, 55–93.

the imperial version of this new Umayyad style (fig. 2).[19] Like the folio in *hijazi* style in the Khalili collection from the Codex Parisino-petropolitanus (fig. 1), the folio in the David Collection has been separated from its parent manuscript, which was a single volume of some 210 folios that is mostly in the Musée des arts islamiques in Kairouan (R38), Tunisia, and still awaits full publication.[20] While it is deplorable that folios such as these have been removed from the original manuscripts and sold to private collectors, the advantage is that the dispersed folios are often more accessible, with better facilities for study and analysis such as carbon-14 dating.

Unlike the earlier manuscript in *hijazi* style, this Umayyad codex is much bigger: it is a folio, rather than a quarto, volume, with the leaves originally measuring 50 × 43 cm. The manuscript would have consumed roughly 80 square meters of parchment, more than four times that needed for the Codex Parisino-petropolitanus. Everything about the Umayyad imperial codex is more uniform. All the pages in it, and in many similar manuscripts, have a standard twenty lines per page of much more upright and regularly spaced script. Words are still divided between lines, but the text has moved from *scriptio defectiva* toward an almost full *scriptio plena* of the type used today.

More visibly noticeable is the addition of colorful illumination. As in the Codex Parisino-petropolitanus, columns of thin diagonal strokes executed in the same color of ink as the text indicate individual verses, but in the Umayyad codex sets of five and ten verses are also marked, the former with red circles and the latter with red squares inscribed with circles containing green knots. Whereas thin diagonal strokes indicate many diacritical marks, red dashes are added to indicate unwritten short vowels. Complex horizontal bands, many geometric and some vegetal, delineate the ends of individual chapters. Decoration is even added to fill out lines of text, as in the arrow at the end of *sūrah* 90 (fig. 2). Braided bands of different colors with small ornaments in the corners frame the individual pages of text at the beginning and end of the manuscript. By filling any vacant space in this and in other contemporary manuscripts,

---

19. David Collection 26/2003; Déroche, *Qur'ans of the Umayyads*, 121–26 and fig. 40.

20. Déroche, *Qur'ans of the Umayyads*, 121–26 and figs. 41–43. A few folios are in other collections as well.

Fig. 2. Recto of a folio from an Umayyad imperial Qur'an manuscript in Kairouan. Source: Copenhagen, David Collection 26/2003.

the calligraphers prevented addition or modification, thus producing a closed protected text.

The parent manuscript, Kairouan R38, is one of the rare codices that has preserved its opening and closing folios. The closing page (fol. 132b) shows a square containing a white vegetal scroll bearing green leaves on a red ground set between two lines of yellow pearls with quatrefoils in the corners.[21] In the center a circle encloses an eight-pointed star filled with circular motifs. This final page of decoration resembles the opening page on an even more ambitious manuscript of the same size in San'a (Dar al-Makhtutat 20–33.1).[22]

The illuminated pages at the beginning and end of imperial Umayyad Qur'an manuscripts readily recall those added in the early sixth century CE to the oldest known and most famous copy of Dioscurides's *De Materia Medica* (Vienna, Österreichische Nationalbibliothek, cod. med. Gr. 1).[23] The circle and eight-pointed star in the center of frontis- and finispieces in the Qur'an manuscripts parallel the shapes used around the donor portrait in the Dioscurides manuscript showing Anicia Juliana, daughter of the emperor Anicius Olybrius (fol. 6v). The frame band of the Kairouan finispiece (R38, f. 132b) is close to that around the author portrait of Dioscurides in the Vienna manuscript (fol. 5v), even using the same colors and design of a white scroll on a red ground with geometric motifs in the corners. In all cases, however, Qur'an manuscripts have only geometric decoration, without the figures typical of the late antique manuscript, for Qur'an codices are never illustrated with pictures of people. Furthermore, the Vienna Dioscurides is much smaller, measuring 37 × 30 cm, about half the area of the folios in the Umayyad imperial Qur'an manuscripts, but with more folios (491) and numerous illustrations (more than four hundred pictures of plants and animals).

Whereas the script in the earlier *hijazi* style was close to that used in regular correspondence, the script in the new Umayyad style can be

---

21. Drawing in Déroche, *Qur'ans of the Umayyads*, fig. 43.

22. Mikhail B. Piotrovsky and John Vrieze, eds., *Earthly Beauty, Heavenly Art: Art of Islam* (Amsterdam: De Nieuwe Kerk, Lund Humphries, 1999), cat. no. 36.

23. Kurt Weitzman, *Late Antique and Early Christian Book Illumination* (London: Braziller, 1977), pls. 15–17. For the revised date for the rest of the manuscript, see Ernst Gamillscheg, "Das Geschenk für Juliana Anicia: Überlegungen zu Struktur und Entstehung des Wiener Dioskurides," in *Byzantina Mediterranea: Festschrift für Johannes Koder zum 65. Geburtstag*, ed. Klaus Belke, Ewald Kislinger, Andreas Külzer, and Maria A. Stassinopoulou (Vienna: Böhlau, 2007), 187–95. Andreas E. Müller, "Ein vermeintlich fester Anker: Das Jahr 512 als eitlicher Ansatz des *Wiener Dioskurides*," *Jahrbuch der Österreichischen Byzantinistik* 62 (2012): 103–9; Alain Touwaide, "Al-Ghāfiqī's *Kitāb fī l-adwiya al-mufrada*, Dioscurides' *De materia medica*, and Mediterranean Herbal Traditions," in *The "Herbal" of al-Ghāfiqī: A Facsimile Edition with Critical Essays*, ed. F. Jamil Ragep, Faith Wallis, Pamela Miller, and Adam Gacek (Montreal: McGill-Queen's University Press, 2014), 87–88 and nn. 20–21.

considered calligraphic with carefully proportioned letters laid on out a grid.²⁴ The new formal style of script provides a new means of dating these Umayyad Qur'an manuscripts: comparison to inscriptions on dated monuments of various types produced under the Umayyad caliph 'Abd al-Malik (r. 685–705).²⁵ One group of inscriptions occurs on a set of milestones measuring the distances from Jerusalem and Damascus. Another example is the long foundation inscription in mosaic around the interior arcade of Dome of the Rock in Jerusalem, dated AH 72/691–692 CE.

A third set of comparative inscriptions is found on gold coins, which offer a precise evolution for the Umayyads' experimentation with figural imagery over the course of the AH 70s/690s CE before adopting a new style exclusively with monumental writing in Arabic script. A trial solidus issued between AH 72–74/692–694 CE copies earlier Byzantine issues, with three standing figures like those on the coins of the Byzantine emperor Heraclius (r. 610–641). These imitative coins were soon replaced by a second trial issue that adapts the model, displaying a single standing figure in Arab dress. This adaptive type of solidus, issued around AH 74–77/693–697 CE, was soon replaced by a revolutionary third type issued from late AH 77/early 697 CE onwards that was entirely epigraphic. Struck to a lower weight standard equivalent to twenty Arabic carats (approximately 4.25 grams), it is called a dinar. Its epigraphic format set the standard until modern times. The dating offered by these stylistic comparisons to dated objects is borne out by carbon-14 testing of the parchment in the Kairouan imperial codex, which established a date between 648 and 691 at a 96 percent probability.²⁶

The formal script used in these imperial Qur'an codices and related objects was the result of 'Abd al-Malik's adoption of Arabic as the language of the chancery as part of a deliberate campaign to refocus on the ideals of the original Community of Believers, with an emphasis on the

---

24. George, *Rise of Islamic Calligraphy*, 95–114, analyzes the grid.

25. Sheila Blair, *Islamic Calligraphy* (Edinburgh: Edinburgh University Press, 2006), 84–94 and figs. 3.3–3.8, illustrating the milestones, Dome of the Rock, and coins. See also Jere Bacharach, "The Shahāda, Qur'anīc Verses, and the Coinage of 'Abd al-Malik," *Muq* 27 (2010): 1–30.

26. Déroche, *Qur'ans of the Umayyads*, 125; despite the results from carbon-14 testing, Déroche dates the manuscript somewhat later (first half of the eighth century) because of its lack of gold.

Qur'an.[27] The caliph and his successors in the Marwanid branch of the Umayyads were keen to create a dynastic image, seen through the erection of public monuments, including the construction of large hypostyle mosques under 'Abd al-Malik's son and successor al-Walid (r. 705–715). The imperial Qur'an manuscripts fit these practices, meeting a new public and propagandistic function.[28] Whereas the earlier codices in *hijazi* style had been intended as records to safeguard the text, these later manuscripts in Umayyad imperial style were designed to promote an officially sponsored text and to remind the audience that the ruler or a member of his circle had commissioned and presented such fine copies for public display.

These imperial Qur'an codices also fit the elaboration of religious practices as described in texts about the Umayyads. The governor of Iraq, al-Hajjaj, for example, is said to have introduced the ritual of public Qur'an recitation in the mosque.[29] Al-Hajjaj is also reported to have distributed codices of the text to the capital cities of the empire. The manuscript al-Hajjaj sent to Medina was said to have been kept in a box (*ṣandūq*) set next to the column to the right of the Prophet's tomb. It was opened on Fridays and Thursdays, when people were supposed to recite from it during morning prayers.[30] The manuscript that al-Hajjaj sent to Egypt provoked the governor there, the caliph 'Abd al-Malik's brother 'Abd al-'Aziz, to commission his own monumental Qur'an codex.[31]

This was also the time when Muslims differentiated themselves from indigenous religions, and the imperial Qur'an manuscripts were clearly intended as bigger and more beautiful variants of contemporary presentation copies of Christian Bibles, such as the Codex Amiatinus (Florence, Biblioteca Medicea-Laurenziana, cod. Aminatino 1). One of the best early examples of Jerome's Vulgate, it was one of three copies commissioned before 716 by Ceolfrith, abbot of the twin monasteries of Wearmouth-Jarrow in Northumbria, and prepared under the supervision of the Venerable

---

27. Fred Donner, *Muhammad and the Believers: At the Origins of Islam* (Cambridge: Harvard University Press, 2010), 194–224.

28. George, *Rise of Islamic Calligraphy*, 55–93; Déroche, *Qur'ans of the Umayyads*, 135–142, esp. 140–42.

29. George, *Rise of Islamic Calligraphy*, 86. The information is given by Egyptian scholar al-Samhudi (d. 1506), in his *Wafa' al-wafa'* (2:256) citing Ibn Zabala (d. early ninth century), whose source is his teacher Malik ibn Anas (d. 796). See also Déroche, *Qur'ans of the Umayyads*, 142.

30. George, *Rise of Islamic Calligraphy*, 86 and n. 84, citing al-Samhudi.

31. George, *Rise of Islamic Calligraphy*, 86.

Bede.[32] The large and heavy volume weighs some 35 kilos without covers and contains 1,030 folios, each measuring 50 × 34 cm and containing forty-three or forty-four lines of round formal uncial script written in two columns by some nine scribes trained to a high and uniform standard. The text is laid out in *per cola et commata*, in which form—specifically the length of the line—clarifies meaning. The imposing codex, which itself may reflect models brought from Rome, was intended as a gift for the pope there and even, as Michele Brown has suggested, as an ambassador of the English nation, demonstrating that the apostolic mission had reached the ends of the known world.[33]

The Codex Amiatinus offers many parallels to Umayyad imperial Qur'an manuscripts such as the one in Kairouan. The Codex Amiatinus too is a single volume with folios about the same height but narrower and therefore of a slightly different proportion from those in the Kairouan codex. The Christian codex consumed the skins of 515 young calves, requiring the monastery to secure a grant of additional land to raise the herd of cattle needed.[34] That is a much a larger flock than the 185 sheep that Déroche estimated were needed to have produced the large Umayyad Qur'an manuscript in San'a (Dar al-Makhtutat 20–33.1), with 370 folios, or the some 105 sheep needed to produce the Kairouan codex of 210 folios.

Like the Umayyad imperial Qur'an manuscripts, the Codex Amiatinus is richly decorated. A full-page depiction of Christ in majesty (796v) and an arcaded canon table (798v) precede the New Testament, but most of the illumination is concentrated at the beginning of the manuscript, which has been much disturbed. The opening pages include a full-page illustration showing the prophet Ezra the Scribe; a purple leaf inscribed with the prologue and the contents of the manuscript; a quincunx arrangement of five medallions set within a large circle, each circle inscribed with a statement

---

32. Lawrence Nees, "Problems of Form and Function in Early Medieval Illustrated Bibles from Northwest Europe," in *Imaging the Early Medieval Bible*, ed. John Williams (University Park: Pennsylvania State University Press, 1999), 121–78.

33. Michelle P. Brown, ed., *In the Beginning: Bibles before the Year 1000* (Washington, DC: Smithsonian Institution, 2006), 279–80.

34. I take my information from Nees, "Problems of Form and Function," 149, following R. L. S. Bruce-Mitford, "The Art of the Codex Amiatinus," *Journal of the British Archaeological Association*, 3/32 (1969): 2. Nees notes also that the manuscript informs us about the Northumbrian diet, following up a suggestion by Christopher De Hamel (*A History of Illuminated Manuscripts* [Boston: Godine, 1986], 84) that the lack of Carthusian manuscripts might be tied to their vegetarian diet.

related to one of the five books of the Pentateuch; and three diagrams showing arrangements of the books of the Bible according to Jerome, Augustine, and Hilary. These decorated pages parallel those in the Umayyad imperial Qur'an codices, which have similar geometric and floral decoration but no figures. The frame around the Ezra scene, for example, has corner pieces like those on the decorated pages in the Qur'an codex; the braided arcades around the prologue and contents recall the braids in the frames around the beginning and end of the Umayyad imperial Qur'an codices.

The largest of the illuminations at the beginning of the Codex Amiatinus is a double-page opening showing a bird's-eye view of the tabernacle in the wilderness, an image probably modeled on one in the Codex Grandior made for the Roman statesman Cassiodorus (d. ca. 585), a codex that was in Northumbria at the time of Bede. Although set horizontally across the gutter of the book, the image of the tabernacle in the Codex Amiatinus was intended to be viewed vertically to take advantage of the frontal perspective of the courtyard and the labels of the objects in it.[35] It calls to mind a similar double-page architectural spread at the beginning of the most ambitious of these Umayyad imperial Qur'an manuscripts, the large manuscript discovered in San'a (Dar al-Makhtutat 20–33.1, fols. 1b–2a).[36] The illustrations show two buildings, usually taken to be mosques, both viewed from the bottom. The images combine the building's floor plans and elevations: the decorated borders can be visualized as mosque walls on a floor plan, while the rows of columns are stacked as in an elevation. The right image shows the type of architecture typical of a Christian basilica and of the Umayyad Mosque of Damascus. Steps at the bottom lead into the courtyard, with two tiers of columns, as at Damascus. A potbellied jug represents the ablution area, actually in front of and not underneath the mosque. It resembles the large two-handled vase with a broad base used to depict the *labrum*, the laver for ceremonial washing that stands in the court of the tabernacle. The similarities between the Codex Amiatinus and the Umayyad imperial Qur'an codices are easily explained, as both were derived from the same late antique models.

Thanks to the work of Déroche and others, we now have a reasonably clear idea of the overall development of Qur'an codices from *hijazi* to Umayyad style during the first centuries of Islam, but the exact dating

---

35. Paul Meyvaert, "Bede, Cassiodorus, and the Codex Amiatinus," *Spec* 71 (1996): 849–53.

36. Piotrovsky and Vrieze, *Art of Islam*, cat. no. 36.

of individual manuscripts is still contentious, and major controversies remain. A good example of the problems is the codex dubbed San'a 1, the only example of a palimpsest known in the three other major collections of early Qur'an codices from Damascus, Fustat, and Kairouan.[37] Most of the manuscript, a total of eighty folios, is in two collections in Yemen, with additional loose folios including one in the David Collection (fig. 3) and another in a private collection in the United States. With the recent find of a large section in a second collection in Yemen, we now have a significant fragment of the entire codex, something on the order of the 45 percent remaining from the Codex Parisino-petropolitanus. San'a 1 is also a quarto, but slightly larger than the Codex Parisino-petropolitanus (36.5 × 28.5 cm versus 33 × 24 cm). As a rough estimate, Déroche suggests San'a 1 might have consumed twenty square meters of parchment, slightly more than the seventeen square meters estimated for the Codex Parisino-petropolitanus, but still only a quarter of that used in the Umayyad imperial manuscripts. Déroche also notes that San'a 1 was transcribed on lower-quality parchment, including some damaged sheets and others with wounds. He therefore suggests that it, like smaller Qur'an codices, might have been produced for a private individual, unlike the officially sponsored codices in Umayyad imperial style. It lacks a public face.

This unusual palimpsest has engendered much discussion, particularly with regard to the dating of the lower text. It is clearly early, for it written in *hijazi* style with a variable number of lines per page (25–30), but scholars have differed on exactly how early. Déroche favors a date in the second half of the seventh century, close to that of the Codex Parisino-petropolitanus. In contrast, Behnam Sadeghi and his coauthors attribute

---

37. Behnam Sadeghi and Uwe Bergmann, "The Codex of a Companion of the Prophet and the Qur'ān of the Prophet," *Arabica* 57 (2010): 343–436; Behnam Sadeghi and Mohsen Goudarzi, "Ṣan'ā' 1 and the Origins of the Qur'an," *Der Islam* 87 (2012): 1–129; Déroche, *Qur'ans of the Umayyads*, 48–56. Déroche (*Qur'ans of the Umayyads*, 55) notes that all the other Arabic palimpsests belong to the Christian Arabic tradition. After I had submitted the text of this article, an important new publication about part of this manuscript appeared: Asma Hilali, *The Sanaa Palimpsest: The Transmission of the Qur'an in the First Centuries AH* (London: Oxford University Press in association with the Institute of Ismaili Studies, 2017). In it, she transcribes the text of both layers of the additional palimpsest folios in the Gharbiyya Library of the Dar al-Makhtutat, Sana'a, to which she had access and argues that the text on the lower one was not a complete manuscript but a fragment used for the scribe's personal use that circulated within the context of a teaching circle in pre-Umayyad times.

it to the first half of the seventh century, within a couple of decades of the Prophet's death. The question is particularly intriguing as the lower text contains a different order of the chapters from the one thought to have been canonized by the third caliph 'Uthman (r. 644–656) and standard today. Rather, the lower text in Sanʿa 1 broadly follows the arrangement used by the Prophet's companion Ubayy ibn Kaʿb (d. 649).

I close here by looking at the arguments laid out by both sides to examine some of the methods of dating used and evaluate some of the problems inherent in them. Déroche's arguments for a date in the second half of the seventh century rest on paleographic concerns. He argued that the use of defective orthography was similar to that found in the Codex Parisinopetropolitanus, itself a copy of a written exemplar. Other features he found indicative of a later date for the lower text in Sanʿa 1 include the counting of the basmala as a verse, the marking of hundredth and two-hundredth verses, examples of *scriptio plena* such as a *qālū* and *kāna/kānū*, the possible detection of a short vowel, and the inclusion of footers separating the chapters, sometimes even with a descriptive title for the preceding sura. Déroche concluded the codex must have been transcribed in a milieu that adhered to a non-'Uthmanic reading of the text long after the 'Uthmanic version had become standard.

Sadeghi, by contrast, relied on radiocarbon analysis, performed several times on the parchment from Sanʿa 1 with mixed results. Some of the testing produced totally implausible results, such as that reported at the Centre de Datation par le Radiocarbone in Lyon, giving a range of 388–535 CE at a 95 percent probability, in other words, before the revelation of Islam. But, as Sadeghi has cogently argued, these aberrant results must be discarded in face of numerous consistent tests carried out repeatedly at other laboratories including Tucson, Oxford, and Zurich, sites known for an established history of dating medieval parchments and other objects such as the Shroud of Turin.[38] Their results give a more plausible and consistent range for the parchment from Sanʿa 1: circa 580–660 CE at a 95 percent probability. Sadeghi argues, rightly in my view, that the Lyon laboratory must have used samples that were contaminated in cleaning with petroleum solvents, the same kind of contamination that occurred when using radiocarbon testing on medieval Islamic silks.[39] Furthermore,

---

38. Behnam Sadeghi, "Testing Sanaa 1 with C-14," forthcoming.
39. Sheila Blair, Jonathan Bloom, and Anne E. Wardwell, "Reevaluating the Date of the 'Buyid' Silks by Epigraphic and Radiocarbon Analysis," *ArsOr* 22 (1992): 1–42.

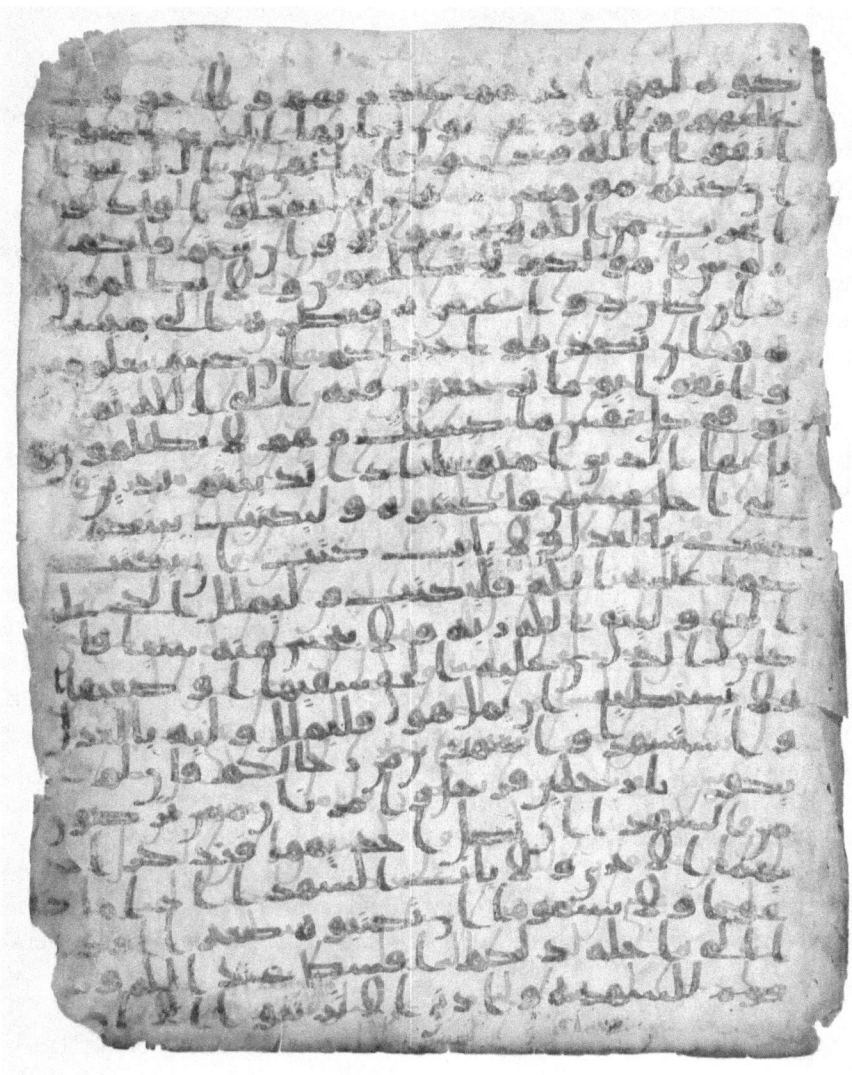

Fig. 3. Recto of a folio from the so-called San'a 1, a palimpsest Qur'an manuscript with lower text in *hijazi* style. Source: Copenhagen, David Collection 86/2003.

as Sadeghi and others have repeatedly noted, it is inaccurate to present the results from radiocarbon testing as specific dates. Rather, they identify a broad range. The repeated radiocarbon testing of Ṣanʿā 1 offers conclusive proof that the parchment dates before 660.

But what of the date of the manuscript? That is, at what date was the parchment transformed into a codex? How much time could have elapsed between slaughtering the animals and preparing the codex? Could the craftsmen who compiled the codex have used old or stockpiled parchment? Such hoarding of parchment does not seem to have been the case with several tested specimens such as the fifteenth-century Vinland Map (dated by radiocarbon analysis between 1411 and 1468 at a 95 percent confidence level, a range compatible with those suggested on historical grounds associating the map with the Council of Basle held between 1431 and 1449) or with Spanish historical manuscripts, in which the results obtained by carbon-14 analysis agreed generally with the paleographical estimates or known ages.[40] Sadeghi argues further the parchment needed for Ṣanʿā 1 was the equivalent in today's terms of a house or luxury car. We are certainly talking about a flock of animals. Thus, Sadeghi recently reaffirmed his original conclusion that the lower text of Ṣanʿā 1 would be contemporary with Ubayy ibn Kaʿb, who had arranged the *sūrahs* in the order found in this copy. Sadeghi's dating also relies on a third methodology using techniques of textual criticism by establishing stemmatics (families of manuscripts), a methodology developed for early Qurʾan manuscripts by Michael Cook, followed by many of his students, and often involving textual comparison of recensions.[41]

The dates proposed by Déroche and Sadeghi do not actually conflict but rather converge in the mid-seventh century. What they show is that we need multiple means of testing to confirm the date of any specific codex. Déroche's careful paleographic analysis presents a plausible evolution for the development of early Qurʾan codices, but it represents a general

---

40. For the Vinland land see D. J. Donohoue, J. S. Olin, and G. Harbottle, "Determination of the Radiocarbon Age of Parchment of the Vinland Map," *Radioc* 44 (2002): 45–52. In general, see Fiona Brock, "Radiocarbon Dating of Historical Parchments," *Radioc* 55 (2013): 353–63.

41. Michael Cook, "The Stemma of the Regional Copies of the Koran," *Graeco-Arabica* 9–10 (2004): 89–104; Sadeghi and Bergmann, "Codex of a Champion of the Prophet"; Intisar Rabb, "Non-canonical Readings of the Qurʾan: Recognition and Authenticity (The Ḥimṣī Reading)," *JQS* 8 (2006): 84–127.

outline. With Umayyad imperial manuscripts, we have a deliberately cultivated style with a uniform aspect, but the *hijazi* material, by contrast, shows much more variability, as individual scribes had much more latitude. San'a 1 also demonstrates that the assumed stylistic evolution toward more elaborate manuscripts does not always hold true, as the lower text has footers, but the upper (and hence later) text does not, thereby complicating or even negating the general progression that later is always more sophisticated.[42]

What all these studies show is the need for more information. We need repeated testing and full publication of the many fragmentary manuscripts. We may well need the collaboration of scholars, since few can control the range of available data. Only then will we not only come to understand the general evolution of early Qur'an codices but also be able to date and perhaps even localize individual ones and put them in context not just in the Islamic lands where they were created but in relationship to early Christian manuscripts and the written materials from other traditions as well.

Bibliography

Bacharach, Jere. "The Shahāda, Qur'anic Verses, and the Coinage of 'Abd al-Malik." *Muq* 27 (2010): 1–30.

Blair, Sheila, Jonathan Bloom, and Anne E. Wardwell. "Reevaluating the Date of the 'Buyid' Silks by Epigraphic and Radiocarbon Analysis." *ArsOr* 22 (1992): 1–42.

Blair, Sheila. *Islamic Calligraphy*. Edinburgh: Edinburgh University Press, 2006.

Brock, Fiona. "Radiocarbon Dating of Historical Parchments." *Radioc* 55 (2013): 353–63.

Brown, Michelle P., ed. *In the Beginning: Bibles before the Year 1000*. Washington, DC: Smithsonian Institution, 2006.

Bruce-Mitford, R. L. S. "The Art of the Codex Amiatinus." *Journal of the British Archaeological Association* 3/32 (1969): 1–25.

Cook, Michael. "The Stemma of the Regional Copies of the Koran." *Graeco-Arabica* 9–10 (2004): 89–104.

---

42. Blair, *Islamic Calligraphy*, 119; Sadeghi and Bergmann, "Codex of a Champion of the Prophet," 359.

De Hamel, Christopher. *A History of Illuminated Manuscripts.* Boston: Godine, 1986.
Déroche, François. *La Transmission écrite du Coran dans les débuts de l'Islam: Le Codex Parisino-petropolitanus.* Leiden: Brill, 2009.
———. *Qur'ans of the Umayyads: A First Overview.* Leiden: Brill, 2014.
Donner, Fred. *Muhammad and the Believers: At the Origins of Islam.* Cambridge: Harvard University Press, 2010.
Donohoue, D. J., J. S. Olin, and G. Harbottle. "Determination of the Radiocarbon Age of Parchment of the Vinland Map." *Radioc* 44 (2002): 45–52.
Dreibholz, Ursula. *Frühe Koranfragmente aus der Grossen Moschee in Sana'a/Early Qur'an Fragments from the Great Mosque in Sana'a.* Hefte zur Kulturgeschichte des Jemen 2. Sana'a: Deutsches Archäologisches Institut Orient-Abteilung Aussenstelle Sana'a, 2003.
Gamble, Harry Y. *Books and Readers in the Early Church: A History of Early Christian Texts.* New Haven: Yale University Press, 1995.
Gamillscheg, Ernst. "Das Geschenk für Juliana Anicia: Überlegungen zu Struktur und Entstehung des Wiener Dioskurides." Pages 187–95 in *Byzantina Mediterranea: Festschrift für Johannes Koder zum 65. Geburtstag.* Edited by Klaus Belke, Ewald Kislinger, Andreas Külzer, and Maria A. Stassinopoulou. Vienna: Böhlau, 2007.
George, Alain. *The Rise of Islamic Calligraphy.* London: Saqi Books, 2010.
Ghabbān, 'Alī Ibrāhīm al-. "The Evolution of the Arabic Script in the Period of the Prophet Muḥammad and the Orthodox Caliphs." Pages 89–102 in *The Development of Arabic as a Written Language.* Supplement to the Seminar for Arabian Studies 40. London: Archeopress, 2010.
Gruendler, Beatrice. *The Development of the Arabic Scripts: From the Nabatean Era to the First Islamic Century according to Dated Texts.* Atlanta: Scholars Press, 1993.
Hilali, Asma. *The Sanaa Palimpsest: The Transmission of the Qur'an in the First Centuries AH.* London: Oxford University Press in association with the Institute of Ismaili Studies, 2017.
Ibn Isḥāq al-Nadim, Muhammad. *The Fihrist of al-Nadīm.* Translated by Bayard Dodge. New York: Columbia University Press, 1970.
Madigan, Daniel A. "Revelation." *EQ* 4:437–48.
Meyvaert, Paul. "Bede, Cassiodorus, and the Codex Amiatinus." *Spec* 71 (1996): 827–83.

Müller, Andreas E. "Ein vermeintlich fester Anker: Das Jahr 512 als eitlicher Ansatz des *Wiener Dioskurides*." *Jahrbuch der Österreichischen Byzantinistik* 62 (2012): 103–9.

Nees, Lawrence. "Problems of Form and Function in Early Medieval Illustrated Bibles from Northwest Europe." Pages 121–78 in *Imaging the Early Medieval Bible*. Edited by John Williams. University Park: Pennsylvania State University Press, 1999.

Piotrovsky, Mikhail B., and John Vrieze, eds. *Earthly Beauty, Heavenly Art: Art of Islam*. Amsterdam: De Nieuwe Kerk, Lund Humphries, 1999.

Rabb, Intisar. "Non-canonical Readings of the Qurʾan: Recognition and Authenticity (The Ḥimṣī Reading)." *JQS* 8 (2006): 84–127.

Rice, David Talbot. *The Illustrations to the "World History" of Rashīd al-Dīn*. Edited by Basil Gray. Edinburgh: Edinburgh University Press, 1976.

Sadeghi, Behnam, and Uwe Bergmann. "The Codex of a Companion of the Prophet and the Qurʾān of the Prophet." *Arabica* 57 (2010): 343–436.

Sadeghi, Behnam, and Mohsen Goudarzi. "Ṣanʿāʾ 1 and the Origins of the Qurʾan." *Der Islam* 87 (2012): 1–129.

Teeter, Timothy. Review of *Books and Readers in the Early Church*, by Harry Y. Gamble. *VC* 50 (1996): 426–28.

Touwaide, Alain. "Al-Ghāfiqī's *Kitāb fī l-adwiya al-mufrada*, Dioscurides' *De materia medica*, and Mediterranean Herbal Traditions." Pages 84–120 in *The "Herbal" of al-Ghāfiqī: A Facsimile Edition with Critical Essays*. Edited by F. Jamil Ragep, Faith Wallis, Pamela Miller, and Adam Gacek. Montreal: McGill-Queen's University Press, 2014.

Webb, Gisela. "Gabriel." *EQ* 2:278–80.

Weitzman, Kurt. *Late Antique and Early Christian Book Illumination*. London: Braziller, 1977.

From Ancient to Medieval Books: On Reading and Illuminating Manuscripts in the Seventh Century

Lawrence Nees

Judging from the surviving evidence, it seems that books of the ancient world were seldom illustrated, but on the basis of what he took to be reflections of lost illustrations in later works, Kurt Weitzmann thought that they were well-nigh universal in scientific, literary, and religious works. He laid out his views in two hugely influential books, *Illustrations in Roll and Codex* of 1947 and *Ancient Book Illumination* of 1959.[1] *Illumination* and *illustration* were used by Weitzmann and most other scholars then and now essentially as synonyms, and the appearance of these different terms in his titles was not meant to draw a distinction between them. Indeed, the terms are still often used as if interchangeable, causing immense confusion, or so it seems to me. I propose to distinguish them, separating illustrations, pictures that in most cases accompany a text, from illumination, decoration that is integrated with the text in a variety of ways.

Whether or not illustration was common in antiquity, and in books produced in the form of papyrus rolls, is debatable and indeed has been much debated. There is, however, no debate about the absence of illumination in the sense that I mean the term from ancient book production. There are no surviving examples, and to the best of my knowledge no one has argued in favor of such a tradition having existed. Illumination begins to appear only with the adoption of the codex form in late antiquity,

---

1. Kurt Weitzmann, *Illustrations in Roll and Codex: A Study of the Origin and Method of Text Illustration*, Studies in Manuscript Illumination 2 (Princeton: Princeton University Press, 1947); Kurt Weitzmann, *Ancient Book Illumination*, Martin Classical Lectures 16 (Cambridge: Harvard University Press, 1959).

already apparently in the second or third century for Christian books, and by the end of the fourth century in almost universal use for all books.[2] The change encompassed many aspects, and ramifications continued to be worked out for centuries. It seems clear that the codex form, especially when combined with the use of parchment rather than papyrus as a material, provided a stable and flat surface suitable for elaborate pictures and thus for what I would term book illustration.[3] Here the change seems to be dramatic, for by the fifth century we have abundant evidence that illustrations were introduced into books of many types, in various places, for various purposes, and according to varying schemes.[4]

In other areas, such as script or reading practices, change seems much less dramatic. Guglielmo Cavallo argues that "the popularity of the codex did not immediately change overall reading strategies."[5] Not all scholars would agree with this formulation, but some aspects of book production offer support. For example, although parchment seems to have been the preferred material already in the fifth century, this may reflect the accidents of survival more than production, papyrus being far less sturdy a material. However, papyrus was still widely available into at least the seventh century, and not only in Egypt, since it was used for many Frankish charters and even for a few codices—such as an Avitus from southern Francia, written in a cursive hand, in a single column on unruled leaves.[6] Perhaps

---

2. There are a great many studies of the issue, but the best introduction is Harry Y. Gamble, *Book and Readers in the Early Church: A History of Early Christian Texts* (New Haven: Yale University Press, 1995). Perhaps I may be permitted to observe here that I was honored to have been invited to the conference at the University of Virginia in his honor, this article being a revised version of the lecture presented on that occasion.

3. Kurt Weitzmann, "Book Illustration in the Fourth Century: Tradition and Innovation," in *Akten des VII: Internationalen Kongresses für Christliche Archäologie, Trier 5-11 September, 1965*, Studi di Antichità Cristiana 27 (Rome: Pontificio istituto di archeologia cristiana, 1969), 257-81.

4. John Lowden, "The Beginnings of Biblical Illustration," in *Imaging the Early Medieval Bible*, ed. John Williams (University Park: Pennsylvania State University Press, 1999), 9-59, is still the best introduction, although not treating non-Christian books.

5. For a recent concise discussion see Guglielmo Cavallo, "Between *Volumen* and Codex: Reading in the Roman World," in *A History of Reading in the West*, ed. Guglielmo Cavallo and Roger Chartier, trans. Lydia G. Cochrane (Boston: University of Massachusetts Press, 1999), 85: "The popularity of the codex did not immediately change overall reading strategies."

6. For Frankish charters on papyrus see Karl August Friedrich Pertz, *Diplomata regum Francorum e stiirpe Merowingica*, ed. Georg Heinrich Pertz, MGH Diplomatum

we have a chancery scribe at work here, for both the material and the script are uncommon in books at this period, at least among those that survive. A remarkable manuscript now divided between Paris, Geneva, and Saint Petersburg shows that the two forms could coexist, for in this manuscript the gatherings of quaternios consist of papyrus leaves but are wrapped in one leaf of tougher parchment to make a quinio.[7] This manuscript is important for this study, for is it closely associated with the decorative styles practiced at the monastery of Luxeuil in Burgundy, whether or not it was actually produced there. Moreover, all parts of the manuscript deploy a hierarchy of scripts and decorative enhancement of some letters,[8] but only the parchment leaves employ the additional features of varying colors and vegetal or zoomorphic ornament that are a prominent feature of what I will term book illumination.

Illumination is associated with changes in the script used for books and in their layout. Through the sixth and into the seventh century, most books were written in a single script, whether capitals (of various types),

---

Imperii 1 (Hannover: Hahn, 1872), nos. 10, 12, 14, 17–20, 32, and 34–37 (the last surviving original on papyrus, dated by Chlotair III 659). The availability of papyrus, and its disappearance, is cited by Henri Pirenne, *Mahomet et Charlemagne* (Paris: Alcan; Brussels: Nouvelle Société d'éditions, 1937), 72–75 and 149 (English translation: *Mohammed and Charlemagne*, trans. Bernard Miall [New York: Barnes & Noble, 1939], 90–93 and 169–70) as one of the factors that made the Muslim conquests of the seventh century the real end of the ancient world. But see Richard Hodges and David Whitehouse, *Mohammed, Charlemagne and the Origins of Europe: Archaeology and the Pirenne Thesis* (Ithaca, NY: Cornell University Press, 1983), which does not, however, take up the issue of papyrus use in Francia. See now also Michael McCormick, *Origins of the European Economy: Communications and Commerce, A.D. 300–900* (Cambridge: Cambridge University Press, 2001), 704–8, who argues that what changed around 700 was not the availability of papyrus from (now Islamic) Egypt but that "the northernmost leg of its distribution into Frankland ceased." For the Ativus codex (Paris, Bibliothèque nationale de France, cod. lat 8913), see *CLA* 5, no. 573.

7. Paris, Bibliothèque nationale de France, cod. lat. 11641 (+ St. Petersburg, RNL cod. F.I.1, and Geneva, Bibl. Publique et Universitaire, cod lat. 16 [97]), Augustine, sermons and letters, central France (Luxeuil or Lyon?), later seventh century. See *CLA* 5, no. 614, and for full codicological description see "Latin 11461," Archives et manuscrits, https://tinyurl.com/SBL4213e, and for digital reproductions http://gallica.bnf.fr/ark:/12148/btv1b8438674r.

8. See Malcolm Parkes, *Their Hands before Our Eyes: A Closer Look at Scribes* (Burlington, VT: Ashgate, 2008), which in the eighth chapter emphasizes that varieties of scripts can have significance.

uncials, or half-uncials. Texts were presented in an almost undifferentiated block of text: no spaces between words, no punctuation, no upper- and lowercase letters, no variation in the size of the script. Carl Nordenfalk demonstrates in a fundamental study that some of these books began to employ decorated letters when beginning a new page, or a new section of text,[9] but these were very much first steps and timid steps, at least before the seventh century. Harry Gamble effectively presented the difficulty of reading such *scriptio continua* in his *Books and Readers*, by presenting five lines of familiar English text in this way.[10] He used this as an introduction to the overwhelming evidence that reading, even private reading, from such a text presupposes and almost demands vocalization, or at least subvocalization, reading being fundamentally an oral and aural practice in antiquity, a point of great importance for the early church and its Scriptures.

A manuscript now in Ivrea announces a different world of books and readers (fig. 1). This opening contains—at the top of the left page, the verso—the end of the list of chapters, the table of contents, written in majuscule "uncial" letters, followed by the *incipit* written in large colored capitals announcing the beginning of Pope Gregory's treatise *Regula Pastoralis*. The first chapter begins on the opposite page, the recto, with a huge initial letter *P* whose vertical stroke stretches the entire length of the page and is richly ornamented.[11] The first three lines of the text are written in colored capital letters before the main text, written in a densely packed cursive minuscule, begins for the rest of the page.[12]

This important manuscript is one of only two written in this distinctive script, long known to palaeographers as "Luxeuil minuscule," which

---

9. Carl Nordenfalk, *Die spätantiken Zierbuchstaben*, Die Bücherornamentik der Spätanike 2 (Stockholm: Egnellska boktr., 1970).

10. Gamble, *Books and Readers*, 203. See also David Crystal, *Making a Point: The Persnickety Story of English Punctuation* (New York: St. Martin's, 2015), esp. 1–10, on ancient and medieval reading and writing practices.

11. See on the decoration of the letters, not an issue addressed here, Jeffrey F. Hamburger, *Script as Image* (Leuven: Peeters, 2014).

12. See on this manuscript Ferruccio Leproni, *Il Liber Regulae Pastoralis di Gregorio I nel codice Merovingio d'Ivrea* (Turin: Arti Grafiche, 1993), pl. VIa (in color), and *CLA* 3, no. 300. See now also the very useful and well-illustrated overview by Babette Tewes, *Die Handschriften der Schule von Luxeuil: Kunst und Ikonographie eines frühmittelalterlichen Skriptoriums*, Wolfenbütteler Mittelalter-Studien (Wiesbaden: Harrassowitz, 2011), 145–47, on the Ivrea manuscript, with earlier literature.

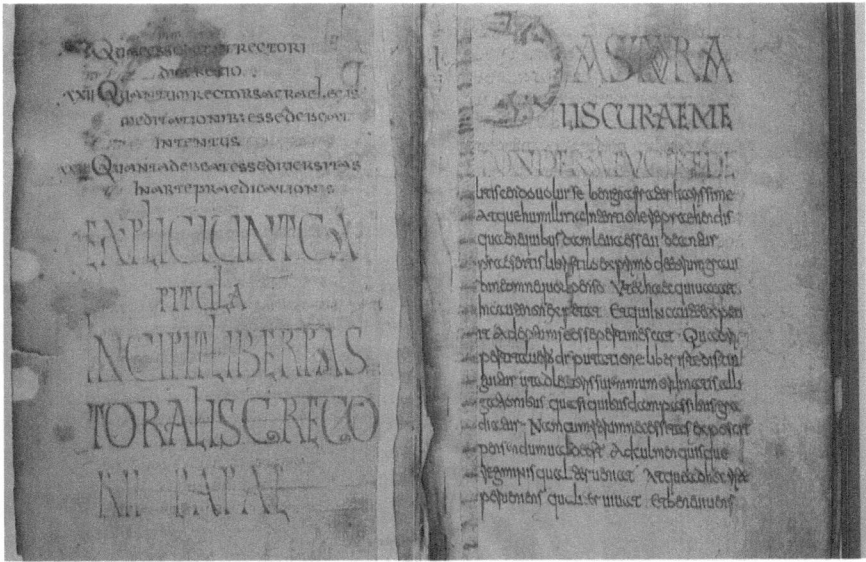

Fig. 1. Ivrea Gregory Regula fols. 3v–4r. Photograph by author.

provides good grounds for relatively close dating.[13] It opens with a large cross page on the first recto and an acrostic dedication to a bishop Desiderius on the verso (fig. 2). Since a bishop of that name in Ivrea participated in a Roman council of 680, circa 680 is a fair date for the book, as long as circa allows for twenty years or so in either direction. It is a remarkable book, one of a group of manuscripts associated with the monastery of

---

13. New York, Morgan 334 is dated to the year 669 but is written in minuscule; see *CLA* 4, no. 433; and Tewes, *Handschriften*, 154–56, no. 9. The other possibly datable manuscript is Rome, Vallicellina cod. B. 62, and an acrostic poem contained in it refers to Basinus, and there was one of that name who was archbishop of Trier 671–697 and died 705, so a date in the last quarter of the seventh century seems most likely. For this manuscript see now David Ganz, "'In the Nets or on the Line': A Datable Merovingian Manuscript and Its Importance," in *Listen, O Isles, unto Me: Studies in Medieval Word and Image in Honour of Jennifer O'Reilly*, ed. Elizabeth Mullins and Diarmuid Scully (Cork: Cork University Press, 2011), 39–46. The fundamental study of the Luxeuil group remains David Ganz, "Texts and Scripts in Surviving Manuscripts in the Script of Luxeuil," in *Ireland and Europe in the Early Middle Ages: Texts and Transmission / Irland und Europa im früheren Mittelalter: Texte und Überlieferung*, ed. Próinséas Ní Chatháin and Michael Richter (Dublin: Four Courts Press, 2002), 186–204. See now also the very useful and well-illustrated overview by Tewes, *Handschriften*.

Fig. 2. Ivrea, Bibl. Cap. 1, fol. 1v. Photograph by author.

Luxeuil, founded in central France in 590, a few dozen of which survive, apparently all, with one possible exception, because they were exported to other centers, as in the case of the Ivrea book, Luxeuil's own library not having survived.[14] In my view, it is with these manuscripts that we begin to see the truly illuminated book, which should be distinguished from the illustrated book. The latter, with pictures inserted, does indeed go back to the fourth or fifth century at the latest, but the illuminated book in my sense, like this Ivrea manuscript, is new in the late seventh century. I will submit that it is a type of book indeed for readers and not for what we might term gazers looking at the pictures. Key to understanding this kind of book and the great medieval tradition that it inaugurates is the integration of text and decoration on several levels, as I hope to show.

---

14. In addition to the studies already cited by Ganz and Tewes, see the still very valuable survey by Rosamond McKitterick, "The Scriptoria of Merovingian Gaul: A Survey of the Evidence," in *Columbanus and Merovingian Monasticism*, ed. H. B. Clarke and Mary Brennan, BARIS 113 (Oxford: B.A.R, 1981), 173–207.

I will concentrate on one manuscript, perhaps the most remarkable in some respects but also a representative of the new type. The Russian National Library in Saint Petersburg preserves a book opening with two remarkable frontispiece pages elaborately decorated with crosses, medallions, birds and many other motifs, to which I shall return (see figs. 8 and 9 below).[15] The book came to Russia in 1793, but for most of the previous thousand years it had been preserved in the great Benedictine abbey at Corbie, near Amiens in northern France. It might have been made at Corbie very shortly after the abbey's foundation in about 660, or it might have been brought there from Luxeuil, the abbey in Burgundy whence came the founders of Corbie. We cannot be certain of its precise date or place of origin, but in the light of scholarship over the last century, especially as clarified in a fundamental recent study by David Ganz, few would challenge its designation as a manuscript produced at Luxeuil or in the orbit of Luxeuil, at the heart of the Frankish kingdom in the forested hills of Burgundy. It is not dated but is likely no more than two or three decades before or after 680. It is small in size, 259 × 183 mm, about the size of a scholarly paperback, so the enormous enlargements you see here are in that sense misleading. It is a book to be held in the hands and read. It is not a book of the Gospels or another text to be used on an altar and set on a lectern, but a copy of Pope Gregory the Great's homilies on Ezekiel, to be used for study and contemplation.

The manuscript is beautifully, indeed most delicately, decorated in a way that can only be appreciated when it is held in one's hands, slowly studied, turning the pages one after another, something that cannot be conveyed even with good-quality color reproduction, so I can give only a pallid impression of its richness (see fig. 3). The scale is minute, and the first block of text in "Luxeuil minuscule" is forbidding. This is among the earliest minuscule hands, in effect lowercase script, used for the writing of books on a large scale, since late Roman books used a variety of majuscule, uppercase scripts. The Luxeuil scribe knows such capital scripts and uses them on this page for the large inscription in colored inks at the bottom of the page, telling you, the reader, that you have reached the end of book 5 and the beginning of book 6. Use of different scripts articulates the contents of the book, a hierarchy of scripts, the forerunner of the varied fonts

---

15. For the most extended description and illustrations of the manuscript see Tewes, *Handschriften*, 171–74, no. 15, figs. 5–13, 149–51, 252, 268.

we have come to expect to see in modern printed books and in unutterable and confusing profusion on the most rudimentary computer. Scribes were clearly aware of the difficulty of this script, especially for readers unaccustomed to it, and provide some welcome assistance. Sometimes there are spaces between words, a phenomenon studied by Paul Saenger emerging just at this time and in this context,[16] and sometimes new sentences begin with a capital letter, a *litera notabilior*, as for example in the large *D*'s in the third and fourth lines from the bottom. Sometimes there are little dots signifying pauses—punctuation also something newly developing and studied by Malcom Parkes as a "grammar of legibility" in his wonderfully titled book *Pause and Effect*.[17] Script and color announce a new section of text unmistakably. The large cross in a circle at the bottom, with the numeral II beside it, tells you that this is the last leaf of the second gathering. In the absence of page numbering, which somehow never occurred to early medieval scribes, this numbering provides a signpost, not only through the numbering but through the graphic ornament, for the decorated quire marks all vary in form.[18] The Luxeuil manuscript is a sophisticated result of thinking about reading, and how reading can be clarified and facilitated by the form in which texts are presented to the eye.

Here is something essential that we also usually take for granted, namely, that reading is a visual rather than an auditory experience. Yet silent reading was unusual in the ancient world, as Harry Gamble discussed in *Books and Readers*, and he drew out some of the consequences of oral reading for literacy and the liturgy.[19] Yet with this marvelous manuscript

---

16. Paul Saenger, *Space between Words: The Origins of Silent Reading* (Stanford, CA: Stanford University Press, 1997).

17. Malcolm Parkes, *Pause and Effect: An Introduction to the History of Punctuation in the West* (Berkeley: University of California Press, 1993).

18. Quire marks in the manuscripts associated with Luxeuil are remarkably interesting but have hitherto escaped serious attention. I will address those in a forthcoming study, "Graphic Quire Marks and Qur'ānic Verse Markers in the Seventh and Eighth Century," in *Visualcy, Literacy, Graphicacy: Graphic Devices and the Early Decorated Book*, ed. Michelle Brown, Ildar Garipzanov and Benjamin Tilghman (Woodbridge: Boydell & Brewer, 2017), 80–99.

19. Gamble, *Books and Readers*, 204–5. There are many other discussions, for example Henri-Jean Martin, *The History and Power of Writing*, trans. Lydia G. Cochrane (Chicago: University of Chicago Press, 1994), 67–69. On silent reading, see, however, the discussion by Jesper Svenbro, "Archaic and Classical Greece: The Invention of Silent Reading," in *History of Reading in the West*, 37–63, esp. at 50.

Fig. 3. Saint Petersburg, Russian National Library, cod. Q. v. I. 14, fol. 48v. Photograph by author.

from late seventh-century Luxeuil, and others like it, we see monastic communities and culture beginning to produce and use different kinds of books that do *not* presuppose, or in some senses do not even permit, oral reading, even private vocalization. Vocalization can perhaps take into account the new marks of punctuation, but not the different colors of script, or the different forms of script, for whether written in uncial or minuscule, a word is sounded the same way. Vocalization cannot capture the decoration of script with ornament, whether vegetal or zoomorphic, and certainly can do nothing with pages that contain no script at all but only decoration, which may speak wonderfully to the eye but which cannot be voiced. It seems not to have been observed that the shift from aural to visual experience of texts is reflected in the language used by contemporaries, for whereas in the early Christian patristic period words for reading such as *legere* and *dicere* can be used interchangeably with verbs for chanting or singing such as *cantare*, by the eighth or ninth century words for writing such as *scribere* can be used interchangeably with words for painting such as *pingere*.[20]

New reading practices, visual and silent, coincide with the new kinds of books that we see in the seventh century. It is my contention that what we today call the illuminated book developed at that time and with this background, the two Luxeuil manuscripts I have shown you being early examples, indeed the earliest in which the implications of the new reading practices have been consistently worked through with regard to the decorative enrichment of the book. In my view, it is probably no coincidence that such a book emerged in a monastic milieu, since monks are enjoined to be silent and also to read regularly.[21] The Rule of Saint Benedict has a chapter

---

20. For several examples of the former set of interchangeable words, see Peter Jeffery, "Monastic Reading and the Emerging Roman Chant Repertory," in *Western Plainchant in the First Millennium*, ed. S. Gallagher, J. Haar, J. Nádas, and T. Striplin (Aldershot, UK: Ashgate, 2003), 45, 48, 50, with references. On the latter set of interchangeable words see Lawrence Nees, "Ultán the Scribe," *ASE* 22 (1993): 132 and 139, with references. Michelle Brown, *The Lindisfarne Gospels: Society, Spirituality and the Scribe* (London: British Library, 2003), esp. 90–104 supports a long tradition that the later colophon's statement that Eadfrith avrát (= Latin *scripsit*) the book "and by implication [executed] the decoration," but also see Lawrence Nees, "Reading Aldred's Colophon for the Lindisfarne Gospels," *Spec* 78 (2003): 355, and Francis L. Newton, Francis L. Newton Jr., and Christopher R. J. Scheirer, "Domiciling the Evangelists in Anglo-Saxon England: A Fresh Reading of Aldred's Colophon in the 'Lindisfarne Gospels,'" *ASE* 41 (2012): 102 and n. 3.

21. From its inception monasticism involved intense scrutiny of all aspects of life.

demanding that monks be silent unless given permission to speak, and the *Regula Monachorum* of Columbanus, founder of Luxeuil, makes *De Taciturnitate* the second of the ten chapters, following only obedience, and begins that chapter with the statement that "the rule of silence is decreed to be carefully observed."[22] Not all important monastic writers enjoined complete silence, for John Cassian writing in the fifth century thought that reading aloud even if only *sotto voce* could aid in meditation,[23] but, of course, he was writing more than a century before Benedict and Columbanus and still in a world where reading aloud was normal and indeed taken for granted. Writing in the seventh century, before 636, Isidore of Seville directly contradicted Cassian's opinion, stating that "the understanding is instructed more fully when the voice of the reader is silent" (*amplius enim intellectus instruitur quando vox legentis quiescit*).[24]

Note that Rebecca Krawiec ("'The Holy Habit and the Teachings of the Elders': Clothing and Social Memory in Late Antique Monasticism," in *Dressing Judeans and Christians in Antiquity*, ed. Kristi Upson-Saia, Carly Daniel-Hughes, and Alicia J. Batten [Farnham, UK: Ashgate, 2014], 56), has referred to how "the 'language' of clothes requires a grammar like writing," referring to Paul Connerton, *How Societies Remember* (Cambridge: Cambridge University Press, 1989), 11, 34–35. Krawiec also discusses John Cassian's work, noting that on several occasions he cites books and writing tools alongside clothing items as things that monks are forbidden to own because of their vows of poverty. I thank Rebecca Krawiec for having provided a copy of the article on short notice, and Thelma Thomas for having brought the article to my attention.

22. The Rule of Saint Benedict 6–7 makes silence the ninth step of humility. See on this point also M. B. Parkes, "Reading, Copying and Interpreting a Text in the Early Middle Ages," in *History of Reading in the West*, 90–102. For Columbanus see *Sancti Columbani Opera*, ed. G. S. M. Walker, Scriptores Latini Hiberniae 2 (Dublin: Dublin Institute for Advanced Studies, 1957), 124–25. It is not specified that reading should be silent, and it is clear that the main objection is to conversation, and the monk should be silent "except for things profitable and necessary," which could of course include vocalized private reading.

23. Cassian *Collationes* 14.10, cited by Parkes, "Reading, Copying and Interpreting," 92.

24. Isidore, *Libri Sent*. 3.14.9, quoted by Parkes, *Pause and Effect*, 21. Whether and to what extent vocalized or subvocalized reading continued during the medieval period, in monasteries or elsewhere, is an issue not addressed here. Of course, I do not mean to imply that vocalized reading stopped in the seventh century. According to Jean Leclercq, *The Love of Learning and the Desire for God: A Study of Monastic Culture*, trans. Catharine Misrahi (New York: Fordham University Press, 1961), 72–73, it continued, especially as what he termed "active reading," resulting in a meditative mastication of the text.

Let me briefly describe how the decoration of the Saint Petersburg Gregory exemplifies this new emphasis on the visual enhancement in such books. Compare several opening or closing frames for the beginnings of books, here Homily 1 and Homily 6 respectively (see figs. 4 and 5). These two both play variations on the same theme, the gable or arch on columns, based on ancient architecture and monumental inscriptions such as the common grave markers used across the Roman world and still in many cases certainly visible in the seventh century. Of course, this is fantasy architecture, freed of any structural requirements, so the frame on the left provides a small pointed gable as if suspended between two upside-down gables, which are in turn suspended between the supporting columns, and that at the right has a single gable, which opens up in great sweeping curves that seem almost as if living things embracing the beginning and end of the title. Other pages show further variations on the theme (fig. 6). Here a triple motif at the top again links the columns, three slightly horseshoe-shaped arches rather than three pointed gables, all right-side up rather than the lateral ones reversed, but with three arches reversed at the bottom of the page. Another page shows a different variation (fig. 7), with a pointed single gable at the top and two arches at the bottom to make up the set of three, unless of course you break down the upper pattern as a triangle divided in three. Such analysis can be taken much further in any one of these pages, and there are many more of them, one for each homily. In part they show scribes at play, I think, and in part they must have functioned as finding tools, allowing the reader to find the passage sought by remembering its visual distinctiveness, as I try to find books on my own shelves by the recalled color and design of the spine.[25]

The opening pair of images, serving as a frontispiece to the volume as a whole, demonstrates how this kind of analysis applies also to the small decorative motifs (figs. 8 and 9). The decoration is very minute, executed

---

25. See the fundamental and extensive discussion by Mary J. Carruthers, *The Book of Memory: A Study of Memory in Medieval Culture* (Cambridge: Cambridge University Press, 1990), esp. 160–61, 242–45, and pl. 10. Carruthers shows that much of the art of memory goes back to Cicero and Quintilian, and most of her examples come from the late medieval period, as do all the texts collected in *The Medieval Craft of Memory: An Anthology of Texts and Pictures*, ed. Mary Carruthers and Jan M. Ziolkowski (Philadelphia: University of Pennsylvania Press, 2002), but she certainly accepts that the function was operative in the early medieval period, giving as an example some of the decorative embellishment in the Book of Kells.

Fig. 4. St. Petersburg, Russian National Library, cod. Q. v. I. 14, fol. 3r. Photograph by author.

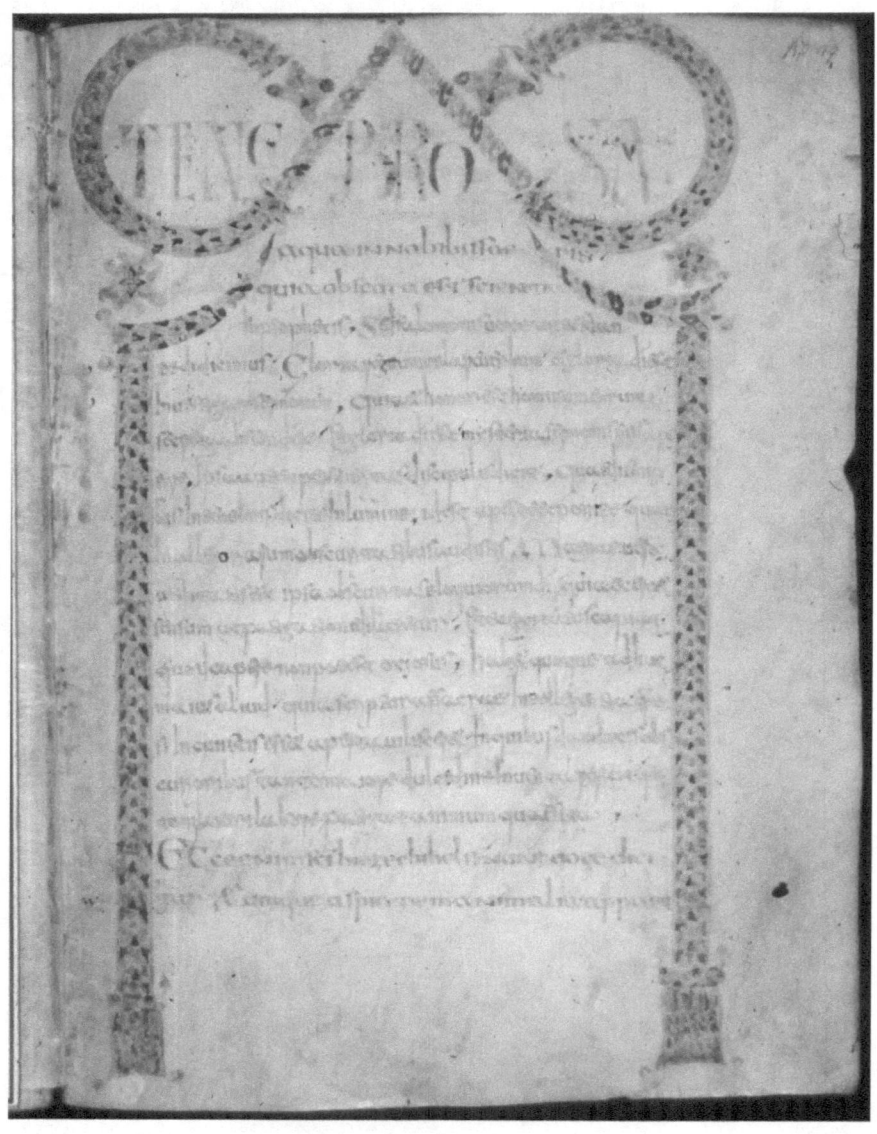

Fig. 5. St. Petersburg, Russian National Library, cod. Q. v. I. 14, fol. 49r. Photograph by author.

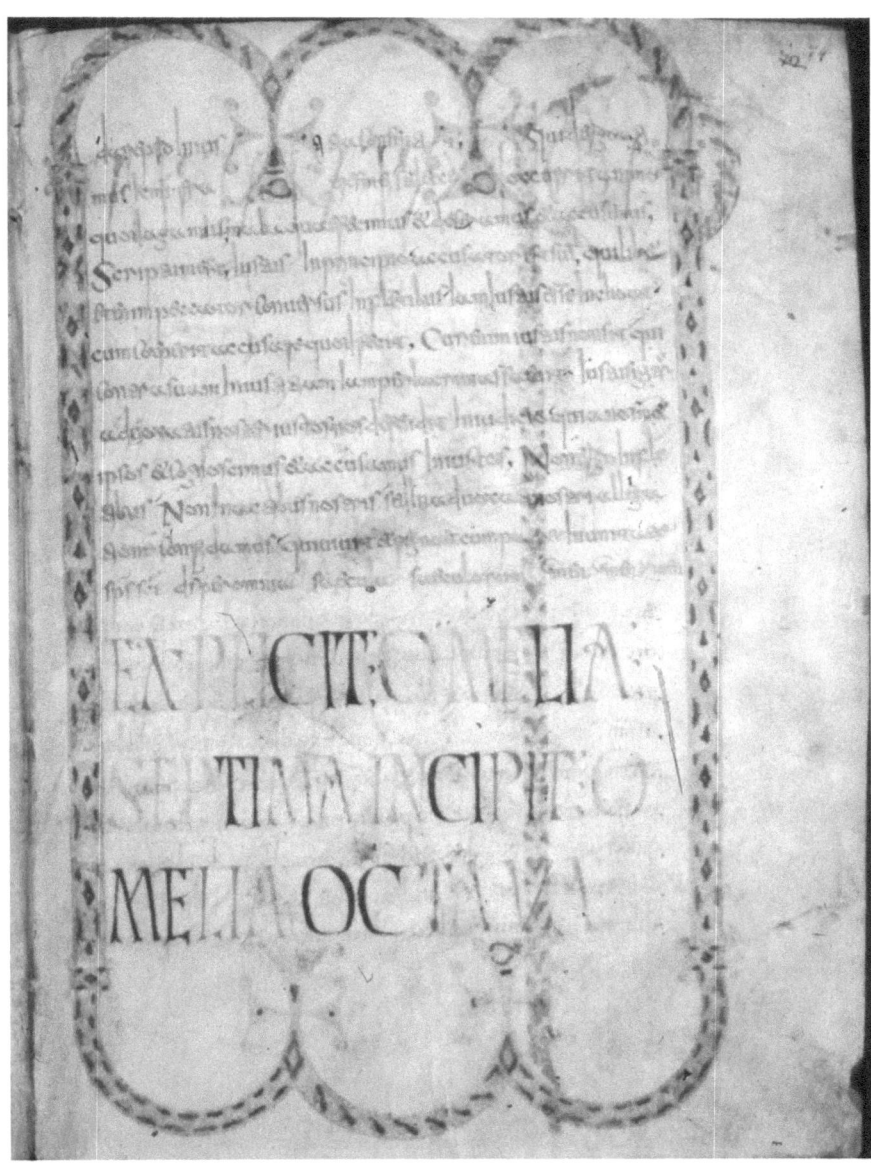

Fig. 6. St. Petersburg, Russian National Library, cod. Q. v. I. 14, fol. 74r. Photograph by author.

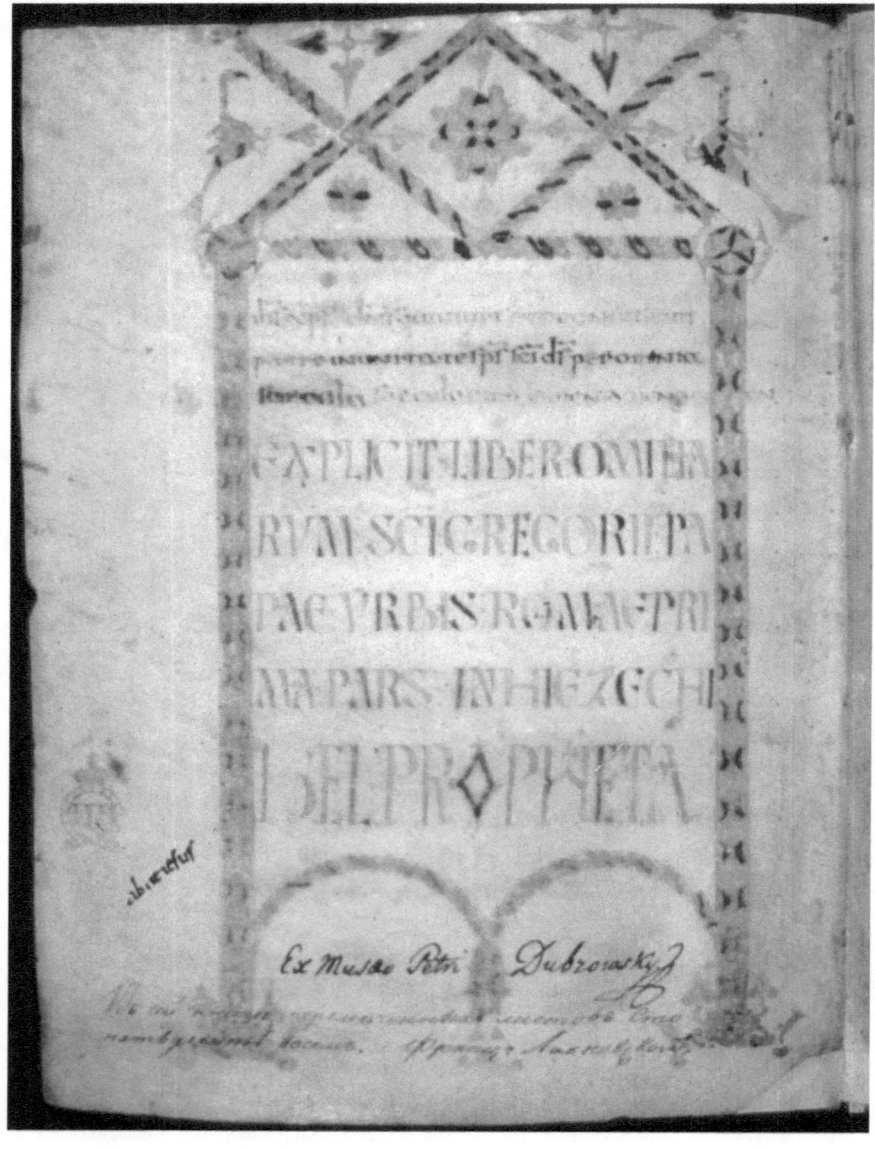

Fig. 7. St. Petersburg, Russian National Library, cod. Q. v. I. 14, fol. 158v. Photograph by author.

in red, yellow, and green pigment as well as the brown ink with which the text is written. Extensive use is made of a compass for the decoration, which includes simple twist patterns, rosettes, birds, and fish as the major motifs. The first miniature, on the left here, has a tall, thin cross, from whose arms are suspended the Greek letters *alpha* and *omega*, commonly used from early Christian times and referring to Christ's statement that "I am *alpha* and *omega*, the beginning and the end" (Rev 1:8 KJV). At the center of the cross is a six-petaled rosette, and around the cross is a large diamond-shaped lozenge frame, whose corners expand into linked pairs of circular segments, forming little fish where they intersect and also forming shapes that repeat the omega four times. The paired segments at the sides are set inside, and those at top and bottom outside the diamond frame. In the corners of the page are four large long-tailed birds. The facing page, on the right here, takes up these themes but varies them, often inverting the pattern. At the center is a large medallion containing a rosette, at whose center is a tiny cross, while four larger medallions with crosses occupy the four corners of the large rectangular frame. The diamond frame recurs but is now doubled, the two twist-pattern diamonds intersecting at the central medallion (which "covers" their merging), while the circular segments are single instead of double and face out rather than in from the corners of the diamonds. The four large birds recur but are here brought to the center of the page from the outer corners and surround the central medallion.

This is very sophisticated decoration, but sophisticated in its structure or what we might call its syntax rather than in its components. The basic ornamental vocabulary of patterns is derived entirely from the themes and ornament and materials of late Roman tradition. Parallels can be readily found across the Mediterranean world of late antiquity, from Visigothic Spain to the great early Islamic complex at Khirbat al-Mafjar near Jericho, in media such as stone carving, stucco work, floor mosaics, and textiles.[26] Perhaps even more to the point, the basic ornamental vocabulary occurs in late antique manuscript decoration. For example, an initial from an important early manuscript of Gregory's *Pastoral Rule* now in Troyes, codex 504, produced probably in Rome close to 600, shows the same color palette of red, yellow, and green used in the Saint Petersburg Gregory, relies on the

---

26. It would be beyond the scope of this article to provide detailed information on this point, which will be addressed *Illuminating the Word: On the Beginnings of Medieval Book Decoration*, which is completed in draft and which I hope to have ready for publication soon.

Fig. 8. St. Petersburg, Russian National Library, cod. Q. v. I. 14, fol. 1v. Photograph by author.

Fig. 9. St. Petersburg, Russian National Library, cod. Q. v. I. 14, fol. 2r. Photograph by author.

same simple twist pattern for its primary ornamental motif, and of course features crosses.[27]

How can we account for what I would term the syntax of the decoration of the Saint Petersburg Gregory, the complex use of themes and variations especially involving inversions and reversals seen in such pages as these? I previously cited a sense of play and the desirability of finding tools, but I think that there is more. It is well to remember that the art of illumination in my sense is very much a book art, and it is thus interesting to consider whether such "syntactical" features as I have described might also be found in texts. Let us consider one example: writings by a contemporary mid-seventh-century author, whose works were copied in monastic schools and who directly addressed the teaching of Latin to the young monks, for many of whom it was an entirely foreign tongue.

Virgilius Maro Grammaticus may have been either Irish or Spanish in origin, the uncertainty itself an interesting example of the difficulty of dividing and characterizing early medieval Latin culture along modern national lines in the absence of clear evidence.[28] Even if we knew his birth name, we should not forget that the nom de plume he adopted and under which his works were transmitted proclaims his primary allegiance to

---

27. Troyes, Bibliothèque communale, cod. 504; see *CLA* 6, no. 838, and Nordenfalk, *Zierbuchstaben*, 159–60, pls. VIIb and 68.

28. See Virgilius Maro Grammaticus, *Opera omnia*, ed. Bengt Löfstedt (Munich: Saur [Bibliotheca Teubneriana], 2003), and the long review by Reinhold F. Glei in *Perit* 19 (2005): 350–59. The latter has lots of bibliography and accepts the arguments of Michael Herren and Dáibhí Ó Cróinín that the author has an Irish background rather than Gaulish. He reports also several articles, including one by Bischoff, suggesting, on the basis of apparent knowledge of some Hebrew words, that Virgilius Maro Grammaticus might have a Jewish background. On this issue see Michael Herren, "Virgil the Grammarian: A Spanish Jew in Ireland?," *Perit* 9 (1995): 51–71, which reiterates his conclusion that the origin and formation and major activity of Virgilius Maro Grammaticus should be seen in Ireland, roughly in the first half of the seventh century (the first citation of his work by name is in a southern Irish computistical text dated 658). See Dáibhí Ó Cróinín, "The Date, Provenance, and Earliest Use of Virgilius Maro Grammaticus," in *Tradition und Wertung: Festschrift für Franz Brunhölzl zum 65. Geburtstag*, ed. Günter Bernt, Fidel Rädle, and Gabriel Silagi (Sigmaringen: Thorbecke, 1989), 13–22. For the earlier editions of Virgilius Maro Grammaticus's *Epitomae* and the *Epistolae*, see Vivien Law, *Grammar and Grammarians in the Early Middle Ages* (New York: Longman, 1997), 240 n. 2; the edition favored and used by Law is *Virgilio Marone grammatico, Epitomi ed Epistole*, ed. Giovanni Polara (Naples: Liguori, 1979).

the great Roman poet Virgil and to the classical Latin tradition. Virgilius Maro Grammaticus's extraordinary and seemingly bizarre inventiveness included making up new words, new forms of verbs, and what he himself termed a *latinitas inussitata* ("the Latin that is not in common use"), and he seems not only to have invented statements from known authorities but to have invented a remarkable series of authorities not otherwise known. Long ago Paul Lehmann suggested that instead of dismissing Virgilius Maro Grammaticus's works as barbaric, the author might better be understood as a parodist.[29] In seeking to understand the "outlandish aspects of his doctrine," Vivien Law analyzed in some detail the technique of *scinderatio fonorum*, which might be rendered by something like "articulation of sounds." The term is difficult to translate, for our author invented the word *scinderatio*, rendered by Law as "scrambling" or "splitting up." His taste for, indeed preference for, perplexing neologisms gives this seventh-century author a remarkably postmodernist quality. *Scinderatio fonorum* is regarded by Law as broadly comparable to the device of *hyperbaton* discussed by earlier grammarians such as Donatus, itself composed of five types, including the inversion of clauses, the inversion of words, and the division of single words.[30] Virgilius Maro Grammaticus tells us why such study, and such a style of writing, is important, attributing the explanation to his teacher, named, typically for this strange author, Aeneas, who said that "utterances are scrambled for three reasons: to test the acuteness of students in seeking out and discovering things that are obscure; for the adornment and improvement of eloquence; and to conceal mystical matters which ought only to be revealed to those able to understand them from base and stupid people."[31]

The complex and to us sometimes peculiar qualities of early medieval Latin prose and early medieval writings about Latin prose have been studied extensively by David Howlett and many other recent scholars,[32] but it is essential to note that such analysis is not itself something invented by the

---

29. Law, *Grammar and Grammarians*, 226, (the chapter is titled "Learning to Read with the *Oculi Mentis*: The Word-Play of Virgilius Maro Grammaticus"), with earlier literature, including Paul Lehmann, *Die Parödie im Mittelalter* (Stuttgart, 1963), 9.

30. Law, *Grammar and Grammarians*, 231.

31. *Epitomae* X [De scinderatio fonorum], 1-13; see Löfstedt, *Virgilius Maro Grammaticus*, 213-25, at 213, discussed by Law, *Grammar and Grammarians*, 231-32.

32. David R. Howlett, *The Celtic Latin Tradition of Biblical Style* (Dublin: Four Courts Press, 1995).

Irish or the Germans or other barbarians. There is no ancient, preclassical, autochthonous, native Irish or Germanic tradition of Latin grammatical study, and the kind of analysis offered by Virgilius Maro Grammaticus rests not only on earlier Latin grammarians firmly within the Roman tradition, such as Servius and Donatus, but also on his namesake Virgil himself and the way Virgil composed his poems in the first place. For just one example, note that Virgil used almost identical hexameter lines for the first line of his first *Eclogue* and for the last line of his last *Georgic*.[33] Further, he uses the same verb, *condere*, for the opening of the Aeneid and for its closing, first for the "planting" of a new city in Latium by Aeneas, and at the end for the "planting" of Aeneas's sword in the breast of the defeated Turnus.[34] This compositional habit, involving antitheses and variations among other rhetorical features, is by no means limited to the ancient world but lived on through commentaries and the grammatical tradition so ably surveyed by Catherine M. Chin.[35]

The interaction between decoration and text in early manuscript illumination is essential, and the entrenched tendency to study them separately is a product not of medieval culture and habits but of modern disciplinary training and organization.[36]

In closing, I would like to call attention to one example from the marvelous manuscript in Saint Petersburg to suggest not only that its decoration is analogous to contemporary habits of reading and writing but also could be directly related to the text itself. The text of the manuscript is Gregory's *Homilies on Ezekiel*, whose second sermon opens with a descrip-

---

33. *P. Vergili Maronis Opera*, ed. R. A. B. Mynors, Scriptorum classicorum Bibliotheca Oxoniensis (Oxford: Clarendon, 1969), 1: *Tityre, tu patulae recubans sub tegmine fagi*; and 101: *Tityre, te patulae cecini sub tegmine fagi*, discussed by Glenn W. Most, "Memory and Forgetting in the Aeneid," *Vergilius* 47 (2001): 156–57, with a number of other examples of this obsessive (and he rightly observes "sometimes obtrusive") structural habit.

34. Mynors, *P. Vergili Maronis Opera, Aeneidos*, 1:5, 12:950.

35. Catherine M. Chin, *Grammar and Christianity in the Late Roman World* (Philadelphia: University of Pennsylvania Press, 2008).

36. Mary Carruthers, *The Craft of Thought. Meditation, Rhetoric and the Making of Images 400–1200* (Cambridge: Cambridge University Press, 1998), 122: "Medieval and ancient writers do not distinguish between what we call 'verbal' and 'visual' memory; that the letters used for writing were considered to be as visual as what we call 'images' today; and that as a result the page as a whole, the complete parchment with its lettering and all its decoration, was considered a cognitively valuable 'picture.'"

tion of the prophet's vision of a whirlwind and fire within cloud, and at the center thereof four living creatures with wings, and the appearance of one wheel with their four faces, and then a wheel within a wheel and wheels lifted up, for the spirit of life was within the wheels.[37] When visualized in figural terms, as in the Syriac Rabbula Gospels dated 586, the four faces of the living creatures, man, lion, bull, and eagle, emerge from the wheels and wings, here of course based on Ezekiel, but used as a way to visualize the ascension of Christ, patently conveying the idea that Christ fulfills the prophecy of Ezekiel.[38] The Ezekiel vision also stands behind compositions of Christ enthroned in majesty surrounded by the four living creatures, now explicitly linked with the four evangelists, as in a book produced in central France, probably not far from Luxeuil in the mid-eighth century.[39] Here, as I have argued elsewhere, the image is meant to be read in conjunction with the text on the facing page and clearly intended to be the basis for detailed thinking about the meaning of the images, *and* of the text, *and* of their relationship.

Returning to the opening frontispiece pages in the St. Petersburg manuscript transmitting Gregory in Ezekiel (see figs. 8 and 9), is it an accident that four living creatures are emphasized in each and that in the second image, on the right, the recto, they are displayed surrounding a wheel? That the Alpha and particularly the Omega are emphasized, alluding to Rev 1:8, suggests a possible reference to that text, in which the four living creatures repeatedly appear. The large text CRUX ALMA FULGIT, "the cross shines, glitters, sparkles," does not derive from the opening vision of Ezekiel, which uses *splendor* instead. *Fulgere* in various forms occurs in many other texts, often associated with the sun (for example, Esth 15:5 and

---

37. For the Latin text, see *Gregorius Magnus, Homeliae in Hiezechielem prophetam*, ed. Marcus Adriaen, CCSL 142 (Turnhout: Brepols, 1971), 17–31.

38. Florence, Biblioteca Mediceaa-Laurenziana, MS Plut. I. 56, fol. 14r; see the facsimile publication Carlo Cecchelli, Giuseppe Furlani, and Mario Salmi, *The Rabbula Gospels* (Olten: Graf, 1959); Lowden, "Beginnings of Biblical Illustration," 26–30 and fig. 9; Michelle P. Brown, *In the Beginning: Bibles before the Year 1000* (Washington, DC: Smithsonian Institution, 2006), no. 62.

39. Autun, Bibliothèque municipale, cod. 3, fol. 12v; see Lawrence Nees, *The Gundohinus Gospels*, Medieval Academy of America Books 95 (Cambridge, MA: Medieval Academy of America, 1987), 177–85, pls. 18 and 19. Note that the identification of the text as a lost work of Jerome suggested by Paul Meyvaert, which I followed, is probably not correct; see Yves-Marie Duval, "Le 'Liber Hieronymi ad Gaudentium': Rufin d'Aquilée, Gaudence de Brescia et Eusèbe de Crémone," *RBén* 97 (1987): 163–86.

Job 31:26); a particularly interesting one in this context is Matt 13:43, a long series of parables, beginning with the sower of seeds, for the disciples do not understand the meaning of the parable, and Jesus explains that the reference is to the end of the world, when some will burn with fire but the just will "shine"—*fulgeret*—like the sun in the kingdom of God. Words need interpretation; parables hide meaning.

Is this all coincidence? Perhaps, but one should look at the text contained in this Saint Petersburg manuscript more closely. Gregory's commentary on Ezekiel opens with a discussion of the three "tenses" of prophecy, past, present, and future. Everything starts with grammar, in a sense, its central place in late Roman Christianity.[40] Gregory quotes Paul (1 Cor 14:25) that prophecy can reveal "secrets of the heart" in the present, continuing: "Thus prophecy is present when something is concealed, not by the spirit, but by the absent word, which however is laid bare by the spirit."[41] This is a less strikingly strange analogue of (or inspiration for?) Vergilius Maro Grammaticus's declaration that "utterances are scrambled … to conceal mystical matters which ought only to be revealed to those able to understand them [*Epit.* X, 1–13]."[42] Gregory's commentary was probably composed during the 590s, just after the foundation of Luxeuil, and probably only a few decades before Vergilius Maro Grammaticus was writing. It is not so strange that these writers' clear expectations for the kind of detailed multilevel intertextual reading in the monastery should be reflected in the decorative embellishment of illuminated manuscripts such as this one.

The text of the fifth homily of book 1 ends on folio 48v (see fig. 3), followed by the *explicit* for that text in large, colored capital letters, alternating colors, and the incipit for the sixth homily in even larger but uncolored capitals. The decorated quire mark at the bottom of the page is remarkably enlarged, and this would be the subject for the connection with the earli-

---

40. Chin, *Grammar and Christianity*.

41. Translation of this work follows *Homilies on the Book of the Prophet Ezekiel by Saint Gregory the Great*, trans. Theodosia Tomkinson, 2nd ed. (Etna, CA: Center for Traditionalist Orthodox Studies, 2008), 28, a translation based on the text in PL 76, cols. 785A–1072C. For the Latin text, see the newer edition *Gregorius Magnus, Homeliae in Hiezechielem prophetam*, ed. Marcus Adriaen, CCSL 142 (Turnhout: Brepols, 1971).

42. Löfstedt, *Virgilius Maro Grammaticus*, 213–25.

est Qur'an manuscripts that I had intended to present here.[43] The facing page (see fig. 5) has the beginning of Homily 6 in a large frame, yet another variant on the arch or arches or gables on columns that I showed earlier, as you may recall. This one is especially odd because the gable floats in the air above the columns, which end in curved points that do not quite touch the superstructure. The gable turns in on itself, making two near circles, and the floating superstructure encapsulates the opening word of the homily, *TENEBROSA*, written in large, colored capital letters. This is a quotation from Ps 17:12, "dark waters in the clouds" (Douay-Rheims), which immediately follows the verse that he "ascended the cherubim, and he flew; he flew upon the wings of the winds" (Douay-Rheims), a Psalms passage that anticipates the subject of this homily, which turns to the vision of the living creatures and the wheel in Ezekiel. Gregory expounds the passage as signifying the darkness of knowledge hidden in prophecies, in what he terms the darkness of allegories. He continues, "The very obscurity of divine speech is of great benefit, because it drills perception to extend itself in weariness, and so exercises it to capture what it could not seize if idle. And it has something still greater because the understanding of Holy Writ, which would become worthless if it were open to all, when found in certain obscure places refreshes with the greater sweetness, the more the search for it wearies the soul" (Gregory the Great, *Hom. Ezek.* 95).

Gregory next takes up the meaning of the wheel, and this certainly might recall to the attentive reader of the text in this manuscript the large round structure at the core of one of the frontispiece miniatures (see fig. 9). The complexity of thought, weaving together quotations from Scripture, is ruminative, as it were, the product of Gregory's meditation about the text and its manifold possible significance going far beyond the written word. Gregory's commentary is vastly longer than the text itself and effectively models the kind of intense contemplative reading that he envisaged for his fellow monks. Few books will be available to the presumptive monastic reader, but Gregory assumes that those books, those manuscripts, will be studied with the greatest intensity. The Rule of Saint Benedict had stipulated a century earlier that each monk should receive a book at the beginning of Lent and should "read it through in its entirety" during the course of the year, with senior brothers circulating during the hours set aside for reading to "see to it that there is no slothful brother who spends

---

43. See n. 18 above.

his time in idleness or gossip and neglects his reading."[44] I would submit that we should consider that the decoration of the opening for this homily (see fig. 5) evokes wheels and the notion of floating in the air on wings, and could serve very effectively as a reader's guide to find this particular passage within the manuscript, since no other homily has this floating effect, or the wheel, or a quire mark that almost looks like a wheel on the facing verso (see fig. 3), with the cross its spokes. The decoration does not illustrate the prophecy directly, certainly not with figures, but evokes or represents it allegorically, as it were, through another mode.[45] The decoration then can not only articulate but also enrich the reader's concentrated attention to the manuscript, so as to reveal its many secrets.

Bibliography

Benedict. *The Rule of Saint Benedict*. Edited and translated by Bruce L. Venarde. Dumbarton Oaks Medieval Library 6. Cambridge: Harvard University Press, 2011.

Brown, Michelle P. *In the Beginning: Bibles before the Year 1000*. Washington, DC: Smithsonian Institution, 2006.

———. *The Lindisfarne Gospels: Society, Spirituality and the Scribe*. London: British Library, 2003.

Carruthers, Mary J. *The Book of Memory: A Study of Memory in Medieval Culture*. Cambridge: Cambridge University Press, 1990.

———. *The Craft of Thought: Meditation, Rhetoric and the Making of Images 400-1200*. Cambridge: Cambridge University Press, 1998.

Carruthers, Mary, and Jan M. Ziolkowski, eds. *The Medieval Craft of Memory: An Anthology of Texts and Pictures*. Philadelphia: University of Pennsylvania Press, 2002.

---

44. Benedict, *The Rule of Saint Benedict*, ed. and trans. Bruce L. Venarde, Dumbarton Oaks Medieval Library 6 (Cambridge: Harvard University Press, 2011), 162-63. The *Regula Monachorum* of Columbanus does not mention reading individually. One could infer from the important production of books in his foundations either that his followers in the seventh century changed or that we should not infer absence of private reading because of Columbanus's silence concerning the subject. On discussions of monastic writing in various rules see Parkes, *Their Hands before Our Eyes*, 6-8.

45. For a more general and extended discussion of the iconography of this and other manuscripts from Luxeuil see Tewes, *Handschriften*, esp. 85-90, on the frames of the Saint Petersburg manuscript, and 125-32, on the iconography of initials, this example not having been discussed.

Cavallo, Guglielmo. "Between *Volumen* and Codex: Reading in the Roman World." Pages 64–89 in *A History of Reading in the West*. Edited by Guglielmo Cavallo and Roger Chartier. Translated by Lydia G. Cochrane. Boston: University of Massachusetts Press, 1999.
Cecchelli, Carlo, Giuseppe Furlani, and Mario Salmi. *The Rabbula Gospels*. Olten: Graf, 1959.
Chin, Catherine M. *Grammar and Christianity in the Late Roman World*. Philadelphia: University of Pennsylvania Press, 2008.
Columbanus. *Sancti Columbani Opera*. Edited by G. S. M. Walker. Scriptores Latini Hiberniae 2. Dublin: Dublin Institute for Advanced Studies, 1957.
Connerton, Paul. *How Societies Remember*. Cambridge: Cambridge University Press, 1989.
Cróinín, Dáibhí Ó. "The Date, Provenance, and Earliest Use of Virgilius Maro Grammaticus." Pages 13–22 in *Tradition und Wertung: Festschrift für Franz Brunhölzl zum 65. Geburtstag*. Edited by Günter Bernt, Fidel Rädle, and Gabriel Silagi. Sigmaringen: Thorbecke, 1989.
Crystal, David. *Making a Point: The Persnickety Story of English Punctuation*. New York: St. Martin's, 2015.
Duval, Yves-Marie. "Le 'Liber Hieronymi ad Gaudentium': Rufin d'Aquilée, Gaudence de Brescia et Eusèbe de Crémone." *RBén* 97 (1987): 163–86.
Gamble, Harry Y. *Book and Readers in the Early Church: A History of Early Christian Texts*. New Haven: Yale University Press, 1995.
Ganz, David. "'In the Nets or on the Line': A Datable Merovingian Manuscript and Its Importance." Pages 39–46 in *Listen, O Isles, unto Me: Studies in Medieval Word and Image in Honour of Jennifer O'Reilly*. Edited by Elizabeth Mullins and Diarmuid Scully. Cork: Cork University Press, 2011.
———. "Texts and Scripts in Surviving Manuscripts in the Script of Luxeuil." Pages 186–204 in *Ireland and Europe in the Early Middle Ages: Texts and Transmission / Irland und Europa im früheren Mittelalter: Texte und Überlieferung*. Edited by Próinséas Ní Chatháin and Michael Richter. Dublin: Four Courts Press, 2002.
Glei, Reinhold F. Review of *Opera omnia*, by Virgilius Maro Grammaticus, edited by Bengt Löfstedt. *Perit* 19 (2005): 350–59.
Gregory the Great. *Gregorius Magnus, Homeliae in Hiezechielem prophetam*. Edited by Marcus Adriaen. CCSL 142. Turnhout: Brepols, 1971.

———. *Homilies on the Book of the Prophet Ezekiel by Saint Gregory the Great*. Translated by Theodosia Tomkinson. 2nd ed. Etna, CA: Center for Traditionalist Orthodox Studies, 2008.

Hamburger, Jeffrey F. *Script as Image*. Leuven: Peeters, 2014.

Herren, Michael. "Virgil the Grammarian: A Spanish Jew in Ireland?" *Perit* 9 (1995): 51–71.

Hodges, Richard, and David Whitehouse. *Mohammed, Charlemagne and the Origins of Europe: Archaeology and the Pirenne Thesis*. Ithaca, NY: Cornell University Press, 1983.

Howlett, David R. *The Celtic Latin Tradition of Biblical Style*. Dublin: Four Courts Press, 1995.

Jeffery, Peter. "Monastic Reading and the Emerging Roman Chant Repertory." Pages 45–103 in *Western Plainchant in the First Millennium*. Edited by S. Gallagher, J. Haar, J. Nádas, and T. Striplin. Aldershot, UK: Ashgate, 2003.

Krawiec, Rebecca. "'The Holy Habit and the Teachings of the Elders': Clothing and Social Memory in Late Antique Monasticism." Pages 55–72 in *Dressing Judeans and Christians in Antiquity*. Edited by Kristi Upson-Saia, Carly Daniel-Hughes, and Alicia J. Batten. Farnham, UK: Ashgate, 2014.

"Latin 11461." Archives et manuscrits. https://tinyurl.com/SBL4213e.

Law, Vivien. *Grammar and Grammarians in the Early Middle Ages*. New York: Longman, 1997.

Leclercq, Jean. *The Love of Learning and the Desire for God: A Study of Monastic Culture*. Translated by Catharine Misrahi. New York: Fordham University Press, 1961.

Lehmann, Paul. *Die Parödie im Mittelalter*. Stuttgart, 1963.

Leproni, Ferruccio. *Il Liber Regulae Pastoralis di Gregorio I nel codice Merovingio d'Ivrea*. Turin: Arti Grafiche, 1993.

Lowden, John. "The Beginnings of Biblical Illustration." Pages 9–59 in *Imaging the Early Medieval Bible*. Edited by John Williams. University Park: Pennsylvania State University Press, 1999.

Martin, Henri-Jean. *The History and Power of Writing*. Translated by Lydia G. Cochrane. Chicago: University of Chicago Press, 1994.

McCormick, Michael. *Origins of the European Economy: Communications and Commerce, A.D. 300–900*. Cambridge: Cambridge University Press, 2001.

McKitterick, Rosamond. "The Scriptoria of Merovingian Gaul: A Survey of the Evidence." Pages 173–207 in *Columbanus and Merovingian*

Monasticism. Edited by H. B. Clarke and Mary Brennan. BARIS 113. Oxford: B.A.R, 1981.

Most, Glenn W. "Memory and Forgetting in the *Aeneid*." *Vergilius* 47 (2001): 148–70.

Nees, Lawrence. "Graphic Quire Marks and Qur'ānic Verse Markers in the Seventh and Eighth Century." Pages 80–99 in *Visualcy, Literacy, Graphicacy: Graphic Devices and the Early Decorated Book*. Edited by Michelle Brown, Ildar Garipzanov, and Benjamin Tilghman. Woodbridge: Boydell & Brewer, 2017.

———. *The Gundohinus Gospels*. Medieval Academy of America Books 95. Cambridge, MA: Medieval Academy of America, 1987.

———. "Reading Aldred's Colophon for the Lindisfarne Gospels." *Spec* 78 (2003): 333–77.

———. "Ultán the Scribe." *ASE* 22 (1993): 127–46.

Newton, Francis L., Francis L. Newton Jr., and Christopher R. J. Scheirer. "Domiciling the Evangelists in Anglo-Saxon England: A Fresh Reading of Aldred's Colophon in the 'Lindisfarne Gospels.'" *ASE* 41 (2012): 101–44.

Nordenfalk, Carl. *Die spätantiken Zierbuchstaben*. Die Bücherornamentik der Spätanike 2. Stockholm: Egnellska boktr., 1970.

Parkes, Malcolm. *Pause and Effect: An Introduction to the History of Punctuation in the West*. Berkeley: University of California Press, 1993.

———. "Reading, Copying and Interpreting a Text in the Early Middle Ages." Pages 90–102 in *A History of Reading in the West*. Edited by Guglielmo Cavallo and Roger Chartier. Translated by Lydia G. Cochrane. Boston: University of Massachusetts Press, 1999.

———. *Their Hands before Our Eyes: A Closer Look at Scribes*. Burlington, VT: Ashgate, 2008.

Pertz, Karl August Friedrich. *Diplomata regum Francorum e stiirpe Merowingica*. Edited by Georg Heinrich Pertz. MGH Diplomatum Imperii 1. Hannover: Hahn, 1872.

Pirenne, Henri. *Mahomet et Charlemagne*. Paris: Alcan; Brussels: Nouvelle Société d'éditions, 1937

———. *Mohammed and Charlemagne*. Translated by Bernard Miall. New York: Barnes & Noble, 1939.

Saenger, Paul. *Space between Words: The Origins of Silent Reading*. Stanford, CA: Stanford University Press, 1997.

Svenbro, Jesper. "Archaic and Classical Greece: The Invention of Silent Reading." Pages 37–63 in *A History of Reading in the West*. Edited by Guglielmo Cavallo and Roger Chartier. Translated by Lydia G. Cochrane. Boston: University of Massachusetts Press, 1999.

Tewes, Babette. *Die Handschriften der Schule von Luxeuil: Kunst und Ikonographie eines frühmittelalterlichen Skriptoriums*. Wolfenbütteler Mittelalter-Studien. Wiesbaden: Harrassowitz, 2011.

Virgilius Maro Grammaticus. *Opera omnia*. Edited by Bengt Löfstedt. Munich: Saur [Bibliotheca Teubneriana], 2003.

———. *P. Vergili Maronis Opera*. Edited by R. A. B. Mynors. Scriptorum classicorum Bibliotheca Oxoniensis. Oxford: Clarendon, 1969.

———. *Virgilio Marone grammatico, Epitomi ed Epistole*. Edited by Giovanni Polara. Naples: Liguori, 1979.

Weitzmann, Kurt. *Ancient Book Illumination*. Martin Classical Lectures 16. Cambridge: Harvard University Press, 1959.

———. "Book Illustration in the Fourth Century: Tradition and Innovation." Pages 257–81 in *Akten des VII: Internationalen Kongresses für Christliche Archäologie, Trier 5–11 September, 1965*. Studi di Antichità Cristiana 27. Rome: Pontificio istituto di archeologia cristiana, 1969.

———. *Illustrations in Roll and Codex: A Study of the Origin and Method of Text Illustration*. Studies in Manuscript Illumination 2. Princeton: Princeton University Press, 1947.

Part 2
Literary Cultures

Books and Private Readers in Early Christian Oxyrhynchus: "A Spiritual Meadow and a Garden of Delight"

AnneMarie Luijendijk

Harry Gamble's *Books and Readers in the Early Church* ushered in an exciting material turn in scholarship on early Christianity and late antiquity, effecting a change of focus from the study of textual variants—important as that is—to manuscripts as "social artifacts."[1] In this paper, I delve deeper into this aspect of social artifacts. I am particularly interested in exploring how the ownership of the Christian texts found at the ancient Egyptian city of Oxyrhynchus can help us to understand better the reception of early Christian literature in a transitional period, from the mid-third to the fourth century. I have identified four cases among the Christian Oxyrhynchus papyri where the individuals who owned and read these texts can be identified (or at least their collection of books), and I conclude that these are evidence for the private possession and study of Christian texts. This conclusion has implications for understanding the

---

My warm thanks go to Karl Shuve and Martien Halvorson-Taylor and the University of Virginia's Religious Studies Department for organizing and sponsoring the conference that allowed me to work on this topic. Brent Nongbri has been a wonderful conversation partner in this topic all along. I am grateful to Jonathan Henry for his help as research assistant. I presented different parts of this paper at the Society of Biblical Literature meeting in San Diego, 2014, in an invited panel on "The Transmission and Reception of Hebrews: Perspectives from Early Manuscripts," at Macquarie University, November 2014, and at the Princeton Society of Fellows, December 2015. I thank the audiences for their questions and feedback.

1. On manuscripts as "social artifact," see Harry Y. Gamble, *Books and Readers in the Early Church: A History of Early Christian Texts* (New Haven: Yale University Press, 1995), 43: "The physical object is also a social artifact.... All aspects of the production, distribution, and use of texts presuppose social functions and forces."

sociology of reading among Christians and also the demise of these texts. I examine here the Oxyrhynchite evidence in light of other clues of reading practices in the early church.

My study of Oxyrhynchite materials builds on and complements Gamble's findings. I admire his ability both to be broad and still to pay attention to detail, although he deliberately refrained from doing a case study.[2] It is precisely this that I will provide in the present essay, zooming in to focus on the individuals who lived in late antique Oxyrhynchus in middle Egypt. This close-up look provides rare glimpses of book collectors and readers within a larger local context. So let me begin by putting Oxyrhynchus on the map.

Oxyrhynchus

Located on a branch of the Nile, some 400 kilometers south of Alexandria, Oxyrhynchus was strategically located on the north-south and east-west trade routes. The city was the capital of the like-named *nome* (or province) and a major Egyptian provincial city with twenty thousand or more inhabitants.[3] Nowadays, Oxyrhynchus is undoubtedly the best-known finding place of classical Greek and early Christian papyri. Well over three thousand fragments of literary works from this site have been published.[4]

Over the course of the third and fourth centuries, Oxyrhynchus turned into an ever more Christian city, in which a large number of texts were composed and copied.[5] So far well over two hundred Christian literary texts

---

2. He states: "It would be far easier to consider Christian literacy and literary culture only in a particular location, at an isolable stage of its development, or in terms of a few Christian writers, but to do so would not yield a sense of the relation of Christianity to the larger societies of which it was a part" (Gamble, *Books and Readers*, 2).

3. See Andrea Jördens and AnneMarie Luijendijk, "Oxyrhynchos," in *Reallexikon für Antike und Christentum: Sachwörterbuch zur Auseinandersetzung des Christentums mit der antiken Welt*, ed. Georg Schöllgen et al. (Stuttgart: Anton Hiersemann, 2014), 685–98.

4. The Leuven Database of Ancient Books (LDAB) lists 3,547 literary manuscripts for Oxyrhynchus (20 March 2018).

5. A collection of all papyri and literary texts relating to Christians at Oxyrhynchus until the year 400 can be found in Lincoln H. Blumell and Thomas A. Wayment, *Christian Oxyrhynchus: Texts, Documents, and Sources* (Waco, TX: Baylor University Press, 2015). For discussions on Christian Oxyrhynchus, see AnneMarie Luijendijk, *Greetings in the Lord: Early Christians and the Oxyrhynchus Papyri* (Cambridge: Har-

have been published. These comprise copies of Septuagint (Old Testament) texts and numerous fragments of writings that later became part of the New Testament, some of them copied quite early. The Gospels of Matthew and John are the best represented. One fragment of the Johannine Gospel once belonged to a deluxe codex (P.Oxy. 15.1780/P^{39}).[6] There are also three fragments of the Gospel of Thomas in Greek from different manuscripts dating to the mid- to late third century (P.Oxy. 1.1, P.Oxy. 4.654 and 4.655); fragments of the Gospel of Mary, Gospel of Peter, and of the Shepherd of Hermas,[7] and many other writings we now call apocryphal. Noteworthy are also an autograph manuscript with a Christian-Jewish dialogue (P.Oxy. 17.2070) and a drawing of Jesus and the apostles from perhaps the sixth century (PSI 8.920v). Furthermore, there are multiple unidentified fragments. These texts together make Oxyrhynchus one of our prime sources for understanding the diversity of earliest Christian literature, including those literary texts that were controversial and eventually did not make it into the Christian Bible of antiquity.

In addition to this corpus of over two hundred Christian literary and subliterary papyri, I work with documentary texts, such as receipts and

---

vard University Press, 2008), and Lincoln H. Blumell, *Lettered Christians: Christians, Letters, and Late Ancient Oxyrhynchus* (Leiden: Brill, 2012).

6. In comparing the remains of the classical library and contemporary New Testament manuscripts from Oxyrhynchus, Barker mentions P.Oxy. 15.1780 as "an exception, both in letter height (c. 5 mm) and the calligraphic nature of the lettering. The Library owner would have considered this book as an expensive deluxe copy. Both the size and the calligraphic nature of the hand suggest that this codex may have been used in a public reading context." See Don C. Barker, "Codex, Roll, and Libraries in Oxyrhynchus," *TynBul* 57 (2006): 139. On this codex, see also Blumell and Wayment, *Christian Oxyrhynchus*, 57–60.

7. See Larry Hurtado, "The Greek Fragments of the Gospel of Thomas as Artefacts: Papyrological Observations on Papyrus Oxyrhynchus 1, Papyrus Oxyrhynchus 654 and Papyrus Oxyrhynchus 655," in *Das Thomasevangelium: Entstehung—Rezeption—Theologie*, ed. Jörg Frey, Enno Edzard Popkes, and Jens Schröter (Berlin: de Gruyter, 2008), 19–32; and AnneMarie Luijendijk, "Reading the Gospel of Thomas in the Third Century: Three Oxyrhynchus Papyri and Origen's Homilies," in *Reading New Testament Papyri in Context/ Lire des papyrus du Nouveau Testament dans leur context*, ed. Claire Clivaz and Jean Zumstein (Leuven: Peeters, 2011), 242. On the large number of Hermas manuscripts from Egypt, see Malcolm Choat and Rachel Yuen-Collingridge, "The Egyptian Hermas: The Shepherd in Egypt before Constantine," in *Early Christian Manuscripts: Examples of Applied Method and Approach*, ed. Thomas J. Kraus and Tobias Nicklas (Leiden: Brill, 2010), 191–212.

private letters. These are more difficult to count. Overall, the literary fragments account for just a fraction, perhaps only 10 percent, of the total find; the bulk consists of documents, of which almost six thousand have been published.[8] These documents make Oxyrhynchus come alive as a city bustling with businesses, temples, and a wide range of human endeavors, insofar as they involve writing. Many of these concern ancient bureaucracy: census declarations, documentation for tax collection, petitions, marriage contracts, divorce papers, and death announcements. Another part consists of private documents, such as letters or party invitations. Individually and as a corpus, these everyday documents are significant for all kinds of historical research: for instance, demography, economy, social and legal history, and in this case religious history.

With so many and such diverse Christian literary papyri from its site, what was Christianity like at Oxyrhynchus? What do these papyri tell us about the theology, beliefs, and religious practices of the Oxyrhynchites? In my book *Greetings in the Lord*, I began to answer these questions using the documentary papyri. Based on Gamble's research in his *Books and Readers*, my specific questions for this paper are: Who owned and read the Christian literary papyri from Oxyrhynchus? To whom did these manuscripts belong? Were they kept in a church library, or did they form part of a library in a family's house? And how do they relate to the larger find of manuscripts at Oxyrhynchus?

Asking questions of ownership is especially important because with their known provenance the Christian Oxyrhynchus papyri (especially the New Testament ones) have become the gold standard of Christian texts.[9] Taken together, the copies of the Gospel of Matthew, Revelation, Hermas,

---

8. The Heidelberger Gesamtverzeichnis der griechischen Papyrusurkunden Ägyptens (HGV) lists 5,886 Greek documents from Oxyrhynchus (20 March 2018).

9. See especially the work of Eldon J. Epp in this regard: "The New Testament Papyri at Oxyrhynchus in Their Social and Intellectual Context," in Epp, *Perspectives on New Testament Textual Criticism: Collected Essays, 1962–2004*, NovTSup 116 (Leiden: Brill, 1997), 47–68; "The Oxyrhynchus New Testament Papyri: 'Not without Honor Except in Their Hometown'?," *JBL* 123 (2004): 5–55; "The Codex and Literacy in Early Christianity and at Oxyrhynchus: Issues Raised by Harry Y. Gamble's *Books and Readers in the Early Church*," *CRBR* 10 (1997): 15–37; "The New Testament Papyri at Oxyrhynchus: Their Significance for Understanding the Transmission of the Early New Testament Text," in *Oxyrhynchus: A City and Its Texts*, ed. Alan K. Bowman, Revel A. Coles, Nikolaos Gonis, Dirk Obbink, and Peter J. Parsons (London: Egypt Exploration Society, 2007), 315–31.

and the Gospel of Thomas witness to the availability of a wide range of Christian literature and the vibrant literary culture in one city. But I want to obtain a more fine-grained picture. Given that Oxyrhynchus was a large city, not all Christian manuscripts found there can be taken together as having belonged to one person or church. My argument in this paper is that the Christian papyri from Oxyrhynchus indicate private ownership and reading of Christian literature.

The Owners of the Papyri from Oxyrhynchus

In order to understand the ownership of the Oxyrhynchus papyri (and other papyri, for that matter), we need to do away with the distinction between literary and documentary papyri, that is, between theological and classical, semiliterary and documentary texts, as Belgian papyrologist Willy Clarysse argues in his article "Literary Papyri in Documentary Archives."[10] No matter how practical for modern publication, on the ground the distinction between literary and documentary papyri is misleading, for it gives the false impression that these texts were separate entities in antiquity. This was, of course, not the case. All indications are to the contrary: literature and documents were preserved together. The people—as well as the institutions (such as churches) to whom they belonged—who possessed literary manuscripts and were sufficiently educated to read them were by and large the same people who kept records about other possessions.

Despite the large size of the find, there is not a whole lot of information from Oxyrhynchus to help answer the question of ownership of the literary papyri. What we do know for sure is that the Oxyrhynchite texts were already discarded in antiquity and not preserved in jars, as the Nag Hammadi or Dead Sea Scrolls codices were.[11] This, of course, seriously limits our ability to find evidence about ownership. Moreover, given the

---

10. Willy Clarysse, "Literary Papyri in Documentary Archives," in *Egypt and the Hellenistic World: Proceedings of the International Colloquium, Leuven 24–26 May 1982*, ed. E. Van't Dack , P. Van Dessel, and W. Van Gucht (Leuven: Orientaliste, 1983), 43–61.

11. AnneMarie Luijendijk, "Sacred Scriptures as Trash: Biblical Papyri from Oxyrhynchus," *VC* 64 (2010): 217–54. On Oxyrhynchus and the provenance of other collections of Christian books, see Brent Nongbri, *God's Library: The Archaeology of the Earliest Christian Manuscripts* (New Haven: Yale University Press, 2018).

excavation techniques at the end of the nineteenth and beginning of the twentieth century, we lack detailed archaeological information for Oxyrhynchus. But although the first excavators, Bernard Grenfell and Arthur Hunt, did not conduct a systematic stratigraphy, occasionally they did note which texts were found together. These instances turn out to be highly important for identifying owners.[12]

In his book *Inside Roman Libraries: Book Collections and Their Management in Antiquity*, classical scholar George Houston discusses five collections of texts from Oxyrhynchus. These (remnants of) libraries could be reconstructed on the basis of archaeological data provided by early excavators.[13] The largest collection comprised sixty-eight rolls, copied by many different professional scribes.[14] Its owner was, in all likelihood, Sarapion alias Apollonianus, *strategos* in the Arsinoite and Hermopolite nomes in the early third century, based on the documents found among the remains of the library.[15] Of particular interest for my research is also a collection with a high percentage of reused rolls, and the library of Aurelia Ptolemais, a woman whom we will meet below.

Yet given the circumstances of the find, it is in most instances impossible to know who owned the papyri found at the Oxyrhynchite trash heaps. For the vast majority of literary papyri from Oxyrhynchus, whether classical or Christian, the actual owners and readers elude us.[16] In four instances, however, owners of Christian literature from Oxyrhynchus can

---

12. For a thorough discussion of the archaeology of Christian books in Egypt in general and also at Oxyrhynchus, see Nongbri, *God's Library*.

13. George W. Houston, *Inside Roman Libraries: Book Collections and Their Management in Antiquity* (Chapel Hill: University of North Carolina Press, 2014), 130–79; George W. Houston, "Papyrological Evidence for Book Collections and Libraries in the Roman Empire," in *Ancient Literacies: The Culture of Reading in Greece and Rome*, ed. William A. Johnson and Holt N. Parker (Oxford: Oxford University Press, 2009) 233–67; and Peter J. Parsons, *City of the Sharp-Nosed Fish: Greek Lives in Roman Egypt* (London: Weidenfeld & Nicolson, 2007), 150–53. Barker published a case study on one of the libraries found in the 1905–1906 season, comparing its contents against Christian manuscripts ("Codex, Roll, and Libraries in Oxyrhynchus"). What is at stake for Barker in this exercise is the Christian adoption of the canon as preferred book format.

14. Houston calls this collection "Breccia + GH3," after the excavators who found it (*Inside Roman Libraries* 4.4, esp. 144).

15. Houston, *Inside Roman Libraries*, 145–46.

16. Roger S. Bagnall, "The Readers of Christian Books: Further Speculations," in *I papiri letterari cristiani: Atti del Convegno internazionale di studi in memoria di*

be identified, albeit with different degrees of detail. It is to these that I now turn.

Leonides

I begin with a man called Leonides, because he was the owner of a Christian papyrus from Oxyrhynchus about whom we possess the most information. Among his papers was a papyrus with the beginning of the Epistle to the Romans (P.Oxy. 2.209 = P^{10}), probably copied as a school exercise or devotional act.[17] Of all 134 New Testament papyri published to date, whether from Oxyrhynchus or elsewhere, only in this one case do we know its owner by name. This is thanks to a short sentence that Grenfell and Hunt noted in their edition of this papyrus: they mention that it was found tied up with a contract dated to the year 316 and other papyri.[18] From his papers, we learn that Leonides, son of Theon, was a flax merchant who belonged to the flax guild and lived in the first half of the fourth century. He was literate and occupied a leadership position in the guild. Of special importance for the present discussion is that this copy of the Epistle to the Romans was a school exercise and that it was tied up with private business documents. The Christian papyrus was not stored in a church building and thus constitutes evidence for the study of the Epistle of the Romans in a private household, using the Pauline letter even as writing exercise.[19] The second example introduces two anonymous Christian book owners.

"My Dearest Lady Sister in the Lord" and Correspondent

This case consists of a reference in a private letter to two books, Ezra and Jubilees, that are now considered apocryphal (P. Oxy. 63.4365). This

---

Mario Naldini, Firenze, 10–11 giugno 2010, ed. Guido Bastianini and Angelo Casanova (Firenze: Istituto papirologico G. Vitelli, 2011), 23–30.

17. On this papyrus and its context, see AnneMarie Luijendijk, "A New Testament Papyrus and Its Documentary Context: An Early Christian Writing Exercise from the Archive of Leonides," *JBL* 129 (2010): 575–96.

18. See Grenfell and Hunt, P.Oxy. 2.209, 8.

19. For an intriguing connection between Leonides and Ammonius, son of Copres, who was a reader in the former church of the village of Chysis, see Luijendijk, "New Testament Papyrus and Its Documentary Context," 587–88.

documentary papyrus gives glimpses into bookish practices and private reading and ownership. Since it is such a short letter, I quote it in full: "To my dearest lady sister in the Lord, greetings. Lend the Ezra, since I lent you the Little Genesis. Farewell from us in God" (τῇ κυρίᾳ μου φιλτάτῃ ἀδελφῇ ἐν κ[υρί]ῳ χαίρειν. χρῆσον τὸν Ἐσδραν, ἐπεὶ ἔχρησά σοι τὴν λεπτὴν Γένεσιν. ἔρρωσο ἡμεῖν ἐν θ[ε]ῷ). This second instance of ownership brings at least one woman to the fore, who remains anonymous.[20] This piece has fascinated many scholars already (and rightly so).[21] For our quest, the address to the sole woman and issue of the lending suggests that these books are privately owned.[22]

The letter is written on the *verso* of a petition from the second half of the third century; this forms the date post quem.[23] According to the phraseology of the address, the reuse must have taken place in the fourth century.[24] The letter presumes previous contact about the lending, since

---

20. Her correspondent also remains anonymous, and scholars debate whether the person was a man or woman. The editor of the papyrus, John Rea, suggests that the handwriting of the letter matches that of the subscription of the document on the recto of the papyrus (P.Oxy. 68.4364), by a woman called Aurelia Soteira, alias Hesychium (P.Oxy. 68.4365, 44). So also Epp, "Oxyrhynchus New Testament Papyri," 28–29; Jean-Luc Fournet, "Femmes et Culture dans l'Égypte Byzantine (Ve–VIIe S.)," in *Les réseaux familiaux: Antiquité tardive et Moyen-Âge; In memoriam A. Laiou et É. Patlagean*, ed. Béatrice Caseau, Centre de Recherche d'Histoire et Civilisation de Byzance—Monographie 37 (Paris: Association des amis du Centre d'histoire et civilisation de Byzance, 2012), 135–45. Epp ("Oxyrhynchus New Testament Papyri," 31–35) considered possible implications of two female correspondents, imagining them to be two female leaders in the Oxyrhynchite church. Blumell (*Lettered Christians*, 262–63 and n. 114) suggests that women more frequently correspond among themselves. My position is that it remains unknown whether her correspondent is female or male (see also Luijendijk, *Greetings in the Lord*, 73 n. 56). There is quite a lot of evidence for exchange of books between men and women; see below.

21. For a list of the scholarship on this papyrus, see Blumell and Wayment, *Christian Oxyrhynchus*, 509–12 (nr. 141). See also Erica Mathieson, *Christian Women in the Greek Papyri of Egypt to 400 CE* (Turnhout: Brepols, 2017), 219–20.

22. At the end of this brief text, the address changes from the singular ("*I lent you*" into the plural: "farewell *from us* in God"). Although this could be interpreted as part of an ecclesiastical context, with the first-person plural referring to a church community, a private context makes more sense, as the papyri preserve many exchanges of families greeting each other.

23. P.Oxy. 63.4365, note to line 7. The petition can be dated to the second half of the third century based on parallel documents that range in date from 241 to 298 CE.

24. Rea writes: "The date range raises the possibility that the letter on the back

the author knows that the addressee, the "dearest lady sister in the Lord," owns a copy of "Ezra."[25] Furthermore, the way the letter is worded presupposes that these correspondents had the choice of more than just one book. Otherwise, would they not have written: "Lend me your book, since I lent you mine"? The specificity of the book titles indicates that the nameless author of the letter could have selected another book from her or his reading partner's library.

For the diversity of early Christian reading practices, the choice of books is fascinating. These correspondents appear to be advanced students of Christian literature, having ventured into apocalyptic literature.[26] These are the kinds of writings that Athanasius did not approve of in his thirty-ninth Festal Epistle from the year 367, a document written probably only somewhat later than our small papyrus letter.[27] The fact that Egyptian Christians were interested in all sorts of Christian texts, of course, exactly prompted Athanasius to delineate what he considered appropriate readings.

Unlike in the other cases discussed in this paper, we do not have the actual manuscripts, just the mention of the books in the letter. So far, the book of Jubilees has not been discovered among the papyri from Oxyrhynchus or elsewhere; as a matter of fact, no Greek manuscripts of this text have been preserved at all as of yet. But among the fragments from Oxyrhynchus there is a small page of 6 Ezra from a miniature codex, measuring 8.4 × 5.6 cm, and dated by palaeography to the fourth century. In his 2016 contribution to the journal *Early Christianity*, Thomas

---

dates from before about 325" (P.Oxy. 63.4364, 43). The vocabulary in line 1 places the date in the fourth century. See Nick Gonis, "Notes on Two Epistolary Conventions," *ZPE* 119 (1997): 148–52. Gonis shows that "in no other private letter from the first three centuries of Roman rule in Egypt does φίλτατος qualify ἀδελφός" (150).

25. On the rather confusing situation of books called Ezra (the canonical Ezra-Nehemiah and 1–6 Ezra), see the table in Bruce M. Metzger, "The Fourth Book of Ezra: A New Translation and Introduction," *OTP* 1:517–60.

26. Epp ("Oxyrhynchus New Testament Papyri," 30) wonders: "Had the study of the 'New Testament' and related Christian books advanced so far in the Oxyrhynchus churches of the third and fourth centuries that some of their inquisitive members had moved beyond—or behind—them to related interests in the Jewish Scriptures?"

27. On this letter, see especially David Brakke, "Canon Formation and Social Conflict in Fourth-Century Egypt: Athanasius of Alexandria's Thirty-Ninth Festal Letter," *HTR* 87 (1994): 395–419; Brakke, "A New Fragment of Athanasius's Thirty-Ninth Festal Letter: Heresy, Apocrypha, and the Canon," *HTR* 103 (2010): 47–66.

Kraus notes about this page: "Obviously, this extra-canonical text meant so much to somebody that they wanted to own a (private) copy of it in this specific format; and the copy was written by a rather competent scribe who knew what to do."[28] Could this fragment be the remains of the very book that was exchanged? Eldon Epp considered such identification too speculative.[29] Indeed, this cannot be proven, but both the book format of miniature codex, as Gamble noticed, and the kind of handwriting would fit well in a private library.[30]

The lack of names in the address of the letter has puzzled scholars—as it is indeed rather uncommon. Epp explained this well, writing: "Obviously a quick communication between close acquaintances, doubtless delivered locally by a personally connected messenger, rendering names

---

28. Thomas J. Kraus, "Miniature Codices in Late Antiquity: Preliminary Remarks and Tendencies about a Specific Book Format," *Early Christianity* 152 (2016): 134–52. Kraus does not mention P.Oxy. 63.4365 in connection with this miniature codex of Ezra here. In his "Bücherleihe im 4. Jh. n. Chr. P. Oxy. LXIII 4365—ein Brief auf Papyrus und die gegenseitige Leihe von apokryph gewordener Literatur," *Biblios* 50 (2001): 285–96, Kraus mentions the codex but does not suggest the possibility of identification: "Wegen eines ebenso in Oxyrhynchos zu Tage geförderten Pergamentblattes eines Miniaturcodex aus dem 4. Jh. (P.Oxy. VII 1010) mit griechischem Rest von IV Esra und der Verwendung ebendieser Bezeichnung in einer Bücherliste aus dem siebten oder achten Jahrhundert (P.Lugd. Bat. XXV 13,36 …) mag der Schluß naheliegen, es handele sich in Z. 3 des Briefes um IV Ezra" (translated to English in his *Ad Fontes: Original Manuscripts and Their Significance for Studying Early Christianity: Selected Essays* [Leiden: Brill, 2007] as "The Lending of Books in the Fourth Century C.E.," 187).

29. Epp, "Oxyrhynchus New Testament Papyri," 29. "It so happens that a fourth-century miniature codex of *6 Ezra* … was found at Oxyrhynchus (P.Oxy. 1010), though *only the wildest speculation* would identify that with the 'Ezra' of our letter" (emphasis added). Blumell and Wayment (*Christian Oxyrhynchus*, 511 n. 3) agree with Epp.

30. Gamble (*Books and Readers*, 235) suggests that small format indicates private reading: "There is a special category of ancient manuscripts that consists of miniature codices, roughly analogous to modern pocket books, and clearly produced for private reading." He distinguishes "two striking features about these miniature codices. First, the large majority … contain Christian texts.… Second, the preponderance of Christian writings found in these small codices are apocryphal.… This underscores the popular nature of the apocryphal literature by showing its use for edifying private reading, and it also shows that official efforts to control what was read privately, whether by drawing up lists or formulating a general principle, were responses to the currency, especially in private hands, of apocryphal books" (236).

superfluous."[31] In this case, the anonymity of the woman is thus not because she was deemed unimportant and voiceless, the kind of anonymity women so often have in texts, but rather because this is a quick note, delivered by a familiar person who had received oral instructions. The fact that there is some formality (why otherwise write the note?) suggests that these are not very close acquaintances.

I propose that it was a household slave who delivered this short, unofficial note without official address, penned on a reused piece of papyrus.[32] Cicero (*Att.* 14.19.1) names a letter carrier called Barnaeus, who was either a slave or a *libertus*, a freedman.[33] In his research on named letter carriers in papyri published in the series The Oxyrhynchus Papyri, Peter Head found that only less than a quarter of the letters in this corpus contained information about the delivery and less than 10 percent mentioned the name of the letter carrier.[34] It seems to me that some of these unnamed deliverers were enslaved people. But in his lengthy study on papyrus letters that mention the sending of goods, Patrick Reinard disputes that enslaved people

---

31. Epp, "Oxyrhynchus New Testament Papyri," 28. The absence of names has, as Epp proposed already, nothing to do with secrecy but rather with the fact that this is "a very personal, local correspondence" (29). Epp (27–28) compares it to party invitations, delivered locally by a slave.

32. About slaves delivering letters, see, e.g., James Albert Harrill, *The Manumission of Slaves in Early Christianity* (Tübingen: Mohr Siebeck, 1995), 63. See also Gamble ("Letters in the New Testament and Greco-Roman World," 193): "The wealthy could enlist their slaves or employees as couriers (*tabellarii*) for their letter."

33. See also Patrick Reinard, *Kommunikation und Ökonomie: Untersuchungen zu den privaten Papyrusbriefen aus dem kaiserzeitlichen Ägypten*, Pharos Studien zur griechisch-römischen Antike 32 (Rahden: Leidorf, 2016), 480. In his epistles, Paul refers to Phoebe (Rom 16:1–2) and Epaphroditus (Phil 2:25–30); Ephesians and Colossians mention Tychicus (Eph 6:21–22; Col 4:7–9). It is not clear what status these had, and the difference with our letter is that the Pauline Epistles were transported over longer distances.

34. Peter M. Head, "Named Letter-Carriers among the Oxyrhynchus Papyri," *JSNT* 31 (2009): 283, writes, "Of the 450 letters published so far in that collection (not date limited), exactly 100 letters provided some relevant information about the delivery of the letter (often this is no more than an address on the back of the letter), and around 40 include reference to named letter carriers." Among these named letter carriers from Oxyrhynchus, Head mentions no slaves; they are presumably among the unnamed carriers. See also Reinard, *Kommunikation und Ökonomie*, 357, esp. 358–66.

were commissioned to deliver letters.³⁵ His arguments, however, pertain to deliveries of letters and goods over longer distances. It makes sense that for short, local communications, such as our letter, slaves functioned as letter carriers.³⁶ In the case of our small missive from Oxyrhynchus, the enslaved person presumably brought back the Ezra manuscript.³⁷

The possible presence of the slave (female or male), visible to us merely as a shadow, suggests an upper-class milieu for the correspondents. This does not surprise since reading was first and foremost an upper-class activity. But it also offers an opportunity to imagine this enslaved person in close proximity to the reading practices in the household. Since ancient reading was a social practice, done in a group and out loud, as William Johnson has shown,³⁸ it seems not unlikely that the slave who delivered the small note and brought back the manuscript was also present when the text was read. We also know from the sermons of preachers such as Chrysostom and Augustine that enslaved people were present in church.³⁹ This piece thereby contributes more broadly to our understanding of household reading practices and religion.

With the third book owner, we meet another woman, this time by name.⁴⁰

---

35. Reinard (*Kommunikation und Ökonomie*, 480) asks: "War das Überbringen von Briefen und Waren eine Tätigkeit, die häufig von Sklaven durchgeführt wurde? Diese Frage ist eindeutig zu verneinen." He argues that only rich people could have afforded slaves and would have been reluctant to send these on the road for fear of flight (481–82).

36. Also, for instance, for the many invitations to celebrations in the papyrological record. Epp ("Oxyrhynchus New Testament Papyri," 28) mentions a "servant or slave" as deliverer for these.

37. As Peter Head notes: "In many examples the primary role of the letter-carrier is as courier of the consignment of goods, the letter functioning as an interpretative supplement to the consignment of goods" ("Named Letter-Carriers among the Oxyrhynchus Papyri," 287).

38. William A. Johnson, "Toward a Sociology of Reading in Classical Antiquity," *AJP* 121 (2000): 593–627.

39. Ramsay MacMullen, "The Preacher's Audience (AD 350–500)," *JTS* (40 (1989): 505–7; Wendy Mayer, "Who Came to Hear John Chrysostom Preach? Recovering a Late Fourth-Century Preacher's Audience," *ETL* 76 (2000): 73–87. On enslaved persons as Christian leaders in a slightly earlier period, see Katherine A. Shaner, *Enslaved Leadership in Early Christianity* (Oxford: Oxford University Press, 2018) (I have not seen this book because it was not yet published when I wrote this piece).

40. Although the woman in our book exchange remains anonymous, we do know

Aurelia Ptolemais

The third known owner of a Christian book from Oxyrhynchus is called Aurelia Ptolemais. Based on another instance where Grenfell and Hunt jotted down succinct information about texts that had been found together, Roger Bagnall identified the owners of a library containing a possibly Christian book.[41] Bagnall builds a convincing case that Aurelia Ptolemais was the owner or heir of these literary papyri, among which is also a papyrus containing the *Kestoi* by the Christian author Julius Africanus (already reused). Even more so than in the archive of Leonides, this collection comprises both documentary and literary papyri. The remains of Aurelia Ptolemais's library consist of six texts written on five pieces of papyrus. In addition to the copy of the *Kestoi*, reused for her father, Hermogenes's, will, it contained a copy of the *History of Sicyon*, two reused papyri with different parts of Homer's *Iliad*, and a land lease.[42]

Ptolemais signed her name at the bottom of the land lease (P.Oxy. 16.1690: Αὐρηλία Πτολεμαῒς καὶ ὡς χρηματ[ίζω] ἔσχον τούτου τὸ ἴσον). Evidently, she was an upper-class and literate woman. Indeed, her father and grandfather both occupied leadership positions in public life, and their

---

other Christian women from Oxyrhynchus by name. A Christian amulet, for instance, citing the incipits of the four New Testament gospels among other scriptural quotations was worn by a woman called Joannia, daughter of Anastasia also known as Euphemia (P.Oxy. 8.1151).

41. Roger S. Bagnall, "An Owner of Literary Papyri," *CP* (1992): 137–40. Bagnall (137–38) writes: "In the description of *POxy*. 14.1690 [a lease of land, AML] (which they did not publish in full), Grenfell and Hunt state that it was 'found with [POxy. 11] 1365, 1386, and 1392.' The last two of these are fragments of the *Iliad*, and thus commonplace, though not without sociological interest. But the first is the fragments of the history of *Sikyon* (Pack² 2181), a far more recherché work." On this collection, see also Houston, *Inside Roman Libraries*, 156–58, and Parsons, *City of the Sharp-Nosed Fish*, 151–52.

42. Published as follows: P.Oxy. 3.412: Julius Africanus, *Kestoi* book 18 (with end title); P.Oxy. 6.907: "Will of Hermogenes," dated 25 June–24 July 276; P.Oxy. 11.1365: History of Sicyon; P.Oxy. 11.1386: Homer, *Il.* 4.257–272 (the recto is a document with two cursive lines; see also J.-L. Fournet, "Homère et les papyrus non littéraires: le poète dans le contexte de ses lecteurs," in *I papiri omerici*, G. Bastianini and A.Casanova, Studi et Testi di Papirologia NS 14 [Florence: Istituto papirologico G. Vitelli, 2012], 126); P.Oxy. 11.1392: Homer, *Il.* 15.303–325 (verso: cursive writing); P.Oxy. 14.1690: "Lease of Land," 19 September 287.

house is located in a well-to-do neighborhood in Oxyrhynchus.⁴³ In such a milieu, women were taught to read and write.⁴⁴ In light of our discussion above about the letter carrier, it is worth noting here that Ptolemais inherited from her father an enslaved woman called Eunoia.

Furthermore, Aurelia Ptolemais and her parents, father Hermogenes alias Eudaimon and mother Isidora alias Prisca, may have been Christians. This is what Edwin Judge and Stewart Pickering suggest, based on a phrase in Hermogenes's will that commends his wife, Aurelia Isidora alias Prisca, for "fitting conduct in married life" (πρεπόντως περὶ τὴν συμβίωσιν ἀναστραφείσῃ). As Judge and Pickering note, the sentence is "not a direct New Testament echo but an idea familiar to its readers."⁴⁵ (If this family is not Christian, then it is interesting that they owned a copy of a text that, although not Christian in content, still was composed by a Christian author.)

For a book collection owned by a family that was probably Christian, the mix of texts is noteworthy. Literary and documentary sources suggest libraries owned by Christians with Homeric and Christian texts side by side on the shelves.⁴⁶ School exercises attest to the fact that (some) Christians continued to be educated with the classical authors in addition to Christian ones.⁴⁷ What strikes me is that this family generated many

---

43. Her father was an *exegetes*, *prytanis*, and councillor of Oxyrhynchus; her mother, Aurelia Isidora alias Prisca, a *matrona stolata* (line 4), and her grandfather Athenaius alias Heracleides had served as *bouleutes*, *kosmetes*, and *tamias* of city funds. See Bagnall, "Owner of Literary Papyri," 139 n. 13.

44. See especially Raffaella Cribiore, *Gymnastics of the Mind: Greek Education in Hellenistic and Roman Egypt* (Princeton: Princeton University Press, 2005), 74–101; Roger Bagnall and Raffaella Cribiore with Evie Ahtaridis, *Women's Letters from Ancient Egypt, 300 BC–AD 800* (Ann Arbor: University of Michigan Press, 2006), 48–49.

45. See Edwin A. Judge and Stewart R. Pickering, "Papyrus Documentation of Church and Community in Egypt to the Mid-Fourth Century," *JAC* 20 (1997): 65: "His wife Isidora, also known as Prisca (the name of a prominent collaborator of St Paul), a matrona stolata, who is praised for >fitting conduct in married life<, not a direct New Testament echo but an idea familiar to its readers." Bagnall ("Owner of Literary Papyri," 139 n. 16) comments: "That suggestion assumes … that the text of Africanus belonged to Hermogenes or one of his children (and was not acquired already as scrap); it also, less compellingly, assumes that the owner of a work written by a Christian, even a work without specifically Christian character, is likely to have been a Christian."

46. For instance, Clement of Alexandria, Basil of Caesarea.

47. Houston (*Inside Roman Libraries*, 178) summarizes the contents of this library

reused rolls: both the Homeric papyri are part of a recycled piece; in one case, the Homeric text is the secondary text, in the other case it is the primary, and also the *Kestoi* roll was turned over for reuse.[48] Such pieces are right at home in a trash heap. This kind of reuse is also what we see in the fourth and final example.

Glimpse of a Diverse Christian Library with Reused Pieces

My last example in this paper constitutes a different case of an Oxyrhynchus papyrus that gives only a slight indication of ownership and libraries, Christian reading practices, and more broadly the formation of the New Testament canon. At the center is a large roll with the Epistle to the Hebrews on its verso (P.Oxy. 4.657 + PSI 1292/P[13], published by Grenfell and Hunt in 1904).[49] Grenfell and Hunt note that they discovered this Hebrews roll, Oxyrhynchus Papyrus 4.657, in the same excavation season as several other early Christian texts, including a copy of Genesis (P.Oxy. 4.656) and two third-century fragments of the Gospel of Thomas (P.Oxy. 4.654 and 655).[50] Before we take a look at this interesting mixture of texts,

---

as follows: "This collection is too small to characterize in any useful way. It is of interest in that it includes Homer, the most basic of authors, but also at least one and probably two very rare works. Perhaps if we had more of the family's collection we would find a wide range of authors both popular and obscure. None of the manuscripts seems to have been kept for more than a century." It makes sense that one would discard both the most basic and also the most spurious works in one's library.

48. Reuse of writing material is common in antiquity and has an economic aspect (but not exclusively so). See, for instance, Houston, *Inside Roman Libraries*, 142 ("money-saving strategy"). On reused texts from Oxyrhynchus more generally, see Mariachiara Lama, "Aspetti di tecnica libraria ad Ossirinco: Copie letterarie su rotoli documentari," *Aegyptus* (1991): 55–120 (not including Christian works).

49. These fragments have evidently not remained unnoticed. In 1994 Junack could already compile an almost page-long list of scholarly references to this item; see Klaus Wachtel and Klaus Witte, *Gal, Eph, Phil, Kol, 1 u. 2 Thess, 1 u. 2 Tim, Tit, Phlm, Hebr*, vol. 2 of *Das Neue Testament auf Papyrus*, ANTF (Berlin: de Gruyter, 1994). P.Oxy. 4.657 + PSI 1292/P[13] is one of three Hebrews papyri from Oxyrhynchus; the others are: P.Oxy. 8.1078/P[17] and P.Oxy. 66.4498/P[114].

50. P.Oxy. 4.656 consists of "parts of four leaves from a papyrus codex of the book of Genesis in the Septuagint version" (28). In other words, this is also quite a substantial piece, although not as large as the Hebrews piece. In the preface to the fourth volume, Grenfell and Hunt (P.Oxy. 4, p. v.) state: "All the theological and most of the classical and the non-literary papyri in this volume were discovered during our

the Hebrews papyrus deserves a closer examination about what it might reveal of its ownership.

Consisting of twelve columns on a reused roll and containing roughly a third of the epistle, P.Oxy. 4.657/P[13] is the most extensive early Christian manuscript from Oxyrhynchus.[51] The recto of the roll contains an epitome of Livy in Latin (published as P.Oxy. 4.668). At a certain moment a Christian scribe repaired damaged sections of the roll with strips of papyrus and penned the Epistle to the Hebrews on the verso. The Hebrews text is written by an unprofessional but educated scribe, who added lectional signs and also made several corrections.[52] Paolo Orsini and Willy Clarysse classify the handwriting as "severe style" and date this papyrus to the fourth century (300–400 CE).[53] But what does this reused roll with lectional

---

second excavations at Oxyrhynchus in 1903.... The rest came from the original Oxyrhynchus find of 1897." As far as I could trace, no other Christian literary fragments have been published from that same excavation season, at least since the editors of the Oxyrhynchus volumes started recording inventory numbers (in vol. 60).

51. See Grenfell and Hunt, P.Oxy. 4.657, 36. This scroll was in all probability discarded at Oxyrhynchus in its entirety; see Luijendijk, "Sacred Scriptures as Trash," 251–52.

52. P[13] features lection signs as well as double points "inserted somewhat freely and not always accurately." At times a single point is used. See Grenfell and Hunt, P.Oxy. 4.657, 37. Common *nomina sacra* such as for πνεῦμα, θεός, χριστός, and Ἰησοῦς appear. Page column numbers are written on the top of the page; preserved are columns 47–50, 61–65, and 67–69. There is "no sign anywhere of a second hand," as Grenfell and Hunt (P.Oxy. 4.657, 37) note. The layout gives an unprofessional impression: the length of the columns varies from twenty-three to twenty-seven lines, and also the width differs significantly. Scholars have drawn attention to the scribe's sloppiness, resulting in numerous singular readings, leading to the conclusion that this papyrus was written by a nonprofessional scribe. See Wachtel and Witte, *Gal, Eph, Phil, Kol, 1 u. 2 Thess, 1 u. 2 Tim, Tit, Phlm, Hebr*, 2:xxxix, and Peter M. Head and M. Warren, "Re-inking the Pen: Evidence from P. Oxy 657 (P 13) concerning Unintentional Scribal Errors," *NTS* 43 (1997): 466–73. In their study on this papyrus, Head and Warren argue that P[13] = P.Oxy. 4.657 provides examples of how the "constant necessity to re-ink one's pen provided the opportunity for scribal distraction at the level of eye, memory, judgment and pen" (473). Yet despite the amateurish copying, let me emphasize (as Head and Warren also note) that the scribe paid attention to content by making corrections and also by reinking at natural points of pause in the text. So, while unprofessional, the scribe still appears to have been educated and engaged.

53. Willy Clarysse and Pasquale Orsini, "Early New Testament Manuscripts and Their Dates," *ETL* 88 (2013): 456–57. Regarding the date of the manuscript, it is worth quoting how Grenfell and Hunt (P.Oxy. 4.657, 37) arrived at their date: "The papyri

signs, copied by an educated but not professionally trained scribe, suggest about the intended purpose of this manuscript and the sociology of reading at Oxyrhynchus? Let me offer here some comments and questions.

First, what are the implications of the reuse, with this Hebrews text penned on a roll that contained a Latin text? We have numerous examples of documentary scrolls turned over for literary texts in antiquity—Mariachiara Lama counted 182 classical Greek texts for Oxyrhynchus alone in her 1991 article, not including Christian ones—whether for Homer, Aristotle (his *Athenaion Politeia* on the verso of P.Lond. 1.131), the Gospel of Thomas (P.Oxy. 4.654; on the back of a still unpublished land register), or the Psalter on the verso of an account of produce.[54] More pertinent to this case, we find the verso of literary rolls reused for letters.[55]

In this case (P.Oxy. 4.668 and 4.657), where a Latin literary roll was turned around for a Christian text, the matter is different. For, as common as the reuse of rolls was in antiquity, the double literary reuse, with a literary roll reused for another literary text, is rare.[56] The intricate notes of punc-

---

with which this [papyrus] was found were predominantly of the third century, and it is not likely to have been separated from them by any wide interval. The fact that the strips of cursive documents which were used to patch and strengthen the papyrus before the verso was used are of the third century and not the fourth points to the same conclusion."

54. Lama, "Aspetti di tecnica libraria ad Ossirinco." For other examples of documentary scrolls reused for literary texts, see Clarysse, "Literary Papyri in Documentary Archives," 45.

55. Clarysse ("Literary Papyri in Documentary Archives," 47) mentions the third-century CE Archive of Heroninus, observing that "several of his correspondents wrote their letters on the verso of used papyrus, usually a discarded document; but some did not shrink from cutting up a roll of Homer, Demosthenes, Menander, or using a fragment of Old Comedy, or even a philosopher." He concedes: "But of course we have no guarantee that these persons had ever read the works they so barbarously mutilated."

56. At least for papyrus rolls. This depends, of course, on how *literary* is defined. One may compare this case with the British Library Hyperides (P.Lond. Lit. 133 descr.) scrawled on the back of a quite nicely produced horoscope. Although the text is not exactly literary, it is not exactly documentary, either. I thank Brent Nongbri for this reference. With parchment codices the matter is different, when text is erased. Scholars long considered another Oxyrhynchus fragment, P.Oxy. 8.1075 and 1079 (= P^{18}), containing the end of Exodus and the beginning of Revelation roll, as such a double literary reuse, but recently Brent Nongbri has convincingly established this as a leaf from a codex ("Losing a Curious Christian Scroll but Gaining a Curious Christian Codex," *NovT* 55 [2013]: 77–88).

tuation point to performance, as they would aid the reader in declaiming the text.[57] Should we imagine this within a household or liturgical setting? The material fact of the reused roll situates this papyrus as more likely produced for private use.[58]

How the ancients reused texts is not yet fully understood, although it was certainly born out of a practical frugality—the kind of frugality that has become rare in our times.[59] To be sure, the Livy epitome belonged in a studious milieu, where obviously Latin was read and perhaps even spoken. Was this manuscript perhaps produced in the Latin West and later brought to Egypt? One might think here of the so-called Amherst papyrus (P^{12}), a letter from Rome that quotes Genesis and Heb 1:1.[60] So do we overhear the owner read the Hebrews scroll with a Latin accent? I can imagine a Roman official who brought the Livy roll from the West, recycling the secular text after becoming Christian. Did the offspring of a Latin-speaking family that had moved to Egypt reuse the roll because they no longer mastered the language or were no longer interested in the

---

57. On the performance of manuscripts, see also Larry W. Hurtado, *The Earliest Christian Artifacts: Manuscripts and Christian Origins* (Grand Rapids: Eerdmans, 2006), 181, and Luijendijk, "Reading the Gospel of Thomas in the Third Century," 241–67.

58. See, for instance, Hurtado, *Earliest Christian Artifacts*, 54–55 and 57 n. 49: "The opisthograph usually made for personal study of literary texts or for documentary texts." According to Claire Clivaz, an opistograph signifies that there was no institutional control over manuscript production and usage. She refers to this papyrus (P^{13}) as an example that "even in Rome itself, there does not exist in the middle of the 2nd century an institutional dominant hold over the production of Christian manuscripts" ("The New Testament at the Time of the Egyptian Papyri: Reflections Based on P12, P72 and P126 (P. Amh. 3b, P. Bod XIV–XV and PSI 1497," in Clivaz and Zumstein, *Reading New Testament Papyri in Context/Lire les Papyrus du Nouveau Testament dans leur context*, 16–55).

59. About P.Oxy. 4.688, Richard Seider (*Texte klassischer Autoren*, part 1 of *Literarische Papyri*, vol. 2 of *Paläographie der lateinischen Papyri* [Stuttgart: Hiersemann, 1978], 91) writes: "Die lateinische Papyrusrolle, deren erhaltene Fragmente—wohl die ältesten Liviusfragmente—uns besonders kostbar sind, scheint für den antiken Besitzer wertlos geworden zu sein. Die Rückseite des Papyrus wurde beschrieben." On reuse, see Lama, "Aspetti di tecnica libraria ad Ossirinco." Also of interest in understanding book reuse is Raymond J. Starr, "The Used-Book Trade in the Roman World," *Phoenix* 44 (1990): 148–57.

60. See P.Amh. 3a–c (including P^{12}) and discussion by Clivaz, "New Testament at the Time of the Egyptian Papyri," 45–51. The letter has Heb 1:1 on the upper margin of the recto and Gen 1:1–5 written on the verso.

subject matter?⁶¹ Or is there no relation between the owner of both texts, and could one buy obsolete scrolls (then still the question remains about who first owned it)?⁶²

A closer look at our scroll, however, suggests, that the Latin roll was probably produced and reused in Egypt rather than in the West. For, as Richard Seider comments, the copyist of Livy, although writing in beautiful script, showed little comprehension of the text and especially botched Latin personal names. In other words, the mistakes in the Latin suggest that the text was not copied in a Latin-speaking region but by a Greek scribe in Egypt.⁶³ Furthermore, in preparation for reuse, the documentary strips used to patch damaged sections in the scroll are written in Greek, suggesting an Egyptian location.⁶⁴

---

61. Philip Wesley Comfort and David P. Barrett (*The Text of the Earliest New Testament Greek Manuscripts* [Carol Stream, IL: Tyndale House, 2001], 84) suggest this, but they refer to "scholars" without citing who proposed this. Another text reaching Egypt (Oxyrhynchus) from the West is Irenaeus, *Adversus Haereses* (P.Oxy. 3.405). The LDAB provides the following data on Latin papyri from Oxyrhynchus: there are fifty-two Latin manuscripts from Oxyrhynchus; of these twenty-three are bilingual texts. Among the bilingual manuscripts, six are school texts; six are word lists (glossaries, lexicons); eight are authored texts by the likes of Cicero, Sallustius, and Virgil (that is, bilingual editions, paraphrases, etc.); and finally, three are miscellaneous (epistolary models, register of imperial constitutions, and legal definitions and maxims). Clivaz suggests that "P13 shows that the owner/scribe tried in the 3rd century to conserve both texts, Livy on the recto and Heb 2–5 and 10–12 on the verso" ("New Testament at the Time of the Egyptian Papyri," 25–26). However, the repair strips over the text suggest the contrary.

62. There exists a large corpus of late antique writing on reused material in Arabic papyri. See Eva Mira Grob, *Documentary Arabic Private and Business Letters on Papyrus: Form and Function, Content and Context*, vol. 29 (Berlin: de Gruyter, 2010). Here, the writing often remains in network, but sometimes even a very personal letter might become reused out of network (Grob, *Documentary Arabic Private and Business Letters on Papyrus*, 103).

63. "Daneben sind dem Schreiber der Liviusrolle aus Oxyrhynchus, der bei der Abschrift dem lateinischen Text nur geringes Verständnis entgegenbrachte, gewiß zahlreiche Verlesungen zuzuschreiben. Manche Verschreibungen lassen sich paläographisch erklären. Sehr schwere und kaum erklärliche Fehler machte der Schreiber, der in schöner kalligraphischer Form zu schreiben verstand, aber hinsichtlich der römischen Eigennamen. Fehler gerade dieser Art könnten vielleicht von einem Griechen verursacht sein" (Seider, *Texte klassischer Autoren*, 92).

64. As is well known among New Testament scholars, the authorship of the Epistle to the Hebrews was debated in antiquity. In Egypt, Origen expressed his doubts

As noted above, the Hebrews scroll came from the same excavation as fragments of two different rolls with the Gospel of Thomas and one of Genesis. This group of texts thus gives an interesting glimpse into the reading practices of the Oxyrhynchite Christians. Oxyrhynchus Papyrus 4.654, a papyrus with the beginning of the Gospel of Thomas, is incidentally also copied on a reused roll. This heavily marked-up papyrus fragment was clearly intended to be performed in a group. This raises the question: Were these texts just spread out in the garbage and accidentally collected in the same garbage heap, or did they belong together in antiquity and therefore constitute the remains of a library or small collection? In his research on libraries from Oxyrhynchus, Houston identified one collection that had a high percentage of reused rolls (37 percent).[65] If these varied texts—Genesis, Hebrews, and the Gospel of Thomas—did form part of the same collection, that would be very interesting for the development of the New Testament canon. It would be a collection with a Septuagint manuscript and several Christian writing in which one Christian text later became authoritative (Hebrews), the other not (Gospel of Thomas), and a library with writings in different formats (whereas early Christian rolls are scarce among the Oxyrhynchus papyri). However, there is no further evidence to support this.

These four examples of Christian owners and thus readers from Oxyrhynchus have in different manners and in different levels of detail all involved private ownership (versus church ownership) and domestic reading of Christian books. As we will see next, church leaders actively promoted study of Christian texts at home.

"A Spiritual Meadow and a Garden of Delight"

Ancient authors such as Clement of Alexandria, Origen of Alexandria/Caesarea, and John Chrysostom recommended Bible study at home. In

---

about the Pauline authorship of the Epistle of the Hebrews. Eusebius mentions that Origen had preached a series of homilies on the text (these are unfortunately lost).

65. Houston, *Inside Roman Libraries*, 142: "The collector of these texts emerges as a serious reader, concerned to obtain correct texts but not necessarily elegant or impressive ones.... An unusually high percentage of the manuscripts—six of about sixteen, or some 37 percent—were copied on the verso of documents, probably as a money-saving strategy." Houston returns to the percentage of reused rolls in this collection and comments on how "exceptional" it is compared to other collections (*Inside Roman Libraries*, 152).

Alexandria, at the turn of the third century, Clement preferred reading over having sex. He instructs married couples to stop having sex ("the mystic rites of nature") during any part of the day and instead to study Scripture or engage in good deeds (*Paed.* 2.10.96).[66] The next example takes us not to the bedroom but to the home. Clement's successor, Origen, in a homily on Leviticus, exhorted his audience that they should "not only hear the word in the church, but also practice it in your homes" ("non solum in ecclesia audire verbum Dei, sed in domibus vestris exerceri"). Indeed, Origen recommended at least two hours of devotion at home.[67] John Chrysostom expresses this most eloquently, and spiritually, in a sermon, when he also exhorts his congregation of Christians to study the Scriptures at home. Chrysostom imagines "the reading of the divine Scriptures" as "a spiritual meadow and a garden of delight" (καὶ γὰρ πνευματικὸς λειμών, καὶ παράδεισος τρυφῆς ἡ τῶν θείων Γραφῶν ἐστιν ἀνάγνωσις)—a paradise of joy that surpasses the garden of Eden.[68] Elsewhere he describes "the reading of

---

66. Ἀλλ' οἷς γε συγκεχώρηται γῆμαι, τούτοις ἐδέησεν παιδαγωγοῦ, ὡς μὴ μεθ' ἡμέραν τὰ μυστικὰ τῆς φύσεως ἐκτελεῖσθαι ὄργια μηδὲ ἐξ ἐκκλησίας, φέρε, ἢ ἀγορᾶς ἥκοντα ἑωθινὸν ἀλεκτρυόνος ὀχεύειν δίκην, ὁπηνίκα εὐχῆς καὶ ἀναγνώσεως καὶ τῶν μεθ' ἡμέραν εὐεργῶν ἔργων ὁ καιρός· (edition: Clement of Alexandria, "Clement, Le pedagogue [par] Clement d'Alexandria. Texte grec.," in *Le Pédagogue, Livre I*, SC 70 [Paris: Cerf, 1960], 2). "Those whom nature has joined in wedlock need the Educator that they might learn not to celebrate the mystic rites of nature during the day, nor like the rooster copulate at dawn, or after they have come from church, or even from the market, when they should be praying or reading or performing the good works that are best done by day" (Clement, *Christ the Educator*, trans. Simon P. Wood, FC 23 [New York: Fathers of the Church, 1954], 174).

67. As Harnack (*Bible Reading in the Early Church*, trans. John Richard Wilkinson [New York: Putnam's Sons; London: Williams & Norgate, 1912], 68–69) puts it: "Origen speaks pretty frequently of the reading of Holy Scripture at home, and strongly commends it. It should be read every day, and even one to two hours seem to him too little to devote to Divine things."

68. John Chrysostom, *Hom. princ. act.* 3.1 [87.33]. Chrysostom compares reading Scriptures at home with a paradisiacal state of joy that surpasses the garden of Eden. Chrysostom writes: "[87.33] The reading of the Divine Scriptures, you see, is a spiritual meadow and a garden of delight [καὶ γὰρ πνευματικὸς λειμών, καὶ παράδεισος τρυφῆς ἡ τῶν θείων Γραφῶν ἐστιν ἀνάγνωσις], a garden of delight better than that garden. God planted this garden, not in the earth, but in the souls of those who believe. He placed this garden not in Eden, nor in the East, enclosing it in one particular spot; rather, he extended it throughout the whole earth, and stretched it out to the ends of the earth. And [to show] that he stretched the Scriptures throughout the whole world, hear what the prophet says, 'Their voice went out into the whole world, and their words to the

the Scriptures [as] a conversation with God" (ἡ δὲ τῶν Γραφῶν ἀνάγνωσις, Θεοῦ ὁμιλία ἐστίν).[69] For Chrysostom, careful, faithful reading practices also have a protective effect against sinning, as he assures his audience that "the reading of the Divine Scriptures rescues the soul from all evil thoughts, as out of the midst of a fire."[70] His sermons contain instances where he advises Scripture reading. In a homily on the Gospel of John, Chrysostom admonishes parishioners to make time to read the weekly gospel section carefully at home in preparation for the church service. The preacher fully expects the richer congregants to possess Christian books. But he also argues that poorer members have no excuse for not owning books, since they also own their tools of trade and should at least become

---

ends of the earth'" (translation from Michael Bruce Compton, "Introducing the Acts of the Apostles: A Study of John Chrysostom's *On the Beginning of Acts*" [PhD diss., University of Virginia, 1996]); Greek from PG 51:87. See also Chrysostom, *Eutrop.* 52.395.54–55: Ἡδὺς μὲν λειμὼν καὶ παράδεισος, πολὺ δὲ ἡδύτερον τῶν θείων Γραφῶν ἡ ἀνάγνωσις; *Hom. Matt.* 9:37 63.19.1: καὶ εἰς τὸν λειμῶνα ὑμᾶς εἰσάξαι πειρασόμεθα τῶν θείων Γραφῶν·; *Stud. praes.* 63.485.10–11: Ὡς ἡδίστη ἡ τῶν Γραφῶν ἀνάγνωσις, καὶ λειμῶνος παντὸς ἡδίων καὶ παραδείσου τερπνοτέρα, καὶ μάλιστα ὅταν γνῶσις τῇ ἀναγνώσει πρόσκειται. For the concept of Scripture as a meadow, see also Philoxenus, *Ep.* 26 (176); Gregory of Nyssa, *Deit.* 46, 556.1: πρὸς τὸν λειμῶνα τῆς Γραφῆς ἀποβλέποντος; Ephraem Syrus, *Encomium in magnum Basilium* 353.3: εἰς λειμῶνα τῶν θεοπνεύστων Γραφῶν; Theodoret, *Eranistes* 253.4: Οὐκοῦν, ὦ ἀγαθέ, ζήλωσον τὰς μελίττας, καὶ τῷ νῷ περιπετόμενος τούς τε λειμῶνας τοὺς τῆς θείας γραφῆς.

69. "[89.54] And if a plague, or assault, or slander, or abuse, or mockery, any sloth, any of the evils of the world, should fall upon such a soul, it easily repels the heat of passions, since it has sufficient consolation from the reading of the Scriptures. For neither greatness of glory, nor weight of sovereignty, nor presence of friends, nor any other human thing will thus be able to comfort someone who is in pain as the reading of the Divine Scriptures can. Why is this so? Because those things are temporary and perishable, and so their comfort is perishable as well. But *the reading of the Scriptures is a conversation with God* [ἡ δὲ τῶν Γραφῶν ἀνάγνωσις, Θεοῦ ὁμιλία ἐστίν]. Whenever, then, God comforts someone who is fainthearted, what created thing is able to cast that person back into faintheartedness?" Chrysostom, *Hom. princ. act.* 3 (trans. Compton); Greek from PG 51:90.3.

70. Chrysostom, *Hom. princ. act.* 3 (trans. Compton). "In just this same way, the one who is seated beside the fount of the Divine Scriptures, even if he might see an annoying flame of improper desire, easily beats off the flame, since through those streams he has purged the soul. And if very hot anger annoys, burning the heart like a boiling kettle, he immediately represses the shamelessness of the emotion. And the reading of the Divine Scriptures rescues the soul from all evil thoughts, as out of the midst of a fire" (Chrysostom, *Hom. princ. act.* 3 [trans. Compton]).

familiar with Scripture through attentive presence in church.[71] In a different sermon, he instructs people to study Scripture after church, saying,

---

71. John Chrysostom, *Hom. Jo.* 11, section 1. NFPF translation: "What then is it that I require of you? That each of you take in hand that section of the Gospels which is to be read among you on the first day of the week, or even on the Sabbath, and before the day arrive, that he sit down at home and read it through, and often carefully consider its contents, and examine all its parts well ...; and when you have tried, in a word every point, so go to hear it read.... How can they, when they have leisure for what is said as a by work, and only in this place, and for this short time? If any lay the fault on business, and cares, and constant occupation in public and private matters, in the first place, this is no slight charge in itself, that they are surrounded with such a multitude of business, are so continually nailed to the things of this life, that they cannot find even a little leisure for what is more needful than all.... There is another most foolish excuse of these sluggards; that they have not the books in their possession. Now as to the rich, it is ludicrous that we should take our aim at this excuse; but because I imagine that many of the poorer sort continually use it, I would gladly ask, if every one of them does not have all the instruments of the trade which he works at, full and complete, though infinite poverty stand in his way? Is it not then a strange thing, in that case to throw no blame on poverty, but to use every means that there be no obstacle from any quarter, but, when we might gain such great advantage, to lament our want of leisure and our poverty? Besides, even if any should be so poor, it is in their power, by means of the continual reading of the holy Scriptures which takes place here, to be ignorant of nothing contained in them." I thank Seumas Macdonald for this reference. See also, much earlier, the Didascalia Apostolurum (200–250 CE?): "[f.i.5] But if thou art rich and hast no need of a craft whereby to live, thou shalt not stray and go about vacantly; but be ever constant in drawing near to the faithful and to them that are like-minded with thee, and be meditating and learning with them the living words. And if not, sit at home and read the Law, and the Book of Kings and the Prophets, and the Gospel the fulfilment of these. [i. 6] But avoid all books of the heathen. For what hast thou to do with strange sayings or laws or lying prophecies, which also turn away from the faith them that are young? For what is wanting to thee in the word of God, that thou shouldst cast thyself upon these fables of the heathen? If thou wouldst read historical narratives, thou hast the Book of Kings; but if wise men and philosophers, thou hast the Prophets, wherein thou shalt find wisdom and understanding more than that of the wise men and philosophers; for they are the words of the one God, the only wise. And if thou wish for songs, thou hast the Psalms of David; but if (thou wouldst read of) the beginning of the world, thou hast the Genesis of the great Moses; and if laws and commandments, thou hast the glorious Law of the Lord God. All strange (writings) therefore, which are contrary (to these), wholly avoid." Translation by Richard Hugh Connolly, *Didascalia apostolorum, the Syriac Version Translated and Accompanied by the Verona Latin Fragments, with an Introduction and Notes by R. Hugh Connolly* (Oxford: Clarendon, 1929), 11–12. See also redaction in the Apostolic Constitutions 1.5: "V. Or if thou stayest at home, read the books of the

"Let each person, after going home, take up the books in their hands."[72] When we combine these exhortations with the Oxyrhynchite evidence examined above, it becomes clear that the papyri provide us with the other side of the exhortations, namely, material evidence of this practice. The four Oxyrhynchite examples are slightly later than Origen and earlier than Chrysostom's exhortations and therefore contribute significantly to our understanding of this practice among third- and fourth-century Christian readers. After examining the late antique evidence, I now turn to the modern time and situate the topic of private reading within the larger academic discussion in order to understand better the scholarly stakes in this debate and therefore the historical significance of these Christian papyri from Oxyrhynchus.

Private Reading of Christian Texts

As Gamble notes in *Books and Readers*, little has been written on the private reading of Christian texts.[73] He attempts to remedy that dearth of scholarship in a section of the book, concluding:

> It seems clear that literate Christians were able to obtain Christian texts for private reading. Because the matter of their cost almost never comes up, expense does not appear to have been an obstacle. Some cost was involved, no doubt, but it was not prohibitive for most. It should probably be assumed that texts were obtained by private transcription, since in all the allusions to private reading there is no mention of a commercial trade in Christian books. Moreover, the church strongly encouraged its literate members to religious cultivation through the private reading of Christian books. The value of private reading, however, depended on what was read, and the currency of apocryphal and heretical texts as well as the persistent aesthetic appeal of pagan literature meant that private reading would not be endorsed as an unqualified good. Yet the worry

---

Law, of the Kings, with the Prophets; sing the hymns of David; and peruse diligently the Gospel, which is the completion of the other" (ANF 7:393).

72. Chrysostom, *Hom. princ. act.* 3 (trans. Compton); *Hom. Act.*, PG 51:65–112.

73. On the private use of Christian books, see Gamble, *Books and Readers*, 231–37. Gamble (231–32) concludes: "The only major barrier to the private acquisition and use of Christian books was the capacity to read them." On the cost of books, see Roger S. Bagnall, *Early Christian Books in Egypt* (Princeton: Princeton University Press, 2009), 50–69.

about what Christians might read privately is itself a telling indication that Christian texts were available in great variety and number.[74]

This is indeed what the materials from Oxyrhynchus suggest.

Since Gamble's *Books and Readers*, the question of private reading evolved in scholarship in two different ways, one conceptual and one technological. First, there is the work of William Johnson, a classicist and papyrologist, on the sociology of reading. Johnson has shown that reading in antiquity was a social occasion, where texts were read out loud and discussed in small groups.[75] Johnson's work on the sociology of reading helps to understand why some of these texts are marked up for reading out loud. This happened also in a small reading group at home. Reading in antiquity was not a solitary occupation. This model helps make sense of the Oxyrhynchus papyri as a larger whole. Second is the development and availability online of the Leuven Database of Ancient Books, a database that collects searchable data on ancient books copied before the year 800, established by Belgian scholar Willy Clarysse.[76] The field of papyrology has been a leader in the development of Digital Humanities, and also my research for this paper has benefitted greatly from it.

In drawing conclusions I return to the Oxyrhynchus papyri examined above.

Conclusions

In this paper, I have probed the ownership of Christian literary papyri from Oxyrhynchus. In four instances, owners of Christian literature from Oxyrhynchus could be identified, with varying degrees of clarity. This is important, because beyond books owned by monastics, we have only very few other instances where the approximate owners appear on the horizon for all Christian papyri.

We encountered a wide range of texts and a diversity of owners: the Epistle to the Romans, the *Kestoi* of Julius Africanus, Jubilees, Ezra, the

---

74. Gamble, *Books and Readers*, 237.
75. William A. Johnson, *Readers and Reading Culture in the High Roman Empire* (New York: Oxford University Press, 2010), 225; Johnson, "Toward a Sociology of Reading in Classical Antiquity."
76. Leuven Database of Ancient Books at http://www.trismegistos.org/ldab/search.php.

Epistle to the Hebrews, and the Gospel of Thomas, with male and female, free and enslaved readers of Greek. These texts were penned on rolls and codices; one was a writing exercise. Leonides's sheet with the opening of the Epistle to the Romans stands out among the other three Christian collections and also with those that Houston discusses. While these other collections all contain multiple literary texts, in the case of Leonides, there is only the school exercise or pious writing sample bound up with his business documents. Perhaps the exemplar for the writing sample belonged in a larger collection of texts, but this we cannot know. Aurelia Ptolemais also had a mixed library with both documents and literature, even some highly specialized literary words.[77] The full extent of the libraries of the "lady sister" and her anonymous correspondent remains unknown, but at least the former seems to have possessed more than one book. The vague contours of a library of Christian texts published in P.Oxy. 4 show a diversity of reading interests. What these textual remains all share is that at one point they were discarded and ended up on the Oxyrhynchite trash heaps.

In the four cases of owners of Christian Oxyrhynchus papyri discussed above, two topics stand out: female owners and reused writing material. Two of the four examples explicitly introduced female owners and readers of Christian literature.[78] As is well known, in literary sources women are frequently left out or silenced. We even have homilies from Oxyrhynchus with rhetoric against women. Fragments from different sermons (both later than our dossiers) preserved at Oxyrhynchus belabor the example of the so-called wicked woman. One dates to the fifth century (P.Oxy. 18.2073), the other to the fifth or sixth century (P.Oxy.

---

77. Just as Sarapion alias Apollonianus, whose first-rate library and papers also ended up among the trash, see Houston, *Inside Roman Libraries*, 145–46. Saving one's literary and documentary texts in one location seems to have been common practice in antiquity.

78. As Jean-Luc Fournet ("Femmes et Culture dans l'Égypte Byzantine [Ve-VIIe S.]," 142) notes, the situation of "femmes en possession de livres qu'elles lisent, est … mal documentée." But Sarit Kattan Gribetz has two excellent articles on women as readers and transmitters of rabbinic and Christian literature: "Consuming Texts: Women as Recipients and Transmitters of Ancient Texts," in *Rethinking "Authority" in Late Antiquity: Authorship, Law, and Transmission in Jewish and Christian Tradition*, ed. Abraham J. Berkovitz and Mark Letteney (London: Routledge, 2018), 178–206; and "Women as Readers of the Nag Hammadi Codices: Historical and Methodological Reflections," *JECS* 26 (2018): 463–94.

13.1603).⁷⁹ But while silenced in sermons and literature, women are very present in the archaeological and documentary record (this is no wonder, since they constituted half of the population). In her delightful and eloquently written book *The Allure of the Archives*, French historian Arlette Farge describes how women show up frequently in eighteenth-century French police archives. She writes: "Women are astonishingly present in the eighteenth century city: they worked, moved around, and fluidly, naturally, took part in the ensemble of urban activity. Finding them is child's play, because they constantly filled the buildings, markets, riverbanks, and fairs."⁸⁰ Encountering female book owners and readers in the material record of the Oxyrhynchus papyri thus stands in this larger context and is, evidently, also attested beyond its boundaries. In a fourth-century papyrus from Lykopolis, for instance, a nun ("always-virgin") is accused of theft of books. It seems that she took more than her fair share of the books in an inheritance (P.Lips. 1.43).⁸¹ Christian literary texts also provide evidence of such Christian female readers. In the martyrological literature, for instance, we encounter the female martyrs from Thessaloniki—Agape, Irene, and Chione—who had multiple Christian books at home.⁸² In a letter, Jerome informs us that Pamphilus of Caesarea, who died in 309 and thus was roughly a contemporary of the correspondents in our book exchange letter and Aurelia Ptolemais, lent books "not only

---

79. On the former sermon, see Amphilochios Papathomas, "Zur byzantinischen Homilie P. Oxy. XVII 2073," *ZPE* (2007): 181–86. Papathomas redates the text to the fifth century (ed. princ. dated it late fourth century) and provides a new edition of the papyrus based on digital images. While Papathomas (186) concedes that it is possible that this is sermon by a local bishop or priest, he does not consider it likely, since it is a learned text and also is already a copy. See also Mathieson, *Christian Women in the Greek Papyri of Egypt*, 148 n. 1. Other Christian sermons with misogynistic content preserved on papyrus are P.Bodl. I 6, BKT IX 175; see Papathomas, "Zur Byzantinischen Homilie P. Oxy. XVII 2073," 184 n. 19. See also Papathomas, "'Keine Bestie auf der Welt gleicht der schlechten Frau.' Frauenfeindliche Polemik aus der ps.-chrysostomischen Homilie In decollationem praecursoris in einem berliner literarischen Papyrus," *MH* 58 (2001): 47–53.
80. Arlette Farge, *The Allure of the Archives* (New Haven: Yale University Press, 2013), 33.
81. See especially María Albarrán Martínez, "Women Reading Books in Egyptian Monastic Circles," in *Eastern Christians and Their Written Heritage: Manuscripts, Scribes and Context*, ed. P. Monferrer, H. Telus, and S. Torallas (Leuven: Peeters, 2012), 199–212, and also Mathieson, *Christian Women in the Greek Papyri of Egypt*, 238–40.
82. See Gamble, *Books and Readers in the Early Church*, 148.

to men, but also to women" from his library in Caesarea.[83] Later and less explicit evidence also points to additional female readers at Oxyrhynchus: fourth-century documents attest to the presence of so-called domestic ascetics at Oxyrhynchus. These women practiced a form of asceticism where they neither retreated into the desert nor lived in a monastery but rather lived as nuns at home. Church leaders specify that these domestic ascetics should spend their days reading and fasting. These women form another demographic for the Christian texts found at Oxyrhynchus, continuing the line of female readers.[84] In her article "Women Reading Books in Egyptian Monastic Circles," María Albarrán Martínez discusses the evidence of the three kinds of female monastics (in addition to domestic virgins, also desert and coenobitic nuns).[85]

Second, it is noteworthy that the four cases presented here contained several documentary texts and multiple reused rolls. With the present evidence from Oxyrhynchus, those are the only instances where we

---

83. "nec solum viris, sed et feminis." See Jerome, *Apology against Rufinus* 1.9 (in *Saint Jerome, Apologie contre Rufin*, ed. and trans. P. Lardet, SC 303 [Paris, 1983], 26). See discussion in Kraus, "Bücherleihe," 292–93. In a non-Christian context, emperor Julian exchanged books with the priestess Theodora. *Ep.* 32: "I have received through Mygdonius the book [τὸ βιβλίον] that you have sent me, and besides, all the letters of recommendation that you forwarded to me throughout the festival" (trans. Wilmer Cave France Wright, *The Works of the Emperor Julian* [Cambridge: Harvard University Press, 1953], 3:108–9); and *Ep.* 33 (Wright, *Works of the Emperor Julian*, 112–13): "I was glad to receive all the books [βιβλία πάντα] that you sent me, and your letters through the excellent Mygdonius." In *Ep.* 34, Julian praises Theodora as being wisdom herself.

84. On domestic virgins in general see Ewa Wipszycka, *Moines et communautés monastiques en Égypte* (Varsovie: Journal of Juristic Papyrology, 2009); Wipszycka, "L'ascétisme féminin dans l'Égypte Tardive: Topoi littéraires et formes d'ascèse," in *Le rôle et le statut de la femme en Égypte hellénistique, romaine et byzantine: Acts du colloque international, Bruxelles-Leuven, 27–29 novembre 1997*, ed. Henri Melaerts, Leon Mooren, and Ewa Wipszycka (Leuven: Peeters, 2016), 355–96; María Jesús Albarrán Martínez, *Ascetismo y monasterios femeninos en el Egipto tardoantiguo: Estudio de papiros y ostraca griegos y coptos* (Barcelona: Publicacions de l'Abadia de Montserrat, 2011); and Wipszycka, "L'ascétisme féminin dans l'Égypte de l'antiquité tardive: un sujet difficile. Sur un livre de María Jesús Albarrán Martínez," *JJP* 42 (2013): 337–52. On domestic virgins at Oxyrhynchus, see AnneMarie Luijendijk, "'Twenty Thousand Nuns': The Domestic Virgins of Oxyrhynchus," in *Christianity and Monasticism in Middle Egypt*, ed. Gawdat Gabra and Hany Takla (Cairo: The American University in Cairo Press, 2015), 57–67.

85. Albarrán Martínez, "Women Reading Books in Egyptian Monastic Circles."

can catch glimpses of owners, and thus they bring a certain bias to the findings, probably a bias toward private ownership. Gamble associates Christian reused rolls with private reading.[86] What do they tell us about their owners? Compared to the professional library of the *strategos* Sarapion alias Apollonianus, these small remnants of Christian collections are more modest and more frugal.[87]

Undoubtedly, the ownership of the Christian papyri from Oxyrhynchus was diverse and included churches. Above I mentioned a papyrus of the Gospel of John (P.Oxy. 15.1780) that must have formed part of a large, expensively produced codex that I can imagine in the possession of a church but just as likely of a wealthy family.[88] But the evidence presented here seems to lead not to church but to the homes of people. To find private owners of Christian papyri at Oxyrhynchus makes sense in a large urban context with wealthy, educated residents. Private ownership perhaps also explains how manuscripts can turn up on trash heaps, as they would probably be more likely to throw out texts than priests at a church (although apparently that happened also). The practice of reading Christian texts at home is recommended in the writings of church leaders. This paper has connected these scattered references to actual manuscripts and even added a few names of actual readers, women and men, of Christian books.

---

86. Gamble, *Books and Readers*, 236: "In addition to pocket codices, opisthographs shed a little light on private reading. Although there are many opisthographs among the papyri, it was unusual to transcribe a text in this way, the only reason for doing so being economic. Most opisthographic manuscripts were either school texts or private copies made by or for persons of limited means. Not many early Christian texts were transcribed on rolls rather than in codices, but of those that were, most are opisthographs. Good examples are a copy of Hebrews written on the back of a roll containing an epitome of Livy (P. Oxy. 657 + P. S. I. 1292), a copy of the Apocalypse on the back of a roll of Exodus [P. Oxy. 1075), and a copy of Hermas (P. Mich. 130) on the back of a documentary text. Such texts were probably private copies made for personal use."

87. According to Houston (*Inside Roman Libraries*, 7): "Since a reused roll should cost less than a new one, it is reasonable to assume that the presence of opisthographs in a collection is ordinarily a sign of an economy-minded collector who hoped to save money by using or buying less expensive materials."

88. For the private sector, at Oxyrhynchus, Sarapion alias Apollonianus (see above) possessed such works.

Bibliography

Albarrán Martínez, María Jesús. *Ascetismo y monasterios femeninos en el Egipto tardoantiguo: Estudio de papiros y ostraca griegos y coptos*. Barcelona: Publicacions de l'Abadia de Montserrat, 2011.

———. "Women Reading Books in Egyptian Monastic Circles." Pages 199–212 in *Eastern Christians and Their Written Heritage: Manuscripts, Scribes and Context*. Edited by P. Monferrer, H. Telus, and S. Torallas. Leuven: Peeters, 2012.

Bagnall, Roger S. *Early Christian Books in Egypt*. Princeton: Princeton University Press, 2009.

———. "An Owner of Literary Papyri." *CP* (1992): 137–40.

———. "The Readers of Christian Books: Further Speculations." Pages 23–30 in *I papiri letterari cristiani: Atti del Convegno internazionale di studi in memoria di Mario Naldini, Firenze, 10–11 giugno 2010*. Edited by Guido Bastianini and Angelo Casanova. Firenze: Istituto papirologico G. Vitelli, 2011.

Bagnall, Roger S., and Raffaella Cribiore with Evie Ahtaridis. *Women's Letters from Ancient Egypt, 300 BC–AD 800*. Ann Arbor: University of Michigan Press, 2006.

Barker, Don C. "Codex, Roll, and Libraries in Oxyrhynchus." *TynBul* 57 (2006): 131–48.

Blumell, Lincoln H. *Lettered Christians: Christians, Letters, and Late Ancient Oxyrhynchus*. Leiden: Brill, 2012.

Blumell, Lincoln H., and Thomas A. Wayment. *Christian Oxyrhynchus: Texts, Documents, and Sources*. Waco, TX: Baylor University Press, 2015.

Brakke, David. "Canon Formation and Social Conflict in Fourth-Century Egypt: Athanasius of Alexandria's Thirty-Ninth Festal Letter." *HTR* 87 (1994): 395–419.

———. "A New Fragment of Athanasius's Thirty-Ninth Festal Letter: Heresy, Apocrypha, and the Canon." *HTR* 103 (2010): 47–66.

Choat, Malcolm, and Rachel Yuen-Collingridge. "The Egyptian Hermas: The Shepherd in Egypt before Constantine." Pages 191–212 in *Early Christian Manuscripts: Examples of Applied Method and Approach*. Edited by Thomas J. Kraus and Tobias Nicklas. Leiden: Brill, 2010.

Clarysse, Willy. "Literary Papyri in Documentary Archives." Pages 43–61 in *Egypt and the Hellenistic World: Proceedings of the Inter National*

Colloquium, Leuven 24–26 May 1982. Edited by E. Van't Dack, P. Van Dessel, and W. Van Gucht. Leuven: Orientaliste, 1983.

Clarysse, Willy, and Pasquale Orsini. "Early New Testament Manuscripts and Their Dates." *ETL* 88 (2013): 456–57.

Clement of Alexandria. *Christ the Educator*. Translated by Simon P. Wood. FC 23. New York: Fathers of the Church, 1954.

———. "Clement, Le pedagogue [par] Clement d'Alexandria. Texte grec." In *Le Pédagogue, Livre I*. SC 70. Paris: Cerf, 1960.

Clivaz, Claire. "The New Testament at the Time of the Egyptian Papyri: Reflections Based on P12, P72 and P126 (P. Amh. 3b, P. Bod XIV–XV and PSI 1497)." Pages 16–55 in *Reading New Testament Papyri in Context/ Lire des papyrus du Nouveau Testament dans leur context*. Edited by Claire Clivaz and Jean Zumstein. Leuven: Peeters, 2011.

Comfort, Philip Wesley, and David P. Barrett. *The Text of the Earliest New Testament Greek Manuscripts*. Carol Stream, IL: Tyndale House, 2001.

Compton, Michael Bruce. "Introducing the Acts of the Apostles: A Study of John Chrysostom's *On the Beginning of Acts*." PhD diss., University of Virginia, 1996.

Connolly, Richard Hugh. *Didascalia apostolorum, the Syriac Version Translated and Accompanied by the Verona Latin Fragments, with an Introduction and Notes by R. Hugh Connolly*. Oxford: Clarendon, 1929.

Cribiore, Raffaella. *Gymnastics of the Mind: Greek Education in Hellenistic and Roman Egypt*. Princeton: Princeton University Press, 2005.

Epp, Eldon J. "The Codex and Literacy in Early Christianity and at Oxyrhynchus: Issues Raised by Harry Y. Gamble's Books and Readers in the Early Church." *CRBR* 10 (1997): 15–37.

———. "The New Testament Papyri at Oxyrhynchus in Their Social and Intellectual Context." Pages 47–68 in *Perspectives on New Testament Textual Criticism: Collected Essays, 1962–2004*. NovTSup 116. Leiden: Brill, 1997.

———. "The New Testament Papyri at Oxyrhynchus: Their Significance for Understanding the Transmission of the Early New Testament Text." Pages 315–31 in *Oxyrhynchus: A City and Its Texts*. Edited by Alan K. Bowman, Revel A. Coles, Nikolaos Gonis, Dirk Obbink, and Peter J. Parsons. London: Egypt Exploration Society, 2007.

———. "The Oxyrhynchus New Testament Papyri: 'Not without Honor Except in Their Hometown'?" *JBL* 123 (2004): 5–55.

Farge, Arlette. *The Allure of the Archives*. New Haven: Yale University Press, 2013.

Fournet, Jean-Luc. "Femmes et Culture dans l'Égypte Byzantine (Ve–VIIe S.)." Pages 135–45 in *Les réseaux familiaux: Antiquité tardive et Moyen-Âge; In memoriam A. Laiou et É. Patlagean*. Edited by Béatrice Caseau. Centre de Recherche d'Histoire et Civilisation de Byzance—Monographie 37. Paris: Association des amis du Centre d'histoire et civilisation de Byzance, 2012.

———. "Homère et les papyrus non littéraires: le poète dans le contexte de ses lecteurs." Pages 125–57 in *I papiri omerici*. Edited by G. Bastianini and A. Casanova. Studi e Testi di Papirologia NS 14. Florence: Istituto papirologico G. Vitelli, 2012.

Gamble, Harry. *Books and Readers in the Early Church: A History of Early Christian Texts*. New Haven: Yale University Press, 1995.

Gonis, Nick. "Notes on Two Epistolary Conventions." *ZPE* 119 (1997): 148–52.

Gribetz, Sarit Kattan. "Consuming Texts: Women as Recipients and Transmitters of Ancient Texts." Pages 178–206 in *Rethinking "Authority" in Late Antiquity: Authorship, Law, and Transmission in Jewish and Christian Tradition*. Edited by Abraham J. Berkovitz and Mark Letteney. London: Routledge, 2018.

———. "Women as Readers of the Nag Hammadi Codices: Historical and Methodological Reflections." *JECS* 26 (2018): 463–94.

Grob, Eva Mira. *Documentary Arabic Private and Business Letters on Papyrus: Form and Function, Content and Context*. Vol. 29. Berlin: de Gruyter, 2010.

Harnack, Adolf von. *Bible Reading in the Early Church*. Translated by John Richard Wilkinson. New York: Putnam's Sons; London: Williams & Norgate, 1912.

Harrill, James Albert. *The Manumission of Slaves in Early Christianity*. Tübingen: Mohr Siebeck, 1995.

Head, Peter M. "Named Letter-Carriers among the Oxyrhynchus Papyri." *JSNT* 31.3 (2009): 279–99.

Head, Peter M., and M. Warren. "Re-inking the Pen: Evidence from P. Oxy 657 (P 13) concerning Unintentional Scribal Errors." *NTS* 43 (1997): 466–73.

Houston, George W. *Inside Roman Libraries: Book Collections and Their Management in Antiquity*. Chapel Hill: University of North Carolina Press, 2014.

———. "Papyrological Evidence for Book Collections and Libraries in the Roman Empire." Pages 233–67 in *Ancient Literacies: The Culture of*

Reading in Greece and Rome. Edited by William A. Johnson and Holt N. Parker. Oxford: Oxford University Press, 2009.

Hurtado, Larry W. *The Earliest Christian Artifacts: Manuscripts and Christian Origins*. Grand Rapids: Eerdmans, 2006.

———. "The Greek Fragments of the Gospel of Thomas as Artefacts: Papyrological Observations on Papyrus Oxyrhynchus 1, Papyrus Oxyrhynchus 654 and Papyrus Oxyrhynchus 655." Pages 19–32 in *Das Thomasevangelium: Entstehung—Rezeption—Theologie*. Edited by Jörg Frey, Enno Edzard Popkes, and Jens Schröter. Berlin: de Gruyter, 2008.

Jerome. *Saint Jerome, Apologie contre Rufin*. Edited and translated by P. Lardet. SC 303. Paris, 1983.

Johnson, William A. *Readers and Reading Culture in the High Roman Empire*. New York: Oxford University Press, 2010.

———. "Toward a Sociology of Reading in Classical Antiquity." *AJP* 121 (2000): 593–627.

Jördens, Andrea, and AnneMarie Luijendijk. "Oxyrhynchos." Pages 685–98 in *Reallexikon für Antike und Christentum: Sachwörterbuch zur Auseinandersetzung des Christentums mit der antiken Welt*. Edited by Georg Schöllgen et al. Stuttgart: Anton Hiersemann, 2014.

Judge, Edwin A., and Stewart R. Pickering. "Papyrus Documentation of Church and Community in Egypt to the Mid-Fourth Century." *JAC* 20 (1997): 47–71.

Kraus, Thomas J. "Bücherleihe im 4. Jh. n. Chr. P. Oxy. LXIII 4365—ein Brief auf Papyrus und die gegenseitige Leihe von apokryph gewordener Literatur." *Biblios* 50 (2001): 285–96.

———. "The Lending of Books in the Fourth Century C.E." Pages 185–206 in Kraus, *Ad Fontes: Original Manuscripts and Their Significance for Studying Early Christianity: Selected Essays*. Leiden: Brill, 2007.

———. "Miniature Codices in Late Antiquity: Preliminary Remarks and Tendencies about a Specific Book Format." *Early Christianity* 152 (2016): 134–52.

Lama, Mariachiara. "Aspetti di tecnica libraria ad Ossirinco: Copie letterarie su rotoli documentary." *Aegyptus* (1991): 55–120.

Luijendijk, AnneMarie. *Greetings in the Lord: Early Christians and the Oxyrhynchus Papyri*. Cambridge: Harvard University Press, 2008.

———. "A New Testament Papyrus and Its Documentary Context: An Early Christian Writing Exercise from the Archive of Leonides." *JBL* 129 (2010): 575–96.

———. "Reading the Gospel of Thomas in the Third Century: Three Oxyrhynchus Papyri and Origen's Homilies." Pages 241–67 in *Reading New Testament Papyri in Context/Lire des papyrus du Nouveau Testament dans leur context*. Edited by Claire Clivaz and Jean Zumstein. Leuven: Peeters, 2011.

———. "Sacred Scriptures as Trash: Biblical Papyri from Oxyrhynchus." *VC* 64 (2010): 217–54.

———. "'Twenty Thousand Nuns': The Domestic Virgins of Oxyrhynchus." Pages 57–67 in *Christianity and Monasticism in Middle Egypt*. Edited by Gawdat Gabra and Hany Takla. Cairo: The American University in Cairo Press, 2015.

MacMullen, Ramsay. "The Preacher's Audience (AD 350–500)." *JTS* (40 (1989): 505–7.

Mathieson, Erica. *Christian Women in the Greek Papyri of Egypt to 400 CE*. Turnhout: Brepols, 2017.

Mayer, Wendy. "Who Came to Hear John Chrysostom Preach? Recovering a Late Fourth-Century Preacher's Audience." *ETL* 76 (2000): 73–87.

Nongbri, Brent. *God's Library: The Archaeology of the Earliest Christian Manuscripts*. New Haven: Yale University Press, 2018.

———. "Losing a Curious Christian Scroll but Gaining a Curious Christian Codex." *NovT* 55 (2013): 77–88.

Papathomas, Amphilochios. "'Keine Bestie auf der Welt gleicht der schlechten Frau.' Frauenfeindliche Polemik aus der ps.-chrysostomischen Homilie In decollationem praecursoris in einem berliner literarischen Papyrus." *MH* 58 (2001): 47–53.

———. "Zur byzantinischen Homilie P. Oxy. XVII 2073." *ZPE* (2007): 181–86.

Parsons, Peter J. *City of the Sharp-Nosed Fish: Greek Lives in Roman Egypt*. London: Weidenfeld & Nicolson, 2007.

Reinard, Patrick. *Kommunikation und Ökonomie: Untersuchungen zu den privaten Papyrusbriefen aus dem kaiserzeitlichen Ägypten*. Pharos Studien zur griechisch-römischen Antike 32. Rahden: Leidorf, 2016.

Seider, Richard. *Texte klassischer Autoren*. Part 1 of *Literarische Papyri*. Vol. 2 of *Paläographie der lateinischen Papyri*. Stuttgart: Hiersemann, 1978.

Shaner, Katherine A. *Enslaved Leadership in Early Christianity*. Oxford: Oxford University Press, 2018.

Starr, Raymond J. "The Used-Book Trade in the Roman World." *Phoenix* 44 (1990): 148–57.

Wachtel, Klaus, and Klaus Witte. *Gal, Eph, Phil, Kol, 1 u. 2 Thess, 1 u. 2 Tim, Tit, Phlm, Hebr.* Vol. 2 of *Das Neue Testament Auf Papyrus.* ANTF. Berlin: de Gruyter, 1994.

Wipszycka, Ewa. "L'ascétisme féminin dans l'Égypte de l'antiquité tardive: un sujet difficile. Sur un livre de María Jesús Albarrán Martínez." *JJP* 42 (2013): 337–52.

———. "L'ascétisme féminin dans l'Égypte Tardive: Topoi littéraires et formes d'ascèse." Pages 355–96 in *Le rôle et le statut de la femme en Egypte hellénistique, romaine et byzantine: acts du colloque international, Bruxelles-Leuven, 27–29 novembre 1997.* Edited by Henri Melaerts, Leon Mooren, and Ewa Wipszycka. Leuven: Peeters, 2016.

———. *Moines et communautés monastiques en Égypte.* Varsovie: Journal of Juristic Papyrology, 2009.

Wright, Wilmer Cave France. *The Works of the Emperor Julian.* Cambridge: Harvard University Press, 1953.

The Bible in the Qur'an; the Qur'an in the Bible: Scriptural Intertextuality in the Language of Islam

Sidney H. Griffith

The Qur'an is a late antique book like no other; for example, it speaks of itself as a book, a "scripture" (*al-kitāb*), sent down to Muhammad even before it was committed to writing!¹ The Qur'an is the recitation, the proclamation of God's Arabic speech (*kalām Allāh*) addressed during the first third of the seventh Christian century at various junctures over a twenty-two year period (610–632 CE) to God's messenger, Muhammad ibn 'Abd Allāh (ca. 570–632 CE), and through Muhammad to the Arabic-speaking inhabitants of the environs of Mecca and Yathrib/Madinah in the Arabian Hijāz. Many of them joined Muhammad as a "Community of Believers," submitting themselves to God as "Muslims." This Qur'an, or "recital," even liturgical "recitative," was collected and redacted in writing from the memories of its first hearers, and from some disparate, written aides de mémoire in their possession, after the death of Muhammad, according to tradition under the direction of the early caliphs, and 'Uthmān ibn 'Affān (r. 644–656) in particular. By early in the second half of the seventh century, therefore, and certainly not long after 660 CE, the Qur'an had come into its final, written form as the first Arabic book, properly so called.²

It is not until almost a century later, after the Arab occupation of much of the Fertile Crescent, that we hear of the Qur'an in texts composed by Greek and Syriac-speaking Christians living on the peripheries of Arabia,

---

1. See, e.g., "[God] has sent down to you [second-person masculine singular; Muhammad] the scripture [*al-kitāb*] in truth, confirming what was before it; He previously sent down the Torah and the Gospel, as guidance for mankind" (Q 'Imran 3:3–4). Translations of the Qur'an are my own or adapted by me.
2. See Nicolai Sinai, *The Qur'ān: A Historical-Critical Introduction* (Edinburgh: Edinburgh University Press, 2017), esp. 40–58.

in Palestine and Syria. For example, a now-unknown Syriac writer of the early eighth century spoke of the Qur'an as the scripture of the Arabs alongside the Torah and the Gospel.[3] The earliest text written by a Christian in Arabic, which was composed around the year 750 CE, purposefully imitates qur'anic diction and quotes passages from the Qur'an for their probative value, along with a chain of biblical testimonies as prooftexts for Christian teaching.[4] Writing in Greek, John of Damascus (d. 749–754) said of Muhammad: "This man, having chanced upon the Old and New Testament, and likely it seems, having conversed with an Arian monk, devised his own heresy."[5] They all noticed the Qur'an's debt to the Bible.

This essay has three main purposes. The first is to explore the ways in which the Qur'an reflects its indebtedness to the Bible, particularly in its evocations of the careers of the biblical patriarchs and prophets as forerunners of the mission of God's messenger and prophet Muhammad. Second is to describe how the Arabic idiom of the Qur'an came to function as virtually the verbal icon of scriptural diction in Arabic and even appeared in Jewish and Christian translations of the Bible into Arabic to impart a certain Islamic cast to the language of the Arabic versions of the biblical books. Third is to discuss briefly how the scriptural intertextuality of Bible and Qur'an exercised a shaping influence on Jewish and Christian religious discourse more generally in the Arabic-speaking milieu of the world of Islam, according it a distinctiveness that marked it off from the modes of expression and reasoning characteristic of their coreligionists elsewhere.

The Bible in the Qur'an

The Qur'an's frequent reminiscences of the careers of God's earlier messengers and prophets are a feature of the Arabic scripture's discourse, which even the most casual reader can scarcely miss. For the most part, but not exclusively, these figures are familiar to the readers of the Bible.

---

3. See Sidney H. Griffith, "Disputing with Islam in Syriac: The Case of the Monk of Bêt Ḥālê and a Muslim Emir," *Hug* 3 (2000): 29–54.

4. See Samir Khalil Samir, "The Earliest Arab Apology for Christianity (c. 750)," in *Christian Arabic Apologetics during the Abbasid Period (750–1258)*, ed. Samir Khalil Samir and Jøgen S. Nielsen, SHR 63 (Leiden: Brill, 1994), 57–114.

5. John of Damascus, *Writings: St. John of Damascus*, trans. F. H. Chase, FC 37 (Washington, DC: Catholic University of America Press, 1958), 153.

And yet much that is said of them in the Qur'an is not to be found in the Bible. In fact, with very few exceptions and only one clear instance (Ps 37:29 in Q Anbya 21:105), there are no real quotations from the Bible in the Qur'an. But readers familiar with biblical and extrabiblical Jewish and Christian traditions about biblical characters will often find elements of their stories recollected in the Qur'an. In the ensemble, these biblical features of the Qur'an's narratives become compelling evidence of the Islamic scripture's participation in the late antique Jewish and Christian thought-world. The lack of explicit quotation bespeaks an oral and not a textual participation, even as there is a persistent mention of books and writing in the Qur'an. They are part of the story, not its medium. The reminiscence of the stories of past messengers and prophets voiced by God himself in the Qur'an is meant to recall a series of admonishers and warners, usually intended to assure Muhammad as well as his audience that he is one of the messengers and prophets, even the last of them. The point is furthermore to disclose the *sunnah* of God's messengers—the profile, the pattern of their careers, the "curve" of their lives (as Louis Massignon [1883–1962] would say), the paradigm that structured Muhammad's own career, the wonder of which showed that "he walked in the way of the prophets," as the Nestorian patriarch Timothy I (r. 780–823) once admitted in the *majlis* of the caliph al-Mahdī (775–785).[6] The Qur'an busily calls one's attention to the wondrous signs (*ayāt*) attending the exploits of the biblical messengers and prophets, testifying to the truth and genuineness of their missions, that they are in accord with the "*Sunnah* of Our Messengers" (Q Isra 17:77), as the Qur'an calls the prophetic paradigm, the "way," according to the Qur'an, of all God's messengers and prophets, including Moses and Jesus the Messiah, and finally in the Qur'an the *sunnah*, or "way," of Muhammad.

The "*Sunnah* of Our Messengers," the Qur'an's distinctive prophetology vis-à-vis that of the Jews and Christians in particular, as it is displayed in a number of *sūrahs*, features several characteristics that when taken in the ensemble compose a pattern or paradigm that not only distinguishes it

---

6. For the quote from Timothy, see Hans Putman, *L'église et l'islam sous Timothée I: Etude sur l'église nestorienne au temps des premiers ʿAbbāsides, avec nouvelle edition et traduction du dialogue entre Timothée et al-Mahdi* [Arabic] (Beirut: Dar El-Machreq, 1975), 31. Massignon's customary expression was "une courbe personnelle de vie." See, e.g., his classic essay, "Étude sur une courbe personnelle de vie, le cas du Hallaj; martyr mystique de l'Islam," *Dieu Vivant* 4 (1945): 11–39.

from the prophetologies of other late antique scriptural communities but also provides a hermeneutical standard or yardstick in reference to which the Qur'an measures and critiques the doctrines and practices of other communities, especially in regard to how they view the lives and teachings of the prophetic figures they share with the Qur'an. This prophetic paradigm may be summarily described as follows. Qur'anic prophetology is *catholic* (God's messengers have come to both biblical and nonbiblical people), *recurrent* (the pattern of apostolic and prophetic experience recurs in the sequence of messengers and prophets), *dialogical* (the messengers and prophets interact in dialogue with their people), *singular* in its message (the one God, who rewards good and punishes evil on the day of judgment; no divinizing of creatures); *triumphant* (God vindicates his messengers and prophets in their struggles with their adversaries; i.e., the so-called punishment stories, accusations of killing the prophets unjustly notwithstanding; see also Q Baqarah 2:61; 'Imran 3:21), and *initiatory* (God's messengers and prophets initiate or reinitiate/renew the religious observance of their own people).[7]

With its disclosure of the "*Sunnah* of Our Messengers," the Qur'an intends to correct the constructions that Jews and Christians had put on the biblical narratives of the patriarchs and prophets. In the case of the Christians, one can readily see that it is especially concerned to set the record straight about the Messiah, Jesus. Whereas contemporaneous late antique Christian homiletic discourses—particularly the Syriac *mêmrê*, which were delivered, like the Qur'an, in cadenced phrases—saw in the narratives of the patriarchs and prophets the signs and symbols (*râzê*) that proleptically present the full truth about Jesus the Messiah as the Son of God, the Qur'an presents him as the messenger of God to the Israelites, to whom the wondrous "signs" (*ayāt*) evident in his career by God's permission unmistakably point and as the one who, among other things, prepares the way for and foretells the coming of Ahmad/Muhammad.[8]

---

7. See this matter discussed in a preliminary fashion in Sidney H. Griffith, *The Bible in Arabic: The Scriptures of the People of the Book in the Language of Islam* (Princeton: Princeton University Press, 2013), 54–96. Further discussion is in Sidney H. Griffith, "The '*Sunnah* of Our Messengers': The Qur'ān's Paradigm for Messengers and Prophets; A Reading of *Sūrah* XXVI *ash-Shuʿarā*," in *Qur'anic Studies Today*, ed. Angelika Neuwrith and Michael Sells (New York: Routledge, 2016), 208–17.

8. "[Remember] when Jesus, the son of Mary, said, 'O Israelites, I am God's Messenger to you, confirming what was before me of the Torah and announcing the good

The principal qur'anic moments in which the names and careers of God's earlier messengers and prophets are recollected seem inevitably to feature Muhammad himself or the believers in his entourage, who, in the face of opposition to their message, are in need of reassurance from their Lord that they are on the right path. In the qur'anic text revealed on these occasions, the Qur'an then typically bids Muhammad to remember when Abraham, Moses, Jesus, or some other biblical or nonbiblical prophet or messenger addressed his own people, calling them to belief in the one God and warning them of the consequences of their unrepentant ways. And in the telling the text reminds Muhammad that God always vindicates his messengers and prophets in their struggles with their adversaries. In addition to biblical figures, who, with one notable exception,[9] are the only ones called prophets in the Qur'an, the text also recalls the careers of other messengers (*ar-rusul*) whom God sent to nonbiblical peoples, otherwise now unknown individuals such as Hūd, Ṣāliḥ, and Shuʿayb, who, like the biblical prophets, are said to have been sent as messengers and warners to their own people. It is clear that in the Qur'an the dominant personal profile for one sent by God to warn his own people is that of the messenger of God (*rasūl Allāh*), a title that occurs some 331 times in the text, whereas the title prophet (*an-nabī*) is found only some seventy-five times.[10]

The most basic thing one notices about the Qur'an and its interface with the Bible is the Islamic scripture's unspoken and pervasive presumption that its audience is thoroughly familiar with the stories of the biblical patriarchs and prophets, to whom and to whose exploits the text refers, confident of audience recognition, without any need for even the most rudimentary form of introduction. The Qur'an presents itself as confirming the truth of the previous scriptures and as safeguarding it. After speaking of the Torah, "in which there is guidance and light," and of Jesus "as confirming the veracity of the Torah before him," and of the Gospel,

---

news of a Messenger who will come after me, whose name is Aḥmad.' When he came to them with clear signs they said, 'This is manifest sorcery'" (Q Saf 61:6).

9. The notable exception is Muhammad himself, whom the Qur'an designates as both messenger and prophet. See, e.g., the dozen of times the title "Prophet" is accorded to Muhammad in Q Saba 33, including the famous verse that speaks of Muhammad as "the Messenger of God and the seal of the Prophets" (v. 40). See also Q Tahrim 66:1–9, where God addresses Muhammad as "O Prophet."

10. See in this connection Willem A. Bijlefeld, "A Prophet and More than a Prophet? Some Observations on the Qurʾānic Use of the Terms 'Prophet' and 'Apostle,'" *MW* 59 (1969): 1–28.

"in which there is guidance and light," God says to Muhammad regarding the Qur'an: "We have sent down to you the scripture in truth, as a confirmation of the veracity of the scripture before it, and as a safeguard for it" (Q Ma'idah 5:44, 46, 48). The previous scriptures were, of course, in the Qur'an's telling, principally the Torah and the Gospel, as is clear here and in other places, where the Qur'an says to Muhammad, "He has sent down to you the scripture in truth, as a confirmation of the veracity of what was before it, and He sent down the Torah and the Gospel" (Q 'Imran 3:3). In these and other passages one might cite, the position of the Qur'an vis-à-vis the Jewish and Christian Bible is clear: the Qur'an confirms the veracity of the earlier scriptures. In other words, the Qur'an not only recognizes the Torah and the Gospel, and the Psalms, too, as authentic scripture sent down by God before it, but it now stands as the warrant for their authenticity.

But the matter does not rest here, for while the Qur'an, following both the concurrent Jewish and Christian view, recognizes the Torah as the scripture God sent down to Moses—"We wrote for him in the Tablets about everything" (Q A'raf 7:145)—the Gospel that the Qur'an confirms is not the Gospel recollected in writing in the gospels according to the four New Testament evangelists—Matthew, Mark, Luke, and John—as Christians encountered it in the time of the Qur'an's delivery.[11] For, following the model of its own distinctive prophetology, the Qur'an speaks of the Gospel as a scripture God gave to Jesus: "We gave him the Gospel, wherein there is guidance and light, confirming what he had before him of the Torah" (Q Ma'idah 5:46; Hadid 57:27). Here the Qur'an apparently intends to criticize and correct what it regards as a mistaken Christian view of its own principal scripture. What is more, by the time of its collection, and principally in criticism of the behavior of the people of the book in regard to their scriptures, the Qur'an is already speaking of the

---

11. Seventh-century Christians were, of course, accustomed to the idea of the one Gospel of Jesus the Messiah as recorded in writing in the four gospels of the evangelists, which is why they spoke of the Gospel according to Matthew, Mark, Luke, or John. Since the Qur'an's evocation of the Gospel is not textual but oral, it is not surprising that it does not mention the gospels. However, it was on its own recognizance, and given its own distinctive prophetology, that the Qur'an then speaks of the Gospel as a "scripture" (*kitāb*) that God sent down to Jesus the Messiah, on the model of the Torah for Moses before him, and of the Qur'an for Muhammad after him. The Qur'an mentions the Torah, the Gospel, and the Qur'an as on a par with one another in Q Tawbah 9:111.

"distortion" and "alteration" of scriptural texts in passages (e.g., in Q Baqarah 2:75-79; 'Imran 3:78; Nisa' 4:46; Ma'idah 5:12-19) that in subsequent Islamic tradition will undergird the doctrine of the corruption of the earlier scriptures,[12] a development that would effectively discount the testimonies drawn by Jews or Christians from their scriptures in proof of the veracity of their teachings.

Against this background of the general recognition of the major scriptures of the Jews and the Christians, the Torah, the Gospel, and the Psalms (*az-Zabūr*), "in which We wrote" (Q Anbiya' 21:105) and which "We brought to David" (Q Nisa' 4:163; Isra 17:55), the Qur'an even advises Muhammad to consult "those who were reading the scripture [*al-kitāb*] before you" (Q Yunus 10:94). In context, the Qur'an speaks of God's instruction to Muhammad for his discourse to his audience, to "relate to them the story of Noah" (10:71), and God goes on to speak of Moses and Aaron, the pharaoh, the exodus from Egypt, and the settlement of the Israelites, and within this frame of reference advises Muhammad, "If you are in doubt about what We have sent down to you, ask those who were reading the scripture before you. The truth has come down to you from your Lord, so you should certainly not be in doubt" (Q Yunus 10:94). In a similar vein, in another place, the Qur'an records God's word to Muhammad: "We have sent out before you only men whom We have inspired, so ask the 'People of remembrance' [*ahl adh-dhikr*] if you do not know;[13] [We have inspired them] with clear evidences and texts [*az-zubur*] and We have sent down the remembrance [*adh-dhikr*] to you so that We might make clear to people what has been sent down to them; perhaps they will reflect" (Q Nahl 16:43-44). Clearly in these passages the Qur'an commends recalling the message of the earlier scriptures, but what catches one's attention here is the phrase "people of remembrance" and the reference to what God sent down to Muhammad as "the remembrance." One notices in the context the parallel between "the remembrance" (*adh-dhikr*) and "the scripture" (*al-kitāb*), so in this context the "scripture people/people of the book" (*ahl al-kitāb*) are the "people of remembrance," and what they remember or recall is God's dealings with the patriarchs and prophets. We now find these dealings recorded in the

---

12. See Jean-Marie Gaudeul and Robert Caspar, "Textes de la tradition musulmane concernant le *taḥrif* (falsification) es écritures," *Islamochristiana* 6 (1980): 61-104; Jane Dammen McAuliffe, "The Qur'ānic Context of Muslim Biblical Scholarship," *ICMR* 7 (1996): 141-58.

13. This exact sentence is also found in Q Anbiya' 21:7.

biblical scriptures and associated literature, the very remembrance that is also recorded in the Qur'an, and this is the reason that the Qur'an itself is referred to in its own text as a "remembrance," here and in the oath formula "By the Qur'an, possessed of remembrance [*dhī adh-dhikr*]" (Q Sad 38:1), and in such epithets of the Qur'an as "a blessed remembrance" (Q Anbiya' 21:50) and as being itself a "reminder" (*tadhkirah*; Q Taha 20:3), a "reminder" (*dhikrā*) for people of the "scripture, the judgment, and the prophethood God had previously sent down (see Q An'ām 6:89–90).

Remembrance suggests orality. And the scriptural remembrance of which the Qur'an speaks has all the marks of a distinctively and primarily oral phenomenon, though what is remembered is said to have been originally recorded in a scripture. The Qur'an remembers, of course, that although its words were spoken by Muhammad under divine inspiration, it is itself also a "book" (*al-kitāb*), like the earlier scriptures, which were inscribed in texts, scrolls, and copies, as the Qur'an itself says. Nevertheless, as an initially oral book, which was sent down to Muhammad, it is important to notice how inevitably in the Qur'an, when the text evokes a biblical narrative or summons up the often-extrabiblical story of a patriarch or prophet, it exhorts its audience to "remember" or to "recall" (*idhkurū*). In many sequences of such narrative in the Qur'an one finds a key term appearing after the initial imperative to remember: it is the simple word "when" (*idh*) or its equivalents, implying a preceding admonition "to remember." Indeed, translators often supply the imperative "remember" in brackets when they encounter a succession of verses in a *sūrah* all beginning simply with the telltale *idh*, *idhā*, or even *lammā*. For example, in Sūrat al-Baqarah the text goes on for a hundred verses and more recalling Israelite salvation history through the remembrance of the experiences of several of the major patriarchs and prophets, Moses in particular, without once quoting the scriptures but nevertheless employing the memory term *idh* and its synonyms some twenty-five times and more, to evoke the biblical and apocryphal scenarios in details familiar not only from the Bible but from Jewish and Christian lore as well, as many recent studies have shown.[14] The remembrance is as if from memory alone, with no explicit textual reference, freely phrased in the telling or retelling of a biblical or

---

14. Such studies are too numerous to list here. Suffice it to cite one that refers to many others in bibliographical notes: Gabriel Said Reynolds, *The Qurʾān and Its Biblical Subtext*, RSQ (London: Routledge, 2010).

prophetic tale that features both narrative and dialogue on the part of both the narrator and the dramatis personae.

The point is that as we find the Bible in the Qur'an, recollecting the patriarchs and prophets of the biblical past, it is for the most part an oral affair, recalling or recollecting biblical narratives and their heroes, usually without reference to a text (Torah or Gospel, even for Joseph [Q Yusuf 12] or Mary [Q Maryam 19]) and never in exact quotation, save in the one instance of Sūrat Al-Anbya' 21:105: "We have written in the Psalms after the reminder that 'My righteous servants will inherit the earth' [Ps 37:29]." One is drawn to the conclusion that while the Torah, the Psalms, and the Gospel are known in the Qur'an and its Arabic-speaking milieu to be scriptures, that is, books or writings, their contents as reflected in the Qur'an seem to have been available in Arabic only orally, as they would have been heard in liturgical proclamations interpreted in the vernacular and in homiletic commentaries, exercises in what would amount to oral *hagaddah* and moral admonitions.[15] Even then, while the Qur'an knows of a long list of biblical figures whom God inspired (see Q Nisa' 4:163–165),[16] it recollects only a relatively small portion of their stories, and that much only as it accords with the Qur'an's own scriptural agenda, set in large part by its own distinctive prophetology, as described above.

Given the fact that neither the Bible nor the extrabiblical lore about the patriarchs and prophets that are recollected in the Qur'an are embedded textually, in translation in the Arabic scripture, but are rather recalled and reported freely, only orally, the question naturally arises about how the narrative details that in many instances can be found otherwise attested only in a disparate array of texts in non-Arabic languages—Hebrew, Aramaic, Greek, Syriac, or Ge'ez—found their way orally into the Arabic-speaking milieu of the Hijāz in the first third of the seventh century. Here

---

15. See in this connection the important study by Andrew B. Bannister, *An Oral-Formulaic Study of the Qur'ān* (Lanham, MD: Lexington Books, 2014).

16. In this passage, the Qur'an addresses Muhammad: "We have brought revelation to you [second-person masculine singular] just as We brought revelation to Noah and the prophets after him, and We brought revelation to Abraham, Ishmael, Isaac, Jacob and the Tribes, [to] Jesus, Job, Jonah, Aaron, Solomon, and We brought David Psalms. We have told you [second-person masculine singular] the stories of Messengers before you [second-person masculine singular] and there were Messengers whose stories We have not told you [second-person masculine singular]. God spoke with Moses directly; Messengers preach and warn so that after the Messengers people would have no case against God; God is mighty and wise" (Q Nisa' 4:163–65).

is not the place to go into the matter in detail; suffice it to say for present purposes that local, Arabic-speaking, Jewish and Christian communities undoubtedly had written scriptures and other texts in their synagogues, churches, and monasteries, not in Arabic but in the canonical languages of their communities. In all likelihood, once passages from them were proclaimed aloud in liturgical settings, they were immediately translated and interpreted in the local, vernacular Arabic language—a custom already well established among both Jews and Christians in Aramaic, in other geographical and cultural settings. In the Christian instance at least, it seems that in Arabia the translations and interpretations were supplemented by expository homilies that drew heavily on the abundant archive of Syriac *mêmrê* that circulated widely in the Syriac-speaking, Christian communities. From the oral recounting of these in translation, Arabic-speaking Christians and others, including the Qur'an itself, seem to have learned about Christian teachings and readings of the biblical and extrabiblical narratives of Old and New Testament patriarchs and prophets as well as other ecclesiastical figures of whom we hear in the Qur'an, such as the "companions of the cave" or elements of the Alexander Romance in Sūrat Al-Kahf.[17]

Independently of the Qur'an's recollection of the stories of the biblical patriarchs and prophets according to the dictates of its distinctive prophetology, the unvarying "*Sunnah* of Our Messengers," as the Qur'an itself puts it (Q Isra' 17:77), there are still numerous passages in the Islamic scripture in which, or behind which, scholars ancient and modern claim to have detected the echo or even the repetition of the very wording in Arabic translation of numerous apocryphal, homiletic, exegetical, hymnic, or hagiographical passages from texts originally written in Greek, Aramaic, Syriac, or Geʿez before the time of the Qur'an.[18] These perceptions

---

17. See these matters discussed in Griffith, *Bible in Arabic*, esp. 41–62. See also Sidney H. Griffith, "Christian Lore and the Arabic Qur'ān: The 'Companions of the Cave' in *Sūrat al-Kahf* and in Syriac Christian Tradition," in *The Qur'ān in Its Historical Context*, ed. Gabriel Said Reynolds, RSQ (London: Routledge, 2008), 109–37; and Kevin Van Bladel, "The Alexander Legend in the Qur'ān 18:83–102," in Reynolds, *Qur'ān in Its Historical Context*, 175–203.

18. The literature that reports these matters is becoming enormous. Suffice it here to cite just a few of the more recent examples that in turn cite earlier studies. See Reynolds, *Qur'ān and Its Biblical Subtext*; Cornelia Horn, "Lines of Transmission between Apocryphal Traditions in the Syriac-Speaking World: Manichaeism and the Rise of Islam; the Case of the *Acts of John*," *ParOr* 35 (2010): 337–55; Guillaume Dye

inevitably raise hermeneutical questions about how deep in the Qur'an's oral or textual background these seeming repetitions or evocations might be supposed to lie, be they allegedly remembered, copied, or transcribed into the Qur'an. The answers to the hermeneutical questions in any given instance depend largely on a given scholar's views of the historiography of Islamic origins: the time, manner, and agency of the collection of the Qur'an and its final recension as the first Arabic book.[19] It is beyond the present purpose to pursue these issues here. The point to be made in the present context is simply that in the view of many researchers, many passages in the Arabic Qur'an can plausibly be seen to have been mapped onto the language and narrative pattern of passages in earlier texts in pre-Islamic Jewish or Christian writings. This is alleged to have been the case especially in reference to narrative themes and modes of discourse otherwise found in biblical and parabiblical literature.

The Bible that is both everywhere and nowhere textually present in the Qur'an is nevertheless also present in another important way in the Islamic scripture. The Qur'an's diction often reflects what one might call a scriptural, that is to say, a biblical, even a liturgical cast of language at many junctures. This feature of qur'anic diction comes to light not only in the matter of wording, where it is perceptible particularly in the numerous instances of the Qur'an's so-called foreign vocabulary,[20] much of which turns out to be biblical or liturgical terminology taken into Arabic either from the scriptural languages themselves, such as Hebrew or Greek, or, more frequently, deriving from wording otherwise found textually in biblical translations and paraphrases in Aramiac, Greek, Syriac, and Ge'ez.

---

and Fabien Nobilio, eds., *Figures bibliques en Islam* (Fernelmont, Belgium: Éditions Modulaires Européennes, 2011); Carlos A. Segovia and Basil Lourié, eds., *The Coming of the Comforter: When, Where, and to Whom? Studies on the Rise of Islam and Various Other Topics in Memory of John Wansbrough* (Piscataway, NJ: Gorgias, 2012); Holger Zellentin, *The Qurʾān's Legal Culture: The Didascalia Apostolorum as a Point of Departure* (Tübingen: Mohr Siebeck, 2013); Paul Neuenkirchen, "Biblical Elements in Koran 89, 6–8 and Its Exegeses: A New Interpretation of 'Iram of the Pillars,'" *Arabica* 60 (2013): 651–700; Neuenkirchen, "Visions et Ascensions: Deux péricopes coraniques à la lumière d'un apocryphe chrétien," *JA* 302 (2014): 303–47.

19. For a discussion of these matters in view of recent historiography, see Angelika Neuwirth, *Der Koran als Text der Spätantike: Ein europäischer Zugang* (Berlin: Verlag der Weltreligionen im Insel Verlag, 2010).

20. See Arthur Jeffrey, *The Foreign Vocabulary of the Qurʾān* (Baroda, India: Oriental Institute, 1938).

In addition, the scriptural and liturgical cast of qur'anic language is also perceptible in the Qur'an's rhetorical style, in oft-repeated set phrases that suggest a liturgical *Sitz im Leben*, especially in the Meccan *sūrahs*, which seemingly owe their inspiration to contemporary synagogue or church practices in the Arabic-speaking milieu. From this perspective, the Qur'an itself might be thought to be a kind of liturgical lectionary, assuming an etymological relationship to the cognate Syriac term, *qeryānâ* (pl. *qeryānê*), which indicates a liturgical lesson, usually a biblical pericope assigned for proclamation and interpretation according to the seasonal and festal liturgical calendars of the Syriac-speaking churches.[21]

The Qur'an in the Bible and in Parabiblical Literature

The Earliest Translations of the Bible into Arabic

There is so far no convincing evidence that any portion of the Bible circulated in writing in an Arabic translation prior to the rise of Islam or in the period of Islamic origins, the first third of the seventh century CE.[22] Among the early Arabic-speaking Christians living outside Arabia in early Islamic times, the translation of the Scriptures into the language of the Qur'an was high on their agenda, but unfortunately the very earliest surviving manuscripts seldom carry the dates of their copying, and the scholars who have studied them have had to make their best judgments on the basis of paleographical considerations. A case in point is the text of Ps 78 (Ps 77 LXX), found in the treasury of the Umayyad Mosque in Damascus.[23] It is a dual-language text, including the psalm written in Greek with an Arabic version written alongside it in Greek script. It seems that the intended reader or interpreter, probably functioning in a liturgical setting, is presumed to have been fluent in Arabic but more familiar with the Greek script than with the Arabic one. On paleographical grounds, scholars have

---

21. See in this connection the essay by Claude Gilliot, "Mohammed's Exegetical Activity in the Meccan Arabic Lectionary," in Segovia and Lourié, *Coming of the Comforter*, 371–98.
22. See the discussion in Griffith, *Bible in Arabic*, 7–53; Griffith, "When Did the Bible Become an Arabic Scripture?," *Intellectual History of the Islamicate World* (2013): 7–23.
23. See Bruno Violet, Ein *zweisprachiges Psalmfragment aus Damaskus* (Berlin: Akademie, 1902).

dated the text to the late eighth century at the earliest, but some have more recently opted for a later date in the ninth century,[24] which would place the text within the range of dates one finds included in the colophons of the dated manuscripts that include the earliest Arabic translations of portions of the Bible so far known.

Not surprisingly, the gospels seem to have been among the earliest biblical texts translated by newly Arabic-speaking Christians, and there are several contending translations that may well have been among the very earliest. What scholars believe to be the earliest known, dated manuscript containing an Arabic translation of a Christian biblical text is a copy of the four gospels in Arabic, now held in the library of the Monastery of Saint Catherine at Mount Sinai, which, according to a scribal note, was completed on the feast of Saint George in the year 859 CE.[25] Sinai Arabic manuscript 151 contains an Arabic version of the Epistles of Paul that according to its colophon was copied in Damascus in the year 867.[26] For the rest, the earliest dated manuscripts cluster in the second half of the ninth century.[27] But it is clear from numerous studies that the earliest dated manuscripts are not in fact the earliest manuscripts, nor are the translations of the Bible they contain necessarily the earliest translations.

---

24. See the discussions by Anton Baumstark, "Der älteste erhaltene Griechisch-Arabische Text von Psalm 110 (109)," *OrChr* 9 (1934): 55–66; Rachid Haddad, "La phonétique de l'arabe chrétien vers 700," in *La Syrie de Byzance a l'Islam: VIIe–VIIIe siècles; Actes du Colloque International Lyon-Maison de l'Orient Méiterranéen, Paris—Institut du Monde Arabe, 11–15 Septembre 1990*, ed. Pierre Canivet and Jean-Paul Rey-Coquais (Damas: Institut Français de Damas, 1992), 159–64; Maria Mavroudi, "Arabic Words in Greek Letters: The Violet Fragment and More," in *Moyen arabe et variétés mixtes de l'arabe à travers l'histoire: Actes dum premier colloque international (Louvain-la-Neuve, 10–14 mai 2004)*, ed. Jérôme Lentin and Jacques Grand'henry, Université Catholique de Louvain, Institut Orientaliste (Leuven: Peeters, 2008), 321–54.

25. See Ioannis Emm. Meimare, Καταλογος των Νεων Αραβικων Χειρογραφων της Ιερας Μονης Αγιας Αικατερινης του Ορους Σινα [List of New Arabic Manuscripts of the Holy Monastery of Saint Catherine of Mount Sinai] (Athens: National Hellenic Research Foundation, 1985), parchment no. 16; see also photos 19–21. See the beautiful photograph of the two pages from this manuscript, including an illustration of St. Luke, in Michelle P. Brown, *In the Beginning: Bibles before the Year 1000* (Washington, DC: Smithsonian Institution, 2006), 166–67, 274–75.

26. See H. Staal, *Mt. Sinai Arabic Codex 151: I Pauline Epistles*, CSCO 452–53 (Leuven: Peeters, 1983).

27. See Griffith, "The Monks of Palestine and the Growth of Christian Literature in Arabic," *The Muslim World* 78 (1988): esp. 13–20.

Judging on the basis of paleographical considerations, scholars have identified several manuscripts containing copies of Arabic translations of the gospels that in their opinion can reasonably be dated to the eighth century, and in one or two instances they even make a case for the seventh century. However, it is important to understand from the outset that a distinction is to be made between the original Arabic translation of a given scriptural text and the surviving copy of it that one finds in the manuscripts. Scholars have often shown that the surviving manuscripts they have studied contain a copy of the original Arabic translation of a biblical text; in no case is it thought that one is dealing with the autograph of the translation as it left the hand of the original translator. The earliest translations of the gospels were made from Syriac and Greek *Vorlagen* into Arabic.[28] In the first instance, they were most likely all produced in the multilingual monastic communities in Syria/Palestine, and particularly in the environs of Jerusalem and the Judean desert, where the first large-scale Arabic translation movement under Christian auspices was undertaken as early as the second half of the eighth century, if not a bit earlier.

The gospels were, of course, not the only portions of the Bible translated by Christians into Arabic in the early period of the ecclesiastical translation movement. As mentioned above, the oldest surviving and dated translation is in fact a gospel text. In the same era translations of the Epistles of Paul were made, and there were translations under Christian auspices of the Torah, the Psalms, and other portions of the Bible. The surviving evidence indicates that in all probability the earliest translations of the Bible into Arabic done by Christians appeared in the eighth century in Syria/Palestine. It is not unreasonable to suppose that in one or two instances one might extrapolate from the evidence in hand back to a date in the late seventh century for the production of the original exemplar of a particular text. Many historians of Christianity among the Arabic-speaking peoples have wanted to find evidence for a pre-Islamic, Arabic translation of the Bible. The trouble is that not only is there so far no completely convincing evidence for the actuality of such a translation, but also the existing evidence argues against its probability.

Without a doubt, the most notable early, Jewish translation of the Hebrew Bible into Arabic is that done by Saʿadya ha-Gaon (882–942),

---

28. See H. Kachouh, "The Arabic Versions of the Gospels: A Case Study of John 1:1 and 1:18," in *The Bible in Arab Christianity*, ed. David Thomas, CMR 6 (Leiden: Brill, 2007), 9–36.

about which more below. But Saʿadya's was certainly not the earliest biblical translation done under Jewish auspices in the early Islamic period, though in all probability Arabic-speaking Jews outside Arabia proper were not as concerned about translating the Bible into Arabic as early as were the newly Arabic-speaking Christians. The concern among Christians to translate the Scriptures into the languages of their several communities, largely for liturgical purposes, had been an imperative for them long before the rise of Islam, whereas among Jews the Hebrew original, along with the Aramaic targums, had long sufficed as the liturgical languages in the synagogues of Syria/Palestine and Mesopotamia. But circumstances seem to have changed in the course of the ninth century as more and more Jews in the Levant adopted Arabic and began to develop the linguistically distinctive "Middle Arabic" state of the language that scholars have come to call Judaeo-Arabic, not only because it was employed by Jews but also because it was written in Hebrew characters and was in many other ways influenced by Hebrew grammar, syntax, and lexicography.[29] The earliest texts in Judaeo-Arabic have been preserved in the Cairo Genizah, an archive that has provided an abundant documentation for the study of Jewish communities and their interactions with others in the Mediterranean milieu from the early Islamic period and well beyond.[30]

As was the case among the Arabic-speaking Christians, so too among the Jews; the earliest texts in Arabic are both translations and original compositions. The earliest of them are dated to the ninth century, and a number of the original compositions are in the apologetic and polemical genres characteristic of the interreligious controversies of the early Islamic period.[31] The earliest Bible translation so far confidently identified seems to be a passage from the book of Proverbs identified by Joshua Blau in a

---

29. Joshua Blau, *The Emergence and Linguistic Background of Judaeo-Arabic: A Study of the Origins of Neo-Arabic and Middle Arabic*; Blau, *A Dictionary of Mediaeval Judaeo-Arabic Texts* (Jerusalem: Israel Academy of Sciences and Humanities, 2006).

30. See the classic study by Goitein, *Mediterranean Society*.

31. See, e.g., Daniel J. Lasker, "*Qiṣṣat Mujādalat al-Usquf* and *Neṣṭor Ha-Komer*: The Earliest Arabic and Hebrew Jewish Anti-Christian Polemics," in *Genizah Research after Ninety Years: The Case of Judaeo-Arabic; Papers Read at the Third Congress of the Society for Judaeo-Arabic Studies*, ed. J. Blau and S. C. Reif (Cambridge: Cambridge University Press, 1992), 112–18; Simone Rosenkranz, *Die jüdisch-christliche Auseinandersetzung unter islamischer Herrschaft: 7.-10. Jahrhundert*, JudChr 11 (Bern: Lang, 2004).

Cairo Genizah fragment.³² Blau points out that the mode of transcription of the Arabic letters into Hebrew ones in the text, the usage characteristic of Judaeo-Arabic, reflects the practice of phonetic spelling common in pre-tenth-century manuscripts, rather than the standard system of transliteration in use from Sa'adya's time onward. This observation pushes the date of the text back into the ninth century. What is more, and again not unlike the case with the earliest surviving Christian Arabic texts, Blau is able to conclude on the basis of his study of the text of Proverbs preserved in the fragment that "its heterogeneous character makes it quite likely that it based itself on other translations preceding it."³³ This probability allows one reasonably to assume that the first translations of portions of the Hebrew Bible were completed quite early in the ninth century. In the meantime, other scholars have identified more fragments of early Bible translations into Judaeo-Arabic in the Cairo Genizah archive, and, again as in the instance of some who have studied the earliest gospel translations, some scholars of the Judaeo-Arabic translations have yielded to the temptation to extrapolate from the state of the texts surviving from the ninth century and to postulate the not-impossible existence of earlier translations, possibly even pre-Islamic ones.³⁴

The problem with extrapolating from the probable ninth-century dating of the earliest surviving Judaeo-Arabic translations of portions of the Bible to a date earlier than the second half of the seventh century as the terminus post quem for written Bible translations in Arabic is that the historian encounters a number of countervailing factors that push the probable date forward from that point, and well into the ninth century for the earliest Judaeo-Arabic translations. There is first of all the fact that the late seventh century is the earliest period from which the available evidence would warrant dating any substantial body of written Arabic, as explored above. But perhaps even more telling in the instance of the Hebrew Bible is the accumulating evidence that even in Arabic-speaking

---

32. See Joshua Blau, "On a Fragment of the Oldest Judaeo-Arabic Bible Translation Extant," in Blau and Reif, *Genizah Research after Ninety Years*, 31–39.

33. Blau, "On a Fragment of the Oldest Judaeo-Arabic Bible," 32.

34. See, e.g., Yosef Tobi, "On the Antiquity of Ancient Judeo-Arabic Biblical Translations and a New Piece of an Ancient Judeo-Arabic Translation of the Pentateuch," in *Ben 'Ever la-'Arav: Contacts between Arabic Literature and Jewish Literature in the Middle Ages and Modern Times*, ed. Y. Tobi and Y. Avishur (Tel Aviv: Afikim Publishers, 2001), 2:17–60.

Jewish communities, the Torah would not have been read individually but proclaimed orally in synagogues and in Hebrew, or in Aramaic targums. Moreover, it appears that the early Bible translations into Judaeo-Arabic were in fact contemporaneous with, and perhaps integral parts of, the cultural shift in Jewish reading and writing practices that occurred in the late eighth century and continued throughout the ninth century, which one recent scholar calls the "codexification" of Judaism.[35] This development was a cultural phenomenon that provides a context for the Judaeo-Arabic translation movement of the same period within the framework of Jewish adjustment to the challenges of early Islam, including the many factors that gave rise to the then-burgeoning controversies within the Jewish communities between Rabbanites and Karaites.[36] In fact, the Karaites seem to have been the earliest Jewish community systematically to produce Arabic translations of the Torah from the late ninth century onward, more for purposes of the close study of the text than for liturgical proclamation.[37]

The major Jewish contribution to the translation of the Bible into Arabic, however, was undoubtedly that of the famous Rabbanite scholar Saʿadyah ben Yosef al-Fayyūmī ha-*Gaʾōn* (882–942).[38] As his name indicates, Saʿadyah came originally from Egypt to Babylonia, with an intervening sojourn in Palestine. He was well known as a scholar even before his arrival in Iraq and in due course, in 928 CE, he was appointed *gaʾōn* of the academy of Sura, now removed to Baghdad. Saʿadyah held the position of *gaʾōn*, not without struggle and controversy, until the end of his life. He made major contributions to Jewish religious and intellectual life, which persist to the present day. And what is more, in his own time he was certainly one of the principal intellectuals involved in the interreligious,

---

35. See David Stern, "The First Jewish Books and the Early History of Jewish Reading," *JQR* 98 (2008): 163–202, esp. 198.

36. Here is not the place to discuss this very important topic. See Daniel Lasker, "Rabbinism and Karaism: The Contest for Supremacy," in *Great Schisms in Jewish History*, ed. R. Jospe and S. M. Wagner (New York: Ktav, 1981), 47–72; Meira Polliack, "Rethinking Karaism: Between Judaism and Islam," *AJS Review* 30 (2006): 67–93.

37. See Meira Polliack, *The Karaite Tradition of Arabic Bible Translation: A Linguistic and Exegetical Study of Karaite Translations of the Pentateuch from the Tenth and Eleventh Centuries CE*, Études sur le Judaïsme Médiéval 17 (Leiden: Brill, 1997).

38. See still Henry Malter, *Saadia Gaon: His Life and Works* (Philadelphia: Jewish Publication Society of America, 1921). See also Robert Brody, *The Geonim of Babylonia and the Shaping of Medieval Jewish Culture* (New Haven: Yale University Press, 1998), 235–48; Haggai Ben-Shammai, "Saʿadya Gaon," *EJIW* 4:197–204.

philosophical, and theological discussions that flourished in the cosmopolitan atmosphere of Baghdad in the tenth century CE. But from the perspective of the present concern, the most important of his works is his translation of the Torah and other books of the Bible into Judaeo-Arabic.

Beyond a doubt, Sa'adyah's *Tafsīr*, as he called his Arabic translations of the Hebrew Bible, stands as an enduring monument of his scholarship; in addition to the Torah, he translated the books of Isaiah, Psalms, Proverbs, Job, Lamentations, Esther, and Daniel.[39] The Arabic title for the translations, a term that means "interpretation," "explanation," or "commentary," bespeaks Sa'adyah's understanding of his project as one in aid of a better understanding of the text of the Hebrew Bible for Jews living in the new, Arabic-speaking milieu. Sa'adyah was concerned, in addition to using good, clear Arabic, to transmit traditional Jewish understandings of the biblical text. As Haggai Ben-Shammai has noted, "His translation of the Pentateuch often follows the Aramaic translation of Onkelos, but not consistently. In matters of lexicography he occasionally follows earlier Judeo-Arabic translations."[40] But in regard to the earlier Judaeo-Arabic usage, it is noteworthy that by means of his biblical translations, which soon became popular throughout the Arabic-speaking Jewish communities, Sa'adyah succeeded not only in overcoming the excessive literalism in the earlier versions and their perceived stylistic clumsiness and infelicity but also in standardizing Judaeo-Arabic spelling, shifting from the earlier phonetic, Hebraized usage to a standard system of transliteration.[41] Moreover, it was Sa'adyah who first introduced Arabic "into the discourse of the

---

39. Sa'adyah's *Tafsīr* and his other works are published in *Ouvres completes de R. Saadia Ben Josef al-Fayyoûmî*, ed. Joseph Derenbourg, 5 vols. (Paris: Leroux, 1893–1899). For further bibliography on more recent editions of Sa'adyah's translations see Richard C. Steiner, *A Biblical Translation in the Making: The Evolution and Impact of Saadia Gaon's Tafsīr*, Harvard University Center for Jewish Studies (Cambridge: Harvard University Press, 2010), esp. 169–70.

40. Ben-Shammai, "Sa'adyah Gaon," 199.

41. Joshua Blau speaks of what he calls "the carelessness" of Judaeo-Arabic style as one of its "chief characteristics." See Blau, *Emergence and Linguistic Background of Judaeo-Arabic*, 97–98. On these and related issues connected with the earlier Jewish Bible translations, see Steiner, *Biblical Translation in the Making*, esp. 5–31. On the standard system of transliteration, see Blau, "On a Fragment of the Oldest Judaeo-Arabic Bible," 31–32.

rabbinic elite.... He also followed the structure of Arabic works, especially in providing systematic theoretical introductions to all his writings."[42]

The perceived Arabic infelicity of earlier Judaeo-Arabic biblical translations along with a number of concerns with translation technique, some of them dictated by important religious considerations, seem to have been among the motives that prompted Saʿadyah to undertake work on his *Tafsīr*. He says himself of his project: "For a long time, in my hometown, I dwelled constantly on my desire, which was to have a translation of the Torah composed by me in use among the people of the true religion, a proper translation that would not be refuted by speculative knowledge or rebutted by tradition; but I refrained from taking that on ... because I thought that in the lands far from my hometown there were translations that were clear and formulated precisely."[43]

Saʿadyah's hometown was in Egypt, and it seems to have been the case that no sooner had he arrived in Palestine that he discovered that the clear and precisely formulated Arabic translations of which he speaks did not in fact yet exist. In all likelihood, then, he started his own long-dreamed-of project already during his sojourn in Tiberias. Richard Steiner makes the case for this position, and he argues that "Saadia's *Tafsīr* was originally nothing more than an annotated translation, perhaps only on the beginning of Genesis." He goes on to explain that on this hypothesis, as Saʿadyah continued work on his project during his years in Baghdad, the annotations became a substantial commentary, leaving the translation engulfed within. Subsequently, according to this view, Saʿadyah, having been persuaded by a request from others, "rectified the situation by reissuing the translation (in a revised version) without any notes at all."[44] So was born the Arabic version of the Torah and other biblical books that quickly found its way throughout the Arabic-speaking Jewish communities in the Islamic world and beyond, even reaching the Samaritans and several Christian communities.

---

42. Ben-Shammai, "Saʿadyah Gaon," 198.

43. Quoted from the preface of Saʿadyah's edition of the *Tafsīr* published without commentary, in Richard Steiner's English translation; Steiner, *Biblical Translation in the Making*, 1.

44. Steiner, *Biblical Translation in the Making*, 93; see also the discussion on 76–93. See Saʿadyah's own remarks on this request and his response to it in the English translation of the relevant passage from the foreword to the unencumbered *Tafsīr*, in Brody, *Geonim of Babylonia*, 302–3.

A Qur'anic Cast of Language in Arabic Bibles and Parabiblical Texts

A very noticeable feature of many of the early Christian and Jewish translations of the Bible into Arabic is what one scholar has called the "Muslim cast" to the language of the translations, by which he means the recurrence of qur'anic diction and obvious Islamic phraseology in the translated texts. Richard Frank first called attention to this phenomenon in his study of the translations of portions of the Bible from Syriac into Arabic by the Nestorian Pethion ibn Ayyūb as-Sahhār, who flourished in Baghdad in the mid-ninth century.[45] The famed Muslim bio-bibliographer of the tenth century, Muḥammad ibn Isḥāq ibn an-Nadīm (d. 905), says in his *Fihrist* that of all the Christian scholars of his day, Pethion "was the most accurate of the translators from the point of view of translation, and also the best of them for style and diction."[46] However true this might have been, Pethion is on record as having translated the biblical books of Job, the Wisdom of Ben Sirach, and the Prophets, all from Syriac into Arabic.[47] Frank edited and translated a portion of Pethion's version of Jeremiah and his version of a Palestinian recension of Ben Sirach into English.[48] And it was in the course of these undertakings that he remarked on the "Muslim cast" to the language. He observed this phenomenon not only in Pethion's translations but also in those by other early translators, and he called attention to what must have been the translators' dilemma in the matter of language. Frank surmised, "To render the Peshitta literally into Arabic or simply to Arabize the Syriac ... would be to produce a rather barbarous Arabic in which the religious tone of the text would be altogether lacking, since the words would have no associations and overtones within themselves but only as seen through another language (Hebrew or Syriac). The book would thus be colorless and devoid of the solemnity which belongs to it."[49]

---

45. On Pethion, see Georg Graf, *Geschichte der christlichen arabischen Literatur*, 5 vols. (Vatican City: Biblioteca apostolica Vaticana, 1944–1953), 2:120–21.
46. Bayard Dodge, ed. and trans., *The Fihrist of al-Nadīm: A Tenth-Century Survey of Muslim Culture* (New York: Columbia University Press, 1970), 1:46.
47. Graf, *Geschichte*, 2:120–21.
48. Richard M. Frank, "The Jeremias of Pethion ibn Ayyūb al-Sahhār," *CBQ* 21 (1959): 136–70; Frank, ed. and trans., *The Wisdom of Jesus Ben Sirach (Sinai ar. 155, IXth/Xth cent.)*, CSCO 357–58 (Leuven: Secrétariat du Corpus SCO, 1974).
49. Frank, "Jeremias of Pethion," 139–40.

The translators solved this dilemma by consistently using Arabic terms with a noticeable Muslim cast, that is to say, they consistently used terms that, though not perhaps exclusively Islamic or qur'anic, are nevertheless thoroughly Muslim and scriptural in their resonance, often by virtue of being stock phrases or oft-repeated invocations from the Qur'an, which soon became common wherever Arabic was spoken. This process inevitably imparted a certain Islamic or qur'anic ring to the biblical diction in the Arabic translations, which enhanced its scriptural quality in the Arabic-speaking milieu, much as the Qur'an had originally purchased a measure of scriptural authority for itself by means of its own adoption of the cadences of biblical language, and even some borrowed biblical vocabulary, in its own recollections of the stories of the Bible's patriarchs and prophets, not to mention its echoes and recapitulations of the phraseology of earlier biblical and parabiblical narratives, as we have mentioned above.

Instances of qur'anic terminology and even phraseology appear broadcast throughout the Jewish and Christian translations and interpretations of biblical books; modern students and editors of these texts routinely call attention to this feature of the Arabic versions. One of the most startling instances of the phenomenon is found in the Samaritan version of Saʿadya ha-Ga'ōn's translation of the Pentateuch, where in rendering Deut 4:35, "The LORD is God; there is no other besides him," the translator, or rather the Samaritan redactor of Saʿadya's *Tafsīr*, has borrowed a qur'anic phrase that lies behind the Islamic *shahādah* to render the biblical phrase: "There is no God but He" (see, e.g., Q Baqarah 2:163, 255; ʿImran 3:2)![50]

Actually, the most notable, early instance of the influence of the Qur'an's language on a post-qur'anic, Christian Arabic composition occurs not in a translated biblical text per se but in a now anonymous, apologetic tract written in the mid-eighth century in support of the credibility of the Christian doctrines of the Trinity and the incarnation. Its first modern

---

50. My thanks to Professor Tamar Zewi, who shared with me her unpublished essay "The Samaritan Version of Saadya Gaon's Translation of the Pentateuch," 10. Professor Zewi proposes that this usage "most probably reflects the Samaritan adoption of the first half of the Islamic creed." In this connection, it is interesting to note that the anonymous author of an early Arab Christian apologetic text, the so-called *Summary of the Ways of Faith*, expressly rejects this accommodation with Islamic language, noting that "they mean a God other than the Father, the Son and the Holy Spirit." See Sidney H. Griffith, *The Church in the Shadow of the Mosque: Christians and Muslims in the World of Islam* (Princeton: Princeton University Press, 2008), 57–58.

editor called the work On the Triune Nature of God.⁵¹ In it the author defends the credibility of the principal articles of the Christian creed, buttressing his reasoning with quotations from the Old Testament, the New Testament, and even from the Qur'an. But the influence of the Qur'an is not limited to quotations used as prooftexts; the whole treatise in its diction and style is suffused with echoes of the Qur'an's language.

In the poetical introduction to the treatise, by allusion and choice of words and phrases the author already echoes the diction and style of the Qur'an.⁵² As Mark Swanson has rightly remarked, "The text simply *is* profoundly Qur'ānic."⁵³ One can see it even in English translation, as in this brief passage from the opening prayer:

> We ask you, O God, by your mercy and your power,
>   to put us among those who know your truth,
>   follow your will, and avoid your wrath,
> [who] praise your beautiful names [Q Aʿraf 7:180],
>   and speak of your exalted similes. [see Q Rum 30:27]
> You are the compassionate One,
>   the merciful, the most compassionate;
> You are seated on the throne [Q Aʿraf 7:54],
>   You are higher than creatures;
>   You fill up all things.⁵⁴

Shortly after this prayer, the author makes a statement that may well serve as an expression of his purpose in composing his work. Again, the attentive reader can hear the qur'anic overtones clearly. The author says,

---

51. Margaret Dunlop Gibson, ed., *An Arabic Version of the Acts of the Apostles and the Seven Catholic Epistles from an Eighth or Ninth Century MS in the Convent of St Catharine on Mount Sinai, with a Treatise on the Triune Nature of God, with Translation, from the Same Codex*, StSin 7 (Cambridge: Cambridge University Press, 1899), 1–36 (English), 74–107 (Arabic); Maria Gallo, trans., *Palestinese anonimo: Omelia arabo-cristiana dell'VIII secolo* (Roma: Città Nuova Editrice, 1994). See Samir, "Earliest Arab Apology for Christianity (c. 750)."

52. See Samir, "Earliest Arab Apology," 69–70; Mark Swanson, "Beyond Prooftexting: Approaches to the Qur'ān in Some Early Arabic Christian Apologies," *MW* 88 (1998): 305–8.

53. Swanson, "Beyond Prooftexting," 308.

54. Adapted from the text and translation in Samir, "Earliest Arab Apology," 67–68.

We praise you, O God, and we adore you and we glorify you in your creative Word and your holy, life-giving Spirit, one God, and one Lord, and one Creator. We do not separate God from his Word and his Spirit. God showed his power and his light in the Law and the Prophets, and the Psalms and the Gospel, that God and his Word and his Spirit are one God and one Lord. We will show this, God willing, in those revealed scriptures, to anyone who wants insight, understands things, recognizes the truth, and opens his breast to believe in God and his scriptures.[55]

One notices straightaway the author's intention to make his case for Christian teaching from the Scriptures; he names the Law, the Prophets, the Psalms, and the Gospel, scriptures that are named as they are named in the Qur'an. Moreover, in emphasizing God, his Word, and his Spirit, the author recalls the Qur'an's own mention of these three names in the oft-quoted phrase "The Messiah, Jesus, Son of Mary, was nothing more than a messenger of God, his word that he imparted to Mary, and a spirit from him" (Q Nisa' 4:171). What is more, the author is willing to include explicit citations from the Qur'an among the scriptural passages he quotes in testimony to the credibility of the Christian doctrine. On the one hand, addressing the Arabic-speaking Christian readers who were his primary audience, the author speaks of what "we find in the Law and the Prophets and the Psalms and the Gospel," in support of the Christian doctrines of the Trinity and the incarnation. On the other hand, several times he rhetorically addresses Muslims; he speaks of what "you will find ... in the Qur'an," and he goes on to cite a passage or a pastiche of quotations from several *surahs*, in support of the doctrines, on behalf of the veracity of which he has been quoting or alluding to scriptural evidence from passages and narratives from the Old or New Testaments.[56] For example, at one point in the argument, in search of testimonies to a certain plurality in the Godhead, the author turns to the Scriptures for citations of passages in which God speaks in the first-person plural. Having quoted a number of such passages, he goes on to say:

You will find it also in the Qur'an that "We created man in misery" [Q Balad 90:4], and "We have opened the gates of heaven with water pour-

---

55. Gibson, *Arabic Version*, 3 (English), 75 (Arabic). Here the English translation has been adapted from Gibson's version.
56. See, e.g., Gibson, *Arabic Version*, 5–6 (English), 77–78 (Arabic). See the passage quoted and discussed in Griffith, *Church in the Shadow of the Mosque*, 55.

ing down" [Q Qamar 54:11], and have said, "And now you come unto Us alone, as We created you at first" [Q An'am 6:94]. It also says, "Believe in God, and in his Word; and also in the Holy Spirit" [see Q Nisa' 4:171]. The Holy Spirit is even the one who brings it down [i.e., the Qur'an] as "a mercy and a guidance from thy Lord" [Q Nahl 16:64, 102]. But why should I prove it from this [i.e., the Qur'an] and bring enlightenment, when we find in the Torah, the Prophets, the Psalms, and the Gospel, and you find it in the Qur'an, that God and his Word and his Spirit are one God and one Lord? You have said that you believe in God and his Word and the Holy Spirit, so do not reproach us, O men, that we believe in God and his Word and his Spirit: we worship God in his Word and his Spirit, one God and one Lord and one Creator. God has made it clear in all of the scriptures that this is the way it is in right guidance and true religion.[57]

Evidently in this passage the Christian author is directly addressing readers of the Qur'an as well as the devotees of the Christian Bible. He speaks of what "we find in the Torah, the Prophets, the Psalms, and the Gospel," and of what "you find ... in the Qur'an." One also notices in this passage the prominence of the author's references to God, his Word, and his Spirit, and how they provide a continual evocation of Q Nisā' 4:171. Like almost every Arab Christian apologetic writer after him, the author of On the Triune Nature of God takes this verse as qur'anic testimony to the reality that the one God is in fact possessed of Word and Spirit and that they are he, the Son of God, and the Holy Spirit, three persons, one God, as the Christians say.

In a further passage, the author of On the Triune Nature of God takes advantage of another verse in the Qur'an to explain how it came about that by the action of the Holy Spirit, God's Word, the Son of God, became incarnate and was clothed, even veiled (*iḥtajaba*),[58] in Mary's human nature. "Thus," he says, "God was veiled [*iḥtajaba*] in a man without sin."[59] The "veiling" language here once again evokes a particular passage in the Qur'an: "God speaks with man only by way of revelation [*waḥy*], or from behind a veil [*ḥijāb*], or he sends a messenger [*rasūl*] and he reveals by His permission what He wishes" (Q Shura 42:51). The author of our treatise likens Jesus's humanity to the veil, from behind which the Qur'an says

---

57. Translation adapted from Gibson, *Arabic Version*, 5–6 (English), 77–78 (Arabic).
58. See Gibson, *Arabic Version*, 11 (English), 83 (Arabic).
59. Gibson, *Arabic Version*, 13 (English), 85 (Arabic).

God might choose to speak to humankind, and in this way he once again evokes qur'anic language in a bid to make use of its probative potential. The perhaps unintended consequence is that he also thereby takes another step in the direction of Islamicizing Christian discourse in Arabic.

INTERTWINED SCRIPTURES, INTERTWINED RELIGIONS

The phenomenon of the Arabic Qur'an's lexical, syntactic, and even topical permeation into the idiom of the Arabic Bible and into early Christian Arabic religious discourse more generally calls attention to an aspect of the process of Oriental Christianity's acculturation into the world of Islam that had a shaping effect on Christian identity formation in the Islamic, Arabic-speaking milieu that not only set Christianity off from Islam but also simultaneously distinguished the cultural profile of the Christian communities living in the world of Islam from the cultural profile of Christians living elsewhere, especially in the contemporary Greek- and Latin-speaking realms. This same phenomenon of acculturation into the new and distinctive social patterns of life in the world of Islam also, mutatis mutandis, as we shall see, shaped the cultural profile of the Jewish communities living in the Arabic-speaking milieu of Islam, simultaneously distinguishing them culturally both from the Muslims among whom they lived as well as from other Jews living in other cultural realms. Historian Albert Hourani memorably describes the distinctive social profile of the new Islamic polity as follows:

> By the third and fourth Islamic centuries (the ninth or tenth century AD) something which was recognizably an "Islamic world" had emerged. A traveler around the world would have been able to tell, by what he saw and heard, whether a land was ruled and peopled by Muslims.... The great buildings above all were the external symbols of the "world of Islam."... By the tenth century, the men and women in the Near East and the Maghrib lived in a universe which was defined in terms of Islam.... Time was marked by the five daily prayers, the weekly sermon in the mosque, the annual fast in the month of Ramadan and pilgrimage to Mecca, and the Muslim calendar.[60]

---

60. Albert Hourani, *A History of the Arab Peoples* (London: Faber & Faber, 1992), 54–57.

This all-encompassing social profile of life in the world of Islam affected all those who were at home in the multireligious but Islamic polity that arose as a result of the Arab territorial occupations beginning in the second half of the seventh century. They eventually extended Islamic hegemony over numerous large non-Muslim communities of Jews, Christians, and others, who in sheer numbers in many places in early Islamic times equaled or surpassed the numbers of local Muslims.[61] It was this demographic feature of the world of Islam that prompted the late historian Marshall Hodgson (1922–1968) to coin a new descriptive adjective, *Islamicate*, to characterize the wider, more comprehensive cultural profile that came to define the lives not only of Muslims but of Jews, Christians, and other subaltern populations as well. He wrote that the neologism "would refer not directly to the religion, Islam itself, but to the social and cultural complex historically associated with Islam and the Muslims, both among Muslims themselves and even when found among non-Muslims."[62] In other words, it is meant to be an inclusive term that indicates a polity or commonwealth dominated by Muslims politically while being religiously diverse, to the distinctive culture of which not only Muslims but Jews, Christians, and others made major contributions.

The Jewish communities of this Islamicate world, like the Christians, eventually adopted the Arabic language as their own, and they not only developed a wide-ranging network of religious and commercial interests throughout this world and beyond[63] but, again like the Christians, also translated their scriptures into the language of Islam, and they produced a large body of Jewish scholarship in Arabic that would in due course come to have a major influence in the thought-world of Jews and others well beyond the world of Islam. One has only to mention the names of major thinkers such as Saʿadyah ha-Gaʾōn (882–942), Moses Maimonides (1134–1204), Abraham ibn Ezra (1089–1164), and Judah ha-Levi (ca. 1075–1141) to make the point. Their work came eventually to enrich Jewish life and

---

61. See in this connection Richard Bulliet, *Conversion to Islam in the Medieval Period: An Essay in Quantitative History* (Cambridge: Harvard University Press, 1979).

62. Marshall G. S. Hodgson, *The Venture of Islam: Conscience and History in a World Civilization* (Chicago: University of Chicago Press, 1974), 1:59.

63. In this connection, see the landmark study by Shelomo Dov Goitein, *A Mediterranean Society: The Jewish Communities of the Arab World as Portrayed in the Documents of the Cairo Geniza*, 6 vols. (Berkeley: University of California Press, 1967–1993).

thought in Europe and elsewhere,[64] where their names are still recognized in the twenty-first century not only by Jews but by all who are interested in the history of philosophy, theology, and intellectual life in general.

Such was not the case with the works of Christian Arabic writers and thinkers in the Islamicate world; their names and works have remained unknown and largely unread by Christians living beyond the borders of their homelands. Their Islamic culture, the Islamic cast of their philosophical and theological writings, and the tendency in the West to view their ecclesial communities as heretical have all conspired to cause Western Christians to view them with disapproval.[65] From the thirteenth century to the present day, Western Christians have continually sent missionaries among the Christians of the world of Islam with the intention of converting them to Western denominations, thereby aiding and abetting the social and historical forces that have reduced them from onetime majorities in many places in early Islamic times to demographic insignificance in modern times, with very few exceptions, such as the case of the Copts of Egypt.

Ironically, the major gift that Oriental Christians gave indirectly to their coreligionists in the West, and particularly to Latin-speaking Christianity in medieval times, was access to Greek logical, philosophical, medical, and scientific works, which in early Abbasid times they had translated into Arabic from their original Greek, and from intervening Syriac translations.[66] These works reached the West in their Arabic versions, where they were promptly translated into Latin, in which language they then came to the attention of the scholastic philosophers and theolo-

---

64. See in this connection the work of Mordechai Cohen, *Three Approaches to Biblical Metaphor: From Abraham ibn Ezra and Maimonides to David Kimhi* (Leiden: Brill, 2003); Cohen, *Opening the Gates of Interpretation: Maimonides' Biblical Hermeneutics in Light of His Geonic-Andalusian Heritage and Muslim Milieu* (Leiden: Brill, 2011). See also Hava Lazarus-Yafeh, *Intertwined Worlds: Medieval Islam and Bible Criticism* (Princeton: Princeton University Press, 1992).

65. Even such a staunch supporter of religious rapprochement between Muslims and Christians as the late Bishop Kenneth Cragg found the Oriental Christians, Islamicized as they were, wanting in their responses to the challenges of Islam. See Kenneth Cragg, *The Arab Christian: A History in the Middle East* (Louisville: Westminster John Knox, 1991; London: Mowbray, 1992).

66. See Dimitri Gutas, *Greek Thought, Arabic Culture: The Graeco-Arabic Translation Movement in Baghdad and Early ʿAbbāsid Society (Second-Fourth/Eighth-Tenth Centuries)* (London: Routledge, 1998).

gians of Europe in the twelfth and thirteenth centuries, who put them to good use as dialogue partners in their own trendsetting works.[67] But this is another story for another time.

Bibliography

Bannister, Andrew B. *An Oral-Formulaic Study of the Qurʾān*. Lanham, MD: Lexington Books, 2014.

Baumstark, Anton. "Der älteste erhaltene Griechisch-Arabische Text von Psalm 110 (109)." *OrChr* 9 (1934): 55–66.

Ben-Shammai, Haggai. "Saʿadya Gaon." *EJIW* 4:197–204.

Bijlefeld, Willem A. "A Prophet and More than a Prophet? Some Observations on the Qurʾānic Use of the Terms 'Prophet' and 'Apostle.'" *MW* 59 (1969): 1–28.

Blau, Joshua. *The Emergence and Linguistic Background of Judaeo-Arabic: A Study in the Origins of Neo-Arabic and Middle Arabic*. 3rd rev. ed. Jerusalem: Ben-Zvi Institute, 1999.

———. "On a Fragment of the Oldest Judaeo-Arabic Bible Translation Extant." Pages 31–39 in *Genizah Research after Ninety Years: The Case of Judaeo-Arabic; Papers Read at the Third Congress of the Society for Judaeo-Arabic Studies*. Edited by J. Blau and S. C. Reif. Cambridge: Cambridge University Press, 1992.

Brody, Robert. *The Geonim of Babylonia and the Shaping of Medieval Jewish Culture*. New Haven: Yale University Press, 2013.

Brown, Michelle P. *In the Beginning: Bibles before the Year 1000*. Washington, DC: Smithsonian Institution, 2006.

Bulliet, Richard. *Conversion to Islam in the Medieval Period: An Essay in Quantitative History*. Cambridge: Harvard University Press, 1979.

Cohen, Mordechai. *Opening the Gates of Interpretation: Maimonides' Biblical Hermeneutics in Light of His Geonic-Andalusian Heritage and Muslim Milieu*. Leiden: Brill, 2011.

———. *Three Approaches to Biblical Metaphor: From Abraham ibn Ezra and Maimonides to David Kimhi*. Leiden: Brill, 2003.

---

67. See Fernand van Steenberghen, *Aristotle in the West: The Origins of Latin Aristotelianism*, trans. Leonard Johnston (New York: Humanities Press, 1970), and more popularly, Richard E. Rubenstein, *Aristotle's Children: How Christians, Muslims, and Jews Rediscovered Ancient Wisdom and Illuminated the Middle Ages* (Orlando: Harcourt, 2003).

Cragg, Kenneth. *The Arab Christian: A History in the Middle East.* Louisville: Westminster John Knox, 1991; London: Mowbray, 1992.
Derenbourg, Joseph, ed. *Ouvres completes de R. Saadia Ben Josef al-Fayyoûmî.* 5 vols. Paris: Leroux, 1893–1899.
Dodge, Bayard, ed. and trans. *The Fihrist of al-Nadīm: A Tenth-Century Survey of Muslim Culture.* 2 vols. New York: Columbia University Press, 1970.
Dye, Guillaume, and Fabien Nobilio, eds. *Figures bibliques en Islam.* Fernelmont, Belgium: Éditions Modulaires Européennes, 2011.
Frank, Richard M. "The Jeremias of Pethion ibn Ayyūb al-Sahhār." *CBQ* 21 (1959): 136–70.
———, ed. and trans. *The Wisdom of Jesus Ben Sirach (Sinai ar. 155, IXth/Xth cent.).* CSCO 357–58. Leuven: Secrétariat du Corpus SCO, 1974.
Gallo, Maria, trans. *Palestinese anonimo: Omelia arabo-cristiana dell'VIII secolo.* Rome: Città Nuova Editrice, 1994.
Gaudeul, Jean-Marie, and Robert Caspar. "Textes de la tradition musulmane concernant le *taḥrīf* (falsification) es écritures." *Islamochristiana* 6 (1980): 61–104.
Gibson, Margaret Dunlop, ed. *An Arabic Version of the Acts of the Apostles and the Seven Catholic Epistles from an Eighth or Ninth Century MS in the Convent of St Catharine on Mount Sinai, with a Treatise on the Triune Nature of God, with Translation, from the Same Codex.* StSin 7. Cambridge: Cambridge University Press, 1899.
Gilliot, Claude. "Mohammed's Exegetical Activity in the Meccan Arabic Lectionary." Pages 371–98 in *The Coming of the Comforter: When, Where, and to Whom? Studies on the Rise of Islam and Various Other Topics in Memory of John Wansbrough.* Edited by Carlos A. Segovia and Basil Lourié. Piscataway, NJ: Gorgias, 2012.
Goitein, Shelomo Dov. *A Mediterranean Society: The Jewish Communities of the Arab World as Portrayed in the Documents of the Cairo Geniza.* 6 vols. Berkeley: University of California Press, 1967–1993.
Graf, Georg. *Geschichte der christlichen arabischen Literatur.* 5 vols. Vatican City: Biblioteca apostolica Vaticana, 1944–1953.
Griffith, Sidney H. *The Bible in Arabic: The Scriptures of the People of the Book in the Language of Islam.* Princeton: Princeton University Press, 2013.
———. "Christian Lore and the Arabic Qurʾān: The 'Companions of the Cave' in *Sūrat al-Kahf* and in Syriac Christian Tradition." Pages 109–37

in *The Qurʾān in Its Historical Context*. Edited by Gabriel Said Reynolds. RSQ. London: Routledge, 2008.

———. *The Church in the Shadow of the Mosque: Christians and Muslims in the World of Islam*. Princeton: Princeton University Press, 2008.

———. "Disputing with Islam in Syriac: The Case of the Monk of Bêt Ḥālê and a Muslim Emir." *Hug* 3 (2000): 29–54.

———. "The Monks of Palestine and the Growth of Christian Literature in Arabic." *The Muslim World* 78 (1988): 1–28.

———. "The '*Sunnah* of Our Messengers': The Qurʾān's Paradigm for Messengers and Prophets; A Reading of *Sūrah* XXVI *ash*-Shuʿarā." Pages 208–17 in *Qurʾanic Studies Today*. Edited by Angelika Neuwrith and Michael Sells. New York: Routledge, 2016.

———. "When Did the Bible Become an Arabic Scripture?" *Intellectual History of the Islamicate World* (2013): 7–23.

Gutas, Dimitri. *Greek Thought, Arabic Culture: The Graeco-Arabic Translation Movement in Baghdad and Early ʿAbbāsid Society (Second–Fourth/Eighth–Tenth Centuries)*. London: Routledge, 1998.

Haddad, Rachid. "La phonétique de l'arabe chrétien vers 700." Pages 159–64 in *La Syrie de Byzance a l'Islam: VIIe–VIIIe siècles; Actes du Colloque International Lyon-Maison de l'Orient Méiterranéen, Paris—Institut du Monde Arabe, 11–15 Septembre 1990*. Edited by Pierre Canivet and Jean-Paul Rey-Coquais. Damas: Institut Français de Damas, 1992.

Hodgson, Marshall G. S. *The Venture of Islam: Conscience and History in a World Civilization*. Vol 1. Chicago: University of Chicago Press, 1974.

Horn, Cornelia. "Lines of Transmission between Apocryphal Traditions in the Syriac-Speaking World: Manichaeism and the Rise of Islam; the Case of the *Acts of John*." *ParOr* 35 (2010): 337–55.

Hourani, Albert. *A History of the Arab Peoples*. London: Faber & Faber, 1992.

Jeffrey, Arthur. *The Foreign Vocabulary of the Qurʾān*. Baroda, India: Oriental Institute, 1938.

John of Damascus. *Writings: St. John of Damascus*. Translated by F. H. Chase. FC 37. Washington, DC: Catholic University of America Press, 1958.

Kachouh, H. "The Arabic Versions of the Gospels: A Case Study of John 1:1 and 1:18." Pages 9–36 in *The Bible in Arab Christianity*. Edited by David Thomas. CMR 6. Leiden: Brill, 2007.

Lasker, Daniel J. "*Qiṣṣat Mujādalat al-Usquf* and *Neṣṭor Ha-Komer*: The Earliest Arabic and Hebrew Jewish Anti-Christian Polemics." Pages

112–18 in *Genizah Research after Ninety Years: The Case of Judaeo-Arabic; Papers Read at the Third Congress of the Society for Judaeo-Arabic Studies*. Edited by J. Blau and S. C. Reif. Cambridge: Cambridge University Press, 1992.

———. "Rabbinism and Karaism: The Contest for Supremacy." Pages 47–72 in *Great Schisms in Jewish History*. Edited by R. Jospe and S. M. Wagner. New York: Ktav, 1981.

Lazarus-Yafeh, Hava. *Intertwined Worlds: Medieval Islam and Bible Criticism*. Princeton: Princeton University Press, 1992.

Malter, Henry. *Saadia Gaon: His Life and Works*. Philadelphia: Jewish Publication Society of America, 1921.

Massignon, Louis. "Étude sur une courbe personnelle de vie, le cas du Hallaj; Martyr mystique de l'Islam." *Dieu Vivant* 4 (1945): 11–39.

Mavroudi, Maria. "Arabic Words in Greek Letters: The Violet Fragment and More." Pages 321–54 in *Moyen arabe et variétés mixtes de l'arabe à travers l'histoire: Actes dum premier colloque international (Louvain-la-Neuve, 10–14 mai 2004)*. Edited by Jérôme Lentin and Jacques Grand'henry. Université Catholique de Louvain, Institut Orientaliste. Leuven: Peeters, 2008.

McAuliffe, Jane Dammen. "The Qurʾānic Context of Muslim Biblical Scholarship." *ICMR* 7 (1996): 141–58.

Meimare, Ioannis Emm. Καταλογος των Νεων Αραβικων Χειρογραφων της Ιερας Μονης Αγιας Αικατερινης του Ορους Σινα [List of New Arabic Manuscripts of the Holy Monastery of Saint Catherine of Mount Sinai]. Athens: National Hellenistic Research Foundation, 1985.

Neuenkirchen, Paul. "Biblical Elements in Koran 89, 6–8 and Its Exegeses: A New Interpretation of 'Iram of the Pillars.'" *Arabica* 60 (2013): 651–700.

———. "Visions et Ascensions: Deux péricopes coraniques à la lumière d'un apocryphe chrétien." *JA* 302 (2014): 303–47.

Neuwirth, Angelika. *Der Koran als Text der Spätantike: Ein europäischer Zugang*. Berlin: Verlag der Weltreligionen im Insel Verlag, 2010.

Polliack, Meira. *The Karaite Tradition of Arabic Bible Translation: A Linguistic and Exegetical Study of Karaite Translations of the Pentateuch from the Tenth and Eleventh Centuries CE*. Études sur le Judaïsme Médiéval 17. Leiden: Brill, 1997.

———. "Rethinking Karaism: Between Judaism and Islam." *AJS Review* 30 (2006): 67–93.

Putman, Hans. *L'église et l'islam sous Timothée I: Etude sur l'église nestorienne au temps des premiers ʿAbbāsides, avec nouvelle edition et traduction du dialogue entre Timothée et al-Mahdi* [Arabic]. Beyrouth: Dar El-Machreq, 1975.

Reynolds, Gabriel Said. *The Qurʾān and Its Biblical Subtext*. RSQ. London: Routledge, 2010.

Rosenkranz, Simone. *Die jüdisch-christliche Auseinandersetzung unter islamischer Herrschaft: 7.–10. Jahrhundert*. JudChr 21. Bern: Lang, 2004.

Rubenstein, Richard E. *Aristotle's Children: How Christians, Muslims, and Jews Rediscovered Ancient Wisdom and Illuminated the Middle Ages*. Orlando: Harcourt, 2003.

Samir, Samir Khalil. "The Earliest Arab Apology for Christianity (c. 750)." Pages 57–114 in *Christian Arabic Apologetics during the Abbasid Period (750–1258)*. Edited by Samir Khalil Samir and Jøgen S. Nielsen. SHR 63. Leiden: Brill, 1994.

Segovia, Carlos A., and Basil Lourié, eds. *The Coming of the Comforter: When, Where, and to Whom? Studies on the Rise of Islam and Various Other Topics in Memory of John Wansbrough*. Piscataway, NJ: Gorgias, 2012.

Sinai, Nicolai. *The Qurʾān: A Historical-Critical Introduction*. Edinburgh: Edinburgh University Press, 2017.

Staal, H. *Mt. Sinai Arabic Codex 151: I Pauline Epistles*. CSCO 452–53. Leuven: Peeters, 1983.

Steenberghen, Fernand van. *Aristotle in the West: The Origins of Latin Aristotelianism* Translated by Leonard Johnston. New York: Humanities Press, 1970.

Steiner, Richard C. *A Biblical Translation in the Making: The Evolution and Impact of Saadia Gaon's Tafsīr*. Harvard University Center for Jewish Studies. Cambridge: Harvard University Press, 2010.

Stern, David. "The First Jewish Books and the Early History of Jewish Reading." *JQR* 98 (2008): 163–202.

Swanson, Mark. "Beyond Prooftexting: Approaches to the Qurʾān in Some Early Arabic Christian Apologies." *MW* 88 (1998): 297–319.

Tobi, Yosef. "On the Antiquity of Ancient Judeo-Arabic Biblical Translations and a New Piece of an Ancient Judeo-Arabic Translation of the Pentateuch." Pages 17–60 in vol. 2 of *Ben ʿEver la-ʿArav: Contacts between Arabic Literature and Jewish Literature in the Middle Ages and Modern Times*. Edited by Y. Tobi and Y. Avishur. Tel Aviv: Afikim Publishers, 2001.

Van Bladel, Kevin. "The Alexander Legend in the Qurʾān 18:83–102." Pages 175–203 in *The Qurʾān in Its Historical Context*. Edited by Gabriel Said Reynolds. RSQ. London: Routledge, 2008.

Violet, Bruno. *Ein zweisprachiges Psalmfragment aus Damaskus*. Berlin: Akademie, 1902.

Zellentin, Holger. *The Qurʾān's Legal Culture: The Didascalia Apostolorum as a Point of Departure*. Tübingen: Mohr Siebeck, 2013.

Unreliable Books: Debates over Falsified Scriptures at the Frontier between Judaism and Christianity

Karl Shuve

This is how the Scriptures acquired [*proselabon*] many falsehoods against God [*polla pseudē kata tou theou*]: After the prophet Moses, by God's will, handed down the Law with its explanations to a certain chosen seventy [*tou prophētou Mōuseōs gnōmēi tou theou eklektois tisin hebdomēkonta ton nomon syn tais epilysesin*] ... not much time elapsed before the Law, having been written down, acquired certain falsehoods against the one and only God [*met' ou polu grapheis ho nomos proselaben tina kai pseudē kata tou monou theou*], who made the heaven and the earth and everything that is in them. (Ps.-Clem. Hom. 2.38)[1]

This provocative statement about the Torah—which asserts that it was corrupted after it was revealed to Moses on Sinai—is placed in the mouth of the apostle Peter in a fourth-century apocryphal text known as the Pseudo-Clementine Homilies.

It is a jarring sentence. We are far more accustomed to Jewish and Christian authors praising their sacred writings. Perhaps one of the most famous examples comes from a pseudonymous letter written in the early decades of the second century, purporting to be from the apostle Paul to his erstwhile disciple Timothy:[2] "All scripture [*pasa graphē*] is inspired by

---

1. Bernard Rehm, *Die Pseudoklementinen I: Homilien*, GCS 42 (Berlin: Akademie, 1953). Translations are adapted, sometimes with significant modification, from *ANF* 8:213–346.

2. An extensive case for the pseudonymity of 2 Timothy is made by Martin Dibelius and Hans Conzelmann, *The Pastoral Epistles*, trans. Philip Buttolph and Adela Yarbro (Minneapolis: Fortress, 1972), 1–5.

God [*theopneustos*] and is useful for teaching, for reproof, for correction, and for training in righteousness" (2 Tim 3:16).³ This text would come to be included in the New Testament canon, and later Christian readers would see in this passage the Bible's own declaration of its inspiration, authority, and complete sufficiency, although its second-century author certainly did not imagine that the letter he was writing would itself be counted as Scripture. Rather, for "Paul," *Scripture* referred to centuries-old texts that had come to be authoritative in Second Temple Jewish communities.⁴ These texts—these *hiera grammata*, "sacred writings," as they are called earlier in the letter (2 Tim 3:15)—are the sole bulwark against "those deceiving others" (2 Tim 3:13), which help their readers to cultivate instruction "for salvation" (2 Tim 3:15) and to be "equipped for every good work" (2 Tim 3:17).

Jewish historian Josephus provides us with a more detailed paean to Scripture in his *Contra Apionem*, which was written at the turn of the second century and is thus contemporaneous with 2 Timothy.⁵ He says that the "books [*biblia*]" of the Jews, which he counts as specifically twenty-two in number, "contain the record of all time" and are in no way "conflicting with each other," even down to the smallest detail. He writes of the Jews that "no one has ventured either to add or to remove, or to alter a syllable; and it is an instinct with every Jew, from the day of his birth, to regard them as the decrees of God [*theou dogmata*], to abide by them, and, if need be, cheerfully to die for them" (*C. Ap.* 1.8).⁶ These five books of the "laws [*nomous*]" of Moses, thirteen books of the prophets, and four books of "hymns [*hymnous*]" and "precepts [*hypothēkas*]" are the unchanging and unchanged archive of the Jewish people—a precious inheritance to be guarded with one's life and to be followed to the letter.

Examples abound. We could point to third-century Alexandrian theologian Origen's startling claim in his work *On First Principles* that Scripture *is* the body of Christ and the only means by which humans can encounter the divine *logos* after the ascension, or the evocative opening passage of the rabbinic midrash Bereshit (Genesis) Rabbah, redacted

---

3. I have used the NRSV translation for biblical quotations, unless otherwise noted.

4. Dibelius and Conzelmann, *Pastoral Epistles*, 119–20.

5. John Barclay, *Against Apion*, FJTC 10 (Leiden: Brill, 2007), xvii.

6. I have made use of the translation in *Josephus: The Life, Against Apion*, trans. H. Thackeray, LCL (Cambridge: Harvard University Press, 1926).

in the fifth century CE, which describes the Torah as the "work-plan" that God consulted when creating the world.[7] But it feels unnecessary to belabor the point, since much scholarship tends to take for granted that late antique Jews and Christians approached their sacred writings as the perfect repository of divine revelation, and this would certainly be the view held by most nonspecialists. It is true that there has been a proliferation of scholarship on biblical interpretation, and much of this has highlighted the intractable interpretive problems faced by their Jewish and Christian readers, who themselves warned about the dangers posed by the polyvalent quality of Scripture; scriptural texts could lead readers astray.[8] But there still generally remains the underlying assumption that late antique Jews and Christians, at least by the fourth century, respected—and were fundamentally constrained by—the limits of their canons.[9] Thus we are interested in learning *when* canons of Scripture were established (including the idea of canon itself), *how* scriptural texts came to be standardized, and *what* techniques were used to bring old writings to bear on new situations.

Many working in the field would, I think, agree with Roland Barthes that for late antique Jews and Christians, when it comes to Scripture, "what has been said cannot be unsaid, *except by adding to it*"—that is,

---

7. Origen, *Princ.* 4.2.2; Gen. Rab. 1.1.2. See especially Karen Jo Torjesen, *Hermeneutical Procedure and Theological Method in Origen's Exegesis* (Berlin: de Gruyter, 1985).

8. Exemplary studies include Daniel Boyarin, *Intertextuality and the Reading of Midrash* (Bloomington: Indiana University Press, 1990); Elizabeth Clark, *Reading Renunciation: Asceticism and Scripture in Early Christianity* (Princeton: Princeton University Press, 1999); David Dawson, *Allegorical Readers and Cultural Revision in Ancient Alexandria* (Berkeley: University of California Press, 1991); Dawson, *Christian Figural Reading and the Fashioning of Identity* (Berkeley: University of California Press, 2002); Steve Fraade, *From Tradition to Commentary: Torah and Its Interpretation in the Midrash Sifre to Deuteronomy* (Albany: SUNY Press, 1991); Frances Young, *Biblical Exegesis and the Formation of Christian Culture* (Cambridge: Cambridge University Press, 1997).

9. There are, of course, exceptions to this. Eva Mroczek, in her important new study *The Literary Imagination in Jewish Antiquity* (New York: Oxford University Press, 2016), attempts to elucidate the literary aspects of early Judaism without presupposing "the Bible's textual centrality" (5). That is, she examines early Jewish literary productions without treating them as steps along an inevitable path to the making of the Bible and closing of the canon (thus she rejects such concepts as rewritten Bible).

only through commentary can Scripture be rewritten.[10] In other words, whatever creativity can be said to exist lies in the technique of *glossing*: there is a fixed, stable, unchanging—*unchangeable*—text, whose meaning can be constrained or manipulated by the practice of writing around it. This is a metaphor, of course, but a metaphor that has a basis in material reality. In medieval glossed Bibles, the biblical text, which was written in a large script in the center of the page, was surrounded with commentaries written by earlier authorities, often transcribed not only in the margins but also literally between the lines.[11] Visually, there is a demarcation between biblical text and commentary—signaled both in the layout and script size—but the act of conjoining them on the page blurs the distinction between the two; indeed, the relative mass of commentary can threaten to overwhelm, and perhaps even displace, the biblical text. It is a potent and revealing metaphor, but one that might obscure other ways of conceptualizing late antique Jewish and Christian approaches to their sacred writings.

This is what makes the Pseudo-Clementine Homilies and its assertion of the falsification of Scripture so fascinating. There are numerous examples—far too many to list comprehensively here—of Jews and Christians expressing disquiet or concern over the apparent meaning of a scriptural passage.[12] But there are few other texts, and none as late as the fourth century, that advocate simply disregarding or eliminating these problematic passages—quite literally unsaying what has been said.[13] Given the sheer

---

10. I borrow this framing directly from Clark, *Reading Renunciation*, 5–6.

11. For a detailed discussion with copious examples, see Lesley Smith, *The "Glossa Ordinaria": The Making of a Medieval Biblical Commentary* (Leiden: Brill, 2009), 91–140.

12. One of the best-known comes from the prologue to Origen's *Commentary on the Song of Songs*: "And there is another practice too that we have received from [the Jews]—namely, that all the Scriptures should be delivered to boys by teachers and wise men, while at the same time the four that they call the *deuteroseis*—that is to say, the beginning of Genesis ... the first chapters of Ezekiel ... the end of that same ... and this book of the Song of Songs—should be reserved for study until the last" (prol. 1.8; trans. Ruth Penelope Lawson [New York: Newman, 1956]).

13. Perhaps the closest parallel—certainly the parallel that receives the most attention—can be found in the late second-century Valentinian teacher Ptolemy's *Letter to Flora*, which is preserved only in the *Panarion* of the fourth-century bishop and heresiologist Epiphanius of Salamis: "First, it must be understood that not all of that Law in the five books of Moses has been made by one legislator. That is, it is not made by

provocativeness of the claim, one would imagine there to be an entire body of scholarship on what has come to be known as the "doctrine of the false pericopes" and how it might disrupt the way we study scriptural interpretation in late antiquity. Yet, it is only in the last few years that it has begun to attract sustained attention, most notably in monographs by Donald Carlson and Patricia Duncan.[14] Duncan's work, the first systematic study of the Homilies (which she refers to as the Klementia) in English, is an especially welcome contribution, deserving of a wide readership.

The reason has much to do with the nature of the Pseudo-Clementine literature itself. There are two extant fourth-century "novels" that feature and are purportedly narrated by a young Clement of Rome: the Homilies and the Recognitions, although the latter is extant only in a Latin translation by Rufinus and in Syriac fragments.[15] Both novels are redactions of various earlier sources, most notably the hypothetical *Grundschrift*, which is taken to be a second-century apocryphal narrative of Clement and the apostle Peter's battles against the nefarious arch-heretic Simon Magus. Through a careful comparison of the Homilies and the Recognitions, scholars have been able to reconstruct, at least in broad strokes, the substance of the *Grundschrift*, and what was of most interest to these scholars was its Jewish Christian character: this source was taken to be a key witness to an early form of Torah-observant Christianity that had been scrubbed from the historical record by later church leaders who deemed it

---

God alone; some of its provisions are made by men.... One division is God himself and his legislation, but another is Moses—not as God legislates through him.... And another division is the elders of the people" (Epiphanius, *Pan.* 33.4.1). Throughout I have made use of the translation of Frank Williams, *The Panarion of Epiphanius of Salamis: Book I (Sects 1–46)*, NHS 35 (Leiden: Brill, 1987). Because the parallel has received extensive consideration by Gilles Quispel in the introduction to his edition of the *Letter to Flora*, I will discuss it only briefly in this essay, focusing instead on other parallels that have received far less, if indeed any, scholarly attention.

14. Donald H. Carlson, *Jewish-Christian Interpretation of the Pentateuch in the Pseudo-Clementine Homilies* (Minneapolis: Fortress, 2013); Patricia Duncan, *Novel Hermeneutics in the Greek Clementine Romance*, WUNT 395 (Tübingen: Mohr Siebeck, 2017).

15. On the Greco-Roman novel, see Tomas Hägg, *The Novel in Antiquity* (Berkeley: University of California Press, 1983); Niklas Holzberg, *The Ancient Novel: An Introduction*, trans. Christine Jackson-Holzberg (London: Routledge, 1995); Tim Whitmarsh, ed., *The Cambridge Companion to the Greek and Roman Novel* (Cambridge: Cambridge University Press, 2008).

heretical. Because the Homilies was primarily studied by those who were interested in Christian origins, it was treated rather like a husk, which could be discarded once its valuable contents had been extracted, rather than as a valuable work of fourth-century literature.[16]

The few earlier scholars who addressed the false pericopes, such as Hans Joachim Schoeps and Gilles Quispel, tended to treat it as a defining feature of primitive Jewish Christianity, in which a primary impulse was to reform the Mosaic law by removing accretions from the supposedly pure original revelation.[17] The problem with this argument is its circularity: there is no independent attestation of this teaching outside the Homilies, and it does not appear at all in the Recognitions. It is true, as Schoeps argues, that fourth-century heresiologist Epiphanius claims in his *Panarion* that the Ebionites, a Torah-observant sect, do not "accept Moses' Pentateuch in its entirety; certain sayings they reject" (30.18.7). But this does not provide independent verification, because Epiphanius asserts that the Ebionites use a corrupted form of "Clement's so-called Peregrenations of Peter" (30.15.1), which almost certainly means that he has learned about the emphasis on falsified Scripture from the Homilies itself. There are thus no external factors that require this teaching to date to the second century, although it cannot be disproven that it was part of the *Grundschrift*.

When I began working on the false pericopes over a decade ago, I approached the teaching as a fourth-century product, since that is the form in which it comes to us, and I situated it as part of a theological and heresiological discourse on the problem of Scripture's unity—that is, how it offers a particular solution to the broader problem that Scripture taken

---

16. A painstakingly thorough history of scholarship on the Pseudo-Clementine literature is offered in F. Stanley Jones, "The Pseudo-Clementines: A History of Research," *SecCent* 2 (1982): 1–33, 63–96. Nichole Kelly, *Knowledge and Religious Authority in the Pseudo-Clementines*, WUNT 2/213 (Tübingen: Mohr Siebeck, 2006), and Annette Yoshiko Reed, "Jewish Christianity after the Partings of the Ways," in *Ways That Never Parted: Jews and Christians in Late Antiquity and the Early Middle Ages*, ed. Adam Becker and Annette Yoshiko Reed (Tübingen: Mohr Siebeck, 2004), 189–231, were responsible for initiating a new trend in scholarship of focusing on the fourth-century context of the novels.

17. Gilles Quispel, *Ptolémée: Lettre à Flora*, SC 24 (Paris: Cerf, 1966), 11–46; Hans J. Schoeps, *Jewish Christianity: Factional Disputes in the Early Church*, trans. Douglas Hare (Minneapolis: Fortress, 1969), 74–98.

as a whole is riven with internal tensions.[18] In an unpublished thesis, I explored the possibility that the Homilies was in fact covertly engaging in debates with other fourth-century Christians over the appropriateness of the allegorical interpretation of Scripture.[19] We know that by the late fourth century, a network of theologians in the environs of Antioch— where the Homilies may well have been redacted—began taking issue with what they perceived to be undisciplined allegorical speculation; the doctrine of the false pericopes could be seen as taking that critique to its logical conclusion, choosing to reject certain passages of the Jewish Scriptures that would otherwise require some form of nonliteral interpretation to make palatable, such as claims of God's ignorance about the extent of human wickedness or God's repentance at having destroyed humanity in the flood.[20]

This claim has been carefully defended in a monograph by Donald Carlson, *The Jewish-Christian Interpretation of the Pentateuch in the Pseudo-Clementine Homilies*.[21] I continue to think that the argument has at least some merit. In books 4–6 of the Homilies, which is a flashback of sorts to Clement's childhood that disrupts the flow of the narrative, there is a fierce polemic against the allegorical interpretation of Greek myths: Clement asserts that allegory is used to covertly promote licentious behavior by justifying the immoral deeds of the gods. This particular textual unit has clearly—and not at all neatly—been stitched into the text by the redactor of the Homilies, and it seems to serve little purpose other than to critique the allegorical reading of sacred texts.[22] Clearly, the author(s)/

---

18. Karl Shuve, "The Doctrine of the False Pericopes and Other Late Antique Approaches to the Problem of Scripture's Unity," in *Nouvelles intrigues pseudo-clémentines*, ed. F. Amsler et al. (Prahins: Éditions du Zèbre, 2008), 437–45.

19. Karl Shuve, "The Pseudo-Clementine *Homilies* and the Antiochene Polemic against Allegory" (MA thesis, McMaster University, 2007).

20. On the existence of and conflict between "Alexandrian" and "Antiochene" schools of biblical exegesis, see especially Young, *Biblical Exegesis*, 161–85.

21. Carlson, *Jewish-Christian Interpretation*, 13–50.

22. William Adler, "Apion's 'Encomium of Adultery': A Jewish Satire of Greek *Paideia* in the Pseudo-Clementine *Homilies*," *HUCA* 64 (1993): 29 n. 37, notes that there are inconsistencies in the number of Peter's companions between Ps.-Clem. Hom. 3.73 and Ps.-Clem. Hom. 8.12 (although the number in 8.12 agrees with Ps.-Clem. Rec. 4.3), which suggests that the narrative of the *Grundschrift* was imprecisely altered to accommodate the addition of the Clement-Apion scene. Carlson, *Jewish-Christian*

redactor(s) of the Homilies were suspicious of allegory, which was widely employed by early Christians in the interpretation of their Scriptures.[23]

But to explain the doctrine of the false pericopes as antiallegorical polemic is to leave the conceptual centrality of canon unchallenged. It is to assume that the primary concern of the Homilies' author(s)/redactor(s) was to ensure the coherence of a fixed written archive, even if it did this by excising problematic passages rather than by explaining them (away) through figural reading practices. In other words, it is to frame the Homilies' approach to Scripture using the metaphor of glossing. What if, instead, we imagined that the doctrine of the false pericopes formed a crucial part of the Homilies' attempt to exert control over this public archive—an archive that is itself fluid, its boundaries ill-defined, accessible in different recensions and translations[24]—by undermining the very reliability of that archive and thereby displacing it as a locus of authority? In the glossing metaphor, the commentator acknowledges that his contribution is secondary to and derivative of the authoritative text, but this is not the case in the Homilies, where most teaching, as we shall see, is articulated apart from any apparent scriptural justification, and where Scripture is framed more as a hindrance in public disputation than as an aid in understanding the divine.

This essay argues that, rather than present its readers with a hermeneutic for interpreting Scripture, the Homilies offers a fictionalized, idealized account of oral transmission as the sole means by which truth can be reliably preserved and disseminated. I am heavily reliant on Martin Jaffee's brilliant exposition of the phenomenon of "Torah in the mouth" (i.e., Oral Torah) in rabbinic Judaism, in which he identifies three dimensions of "oral-literary tradition": the "*textual substance of the tradition*"; the "*social settings in which the texts are composed, stored and transmitted*"; and the "*ideological system by which the texts and their social settings are repre-*

Interpretation, concurs that this scene is included to polemicize against the allegorical reading of sacred texts (26–40).

23. See, e.g., Dawson, *Allegorical Readers*; Young, *Biblical Exegesis*.

24. See, e.g., Adam Kamesar, *Jerome, Greek Scholarship, and the Hebrew Bible: A Study of the Quaestiones Hebraicae in Genesim* (Oxford: Clarendon, 1993); Mroczek, *Literary Imagination*; Annette Yoshiko Reed, *Fallen Angels and the History of Judaism and Christianity: The Reception of Enochic Literature* (Cambridge: Cambridge University Press, 2006).

sented within the culture."²⁵ He distinguishes the content and praxis of oral tradition, on the one hand, from the "ideological constructions that frame the cultural meaning of that praxis," on the other, identifying the *concept* of Torah in the mouth with the latter. Jaffee continues to say that this ideological dimension is not a necessary aspect of oral tradition but emerges only when "the distinction between written and oral-literary tradition has become crucial to some sort of social undertaking that distinguishes the bearers of the oral tradition from those who do not bear it."²⁶ I assert that much like Torah in the mouth, the doctrine of the false pericopes serves an *ideological* function. The Homilies, of course, contains specific teachings, doctrinal statements, and reflections on a limited number of passages from the Torah, but more fundamentally it offers, through the immediacy of "Clement's" first-person authorial voice, a way for its fourth-century readers/hearers to understand and respond to their situation in a world rife with sectarian conflict and cut off, by the passage of centuries, from the golden age of Jesus and the apostles.²⁷

Fundamental to the Homilies' narrativized portrayal of oral transmission is its intense, if somewhat paradoxical, suspicion of writing and of books. Scripture—indeed, any text—can be manipulated in all sorts of ways once it is out of the hands of its author and is publicly available. Books can certainly be read badly, but, more troublingly, they can be transmitted badly, subject to interpolation and falsification. The Homilies thus exploits anxieties over textual manipulation in antiquity to claim for its readers a privileged access to the truth. The public archive of Scripture is thus presented as an inadequate, if not entirely deceptive, source of authority, and the Homilies counters it with its own private archive of Petrine teachings, which has been assiduously and secretly handed down through the generations. Thus while there is a contrast between the oral

---

25. Martin Jaffee, *Torah in the Mouth: Writing and Oral Tradition in Palestinian Judaism, 200 BCE–400 CE* (Oxford: Oxford University Press, 2001), 9, emphasis original.

26. Jaffee, *Torah in the Mouth*, 10.

27. Annette Yoshiko Reed, "'Jewish Christianity' as Counterhistory? The Apostolic Past in Eusebius' *Ecclesiastical History* and the Pseudo-Clementine *Homilies*," in *Antiquity in Antiquity: Jewish and Christian Pasts in the Greco-Roman World*, ed. Greg Gardner and Kevin Osterloh, TSAJ 123 (Tübingen: Mohr Siebeck, 2008), 173–216, charts the emergence of what she terms the "third privileged space in the Christian imagination—namely, the 'apostolic past'" (174), and she finds in the Homilies the elevation of this apostolic (specifically, Petrine) past to the level of the biblical past.

and the written, the more important one seems to be between the private and the public, although these two binaries are frequently linked together. Rather than imagine that this private oral archive serves as an interpretive key that unlocks the mysteries of the public written archive, it seems better to understand it as a creative exercise whose primary purpose is to resist archival closure. Because of the unreliability of Scripture and the competing claims laid to it by various sects, new bodies of authoritative teaching will need to be produced (or discovered). The Homilies, in my view, does not present itself as the final word but as authorizing the imaginative production of apostolic literature.

In what follows I give a brief overview of the problems associated with the circulation of texts in late antiquity, followed by a lengthy analysis of oral and written traditions in the Homilies, and conclude with some remarks on the relationship between the Homilies and other late antique Jewish and Christian groups.

Books and Their Reliability in Late Antiquity

In a rich chapter on the publication and circulation of early Christian literature in his *Books and Readers in the Early Church*, Harry Gamble gives a detailed and compelling account of how publication functioned in the world of late antiquity.[28] A book would be "published" once its author distributed one or more copies to patrons, dedicatees, and friends—an act that would often be accompanied by a public reading, which was to give "a literary work immediate and wide publicity."[29] After this point, as Gamble notes, the author

> effectively surrendered further personal control over the text. A recipient might make her copy available to another, who could then make a copy in turn.... In this way copies multiplied and spread seriatim, one at a time, at the initiative of individuals who lay beyond the author's acquaintance. Since every copy was made by hand, each was unique, and every owner of such a copy was free to do with it as he or she chose. In this way a text quickly slipped beyond the author's reach. There were no means of making authoritative revisions, of preventing others from transcribing it

---

28. Harry Y. Gamble, "The Publication and Circulation of Early Christian Literature," in *Books and Readers in the Early Church: A History of Early Christian Texts* (New Haven: Yale University Press, 1995), 82–143.

29. Gamble, *Books and Readers*, 84.

or revising it as they wished, of controlling the numbers of copies made, or even assuring that it would be properly attributed to its author.[30]

Ancient authors were keenly aware of the vulnerability of their work. Perhaps the most interesting and well-known example comes from a letter that Augustine of Hippo wrote in 416 to Aurelius, the bishop of the North African city of Carthage, complaining that his work *On the Trinity* had been put into circulation without his consent while he was still in the midst of dictating it, forcing him to delay its completion and to write the final books so that they matched the ones that "have been surreptitiously in circulation for some time," even though he wished that he could have corrected them further.[31] According to Augustine, the fragmentary portions of the *De Trinitate* that had circulated without his knowledge were unreliable, even though they were his own words, because they need to be placed within the overarching argument of the book in order to be properly understood. Books are thus an inadequate, and potentially misleading, substitute for the magisterial voice, even when they have not been adulterated.

Of course, there are many examples of ancient authors expressing concern over the falsification of their texts. There are the famous closing lines of the Revelation to John: "I warn [*martyrō*] everyone who hears the words of the prophecy of this book: if anyone adds to them, God will add to that person the plagues described in this book; if anyone takes away from the words of the book of this prophecy, God will take away that person's share in the tree of life and in the holy city, which are described in this book" (Rev 22:18-19). John's Apocalypse is particularly preoccupied with the phenomenon of writing, and so it is fitting that he expresses a particular anxiety about the possible interpolation or manipulation of his text, cursing those who omit or add anything to what he has written.[32] Gamble directs our attention to similar warnings in Irenaeus and Rufinus.[33] In a fragment from a lost treatise preserved by church historian

---

30. Gamble, *Books and Readers*, 84-85.
31. Cited and discussed in Gamble, *Books and Readers*, 133-34.
32. Gamble, *Books and Readers*, 104, suggests that it "is not too much to say that the author of the Apocalypse, despite his idiosyncratic grammar and style, may be the most textually self-conscious Christian writer of the early period. In no other early Christian text do the notions of books, writing, and reading occur so prominently."
33. Gamble, *Books and Readers*, 124.

Eusebius of Caesarea, Irenaeus presents copyists with an oath that they must transcribe in their copy, adjuring them to "collate ... and correct it against this copy [*antigraphon*]" (in Euesbius, *Hist. eccl.* 5.20.2 [Lake]). Likewise, in the preface to his translation of Origen's *On First Principles*, Rufinus has copyists swear by their belief in the "faith of the coming kingdom [*per futuri regni fidem*]," "the mystery of the resurrection from the dead [*per resurrectionis ex mortuis sacramentum*]," and the "everlasting fire [*aeternum ignem*]" that they will "add [*addat*] nothing to what is written and take nothing away [*auferat*] from it"—including the punctuation—strongly echoing the words of Revelation (*Orig. Princ.* praef. 4).[34] The Rufinus example appears to be even more salient when we consider that he was accused—credibly—by Jerome of having made significant alterations to the Greek text when translating it into Latin in order to save Origen from charges of heresy.[35]

Texts could be circulated prematurely without authorial permission, they could be interpolated and emended by subsequent copyists, and they could even be faked outright. Ancient readers needed to be sensitive to the possibility not only that the copy that they possessed had been altered, perhaps substantially, but also that the person to whom it was attributed did not in fact write it. As Bart Ehrman has demonstrated in his recent monograph *Forgery and Counterforgery*, "arguably the most distinctive feature of the early Christian literature is the degree to which it was forged."[36] Setting aside the polemical thrust of Ehrman's book—to argue that Christian authority was constructed, to an unusual degree for the ancient world, on a foundation of "lies"—his analysis helpfully demonstrates that while late antique Christians produced a large volume of pseudonymous literature, the act of writing pseudonymously was almost universally condemned.[37]

---

34. Latin text is from the edition in *Origène: Traité des principes I*, ed. and trans. Henri Crouzel and Manlio Simonetti, SC 252 (Paris: Cerf, 1978), my translation.

35. Jerome, *Ruf.* 1.6. Rufinus, for his part, asserted that he was removing heretical interpolations in Origen's treatise. For a detailed analysis, see Elizabeth Clark, *The Origenist Controversy: The Cultural Construction of an Early Christian Debate* (Princeton: Princeton University Press, 1992), 159–93.

36. Bart D. Ehrman, *Forgery and Counterforgery: The Use of Literary Deceit in Early Christian Polemics* (Oxford: Oxford University Press, 2013), 1.

37. That Christian authority was constructed on a foundation of lies is most forcefully articulated in his closing chapter, "Lies and Deception in the Cause of Truth" (*Forgery and Counterforgery*, 529–48). On pseudonymous literature see especially Ehrman, *Forgery and Counterforgery*, 69–92.

Indeed, early Jewish and Christian discussions of scriptural authority often turned on the question of genuine authorship.[38] Perhaps the most revealing example is the treatment of the Book of the Watchers, an apocalypse written in the third century BCE that is attributed to the antediluvian patriarch Enoch.[39] This text and its traditions about fallen angels were widely known and achieved authoritative status in early Christian communities, appearing not only in the writings of Justin Martyr (*2 Apol.* 5), Irenaeus (*Haer.* 1.15.6), Tertullian (*Cult. fem.* 1.2), and even the Pseudo-Clementine Homilies (8.12–16) but also in texts that would later be included as part of the New Testament canon—most notably the epistle of Jude, in which a portion of the Book of the Watchers is cited (Jude 14–15). Its later repudiation by Christian theologians would be rooted in their rejection of Enochic authorship.[40] Augustine, in the fifteenth book of his *City of God*, denies "canonical authority [*canonica auctoritas*]" to the Book of the Watchers, because it was not passed down "by a most certain and known succession [*certissima et notissima successione*]" by the church fathers and also was not among the "canon of the Scriptures [*canone scripturarum*] which was preserved in the temple of the Hebrew people" (*Civ.* 15.23).[41] He does acknowledge that Enoch did indeed write things "by divine inspiration [*divine*]," since Jude says so in his "canonical epistle [*epistula canonica*]," but the books of Enoch that are circulating in his day are "judged to be of suspect credibility on account of their antiquity [*ob antiquitatem suspectae fidei iudicata sunt*]"—that is, because they would have been written before the flood, which would have disrupted their transmission. More specifically, he argues that since they were not preserved "with due rigor [*rite*] through a clear succession [*per seriem successioni*]," it is not possible to believe that "Enoch is the author of the works attributed to him," as is also the case with many other books put forward under the names of "prophets" and "apostles" (*Civ.* 15.23). Here, authorship, transmission, and authority are inseparably bound together. Augustine could accept the reliability of the canonical writings because they were handed down in clear, rigorous, and unbroken succession, with

---

38. As Ehrman notes, "Since authority resided in authorship, the easiest way to deny authority was to reject authorship" (*Forgery and Counterforgery*, 92).

39. Reed, *Fallen Angels*, provides the definitive account of the composition and reception history of the Book of the Watchers.

40. Reed, *Fallen Angels*, 194–205.

41. Latin text from CSEL 40/2. English translations are my own.

each generation of custodians ensuring their accuracy. When he wishes to deny canonical authority to a particular text, he does so by placing it outside this line of transmission and thus leaving it exposed to corruption, interpolation, and the possibility of outright forgery.

FALSIFIED SCRIPTURE IN THE PSEUDO-CLEMENTINE HOMILIES

The doctrine of the false pericopes occupies a prominent place in the opening narrative sequence of the Homilies, which runs from books 1–3. The entirety of the Homilies is narrated in the voice of Clement, who introduces himself to the reader with the first two words of the text: *egō Klēmēs*, "I, Clement." He will serve as the reader's guide through the tumultuous events of his youth, when he converted to the religion of the "true prophet"—the term that is most frequently used to refer to Jesus—and accompanied the apostle Peter on a journey around the eastern shore of the Mediterranean in pursuit of the arch-heretic Simon Magus, with whom they engaged in frequent public disputation.[42] In the course of these travels, Clement is reunited with the family from which he has been separated—not only his mother and father but also his two brothers, who, by a stroke of fate, have already become disciples of Peter and welcome him into their circle, unaware of their relation to him. These themes of recognition and reunification, which display strong generic similarity with the Hellenistic novels, emerge only in the second half of the Homilies.[43] The first three books, which are of most direct interest to us, consist almost entirely of philosophical dialogue and disputation.

The first book serves primarily as a critique of Greek philosophy, which is essentially reduced to Aristotelian logic, although there is also a brief polemic against what we might term magic. We meet Clement as a young man, austere and conflicted, living in Rome. There are no references to the missing family, which will later occupy such a central role in the plot. Instead, Clement's sole focus is how he was tormented by the problem of the immortality of the soul. He sought to resolve this by attending the "schools of the philosophers [*tōn philosophōn diatrabas*],"

---

42. On the figure of Simon Magus in the *Homilies*, see Dominique Côté, *Le thème de l'opposition entre Pierre et Simon dans les Pseudo-Clémentines* (Paris: Institut d'Études Augustiniennes, 2001).

43. On the novelistic features of the Homilies, see Mark J. Edwards, "The Clementina: A Christian Response to the Pagan Novel," *CQ* 42 (1992): 459–74.

but there he found only the "setting up and tearing down of doctrines [*dogmatōn anaskeuas kai kataskeuas*]" (1.3.1). His elation at hearing an argument for the soul's immortality would be quickly dashed by an equally plausible argument for its mortality. Clement concludes that such philosophical inquiry reveals only the skill of those making the arguments (*tous ekdikountas*), and not the truth of the opinions (*doxai*) under examination (1.3.3). He briefly flirts with the idea of traveling to Egypt to persuade a *magos* to "raise up a soul [*psychēs anapompēn ... poiēsē*]," so that he might settle once and for all the question of whether it is immortal, but he is talked out of the idea by a friend—a philosopher, no less—on the grounds that it is a violation of "piety [*eusebeia*]" (1.5.1, 7).

The answer to Clement's dilemma ultimately comes in the form of an itinerant preacher, who proclaims that the "son of God [*ho tou theou huios*]" has appeared in Judea and offers the possibility to human beings of "becoming eternal [*aidioi genomenoi*]" if they live according to the "counsel [*boulēsin*]" of the "one God [*hena theon*]" (1.7.1-6). Although the citizens of Rome ignore his message, Clement is inspired to travel to Judea. His ship is ultimately blown off course and makes harbor in Alexandria, where he meets Barnabas and becomes an adherent of this new movement. Barnabas seems to be introduced into the narrative only to further the critique of Greek philosophy, since all that we learn of him is that he spoke "not by making use of dialectic [*dialektikēi*], [and] he expounded without guile or preparation [*akakōs kai aparaskeastōs*] the things that he heard and saw the one who was revealed to be the son of God do and say" (1.9.2). While the crowds (*ochloi*) respond positively to Barnabas's preaching, the philosophers—men of "worldly *paideia*"—mock (*gelan*) him, attempting to rebut his arguments with "syllogisms [*syllogismois*]" (1.10.1-2). In a lengthy speech, Clement upbraids the philosophers for not in fact being philosophers at all: they are "word-lovers [*philologoi*]" and not "truth-lovers [*philalētheis*]" or "wisdom-lovers [*philosophoi*]" (1.11.7).

In this opening book the Homilies sets up a contrast between prophetic revelation conveyed in plain, artless speech, which is presented as a sure guarantor of the truth, and formal (Aristotelian) logic, which is derided as nothing more than a game of words that leads the arrogant astray—presented, of course, using technical terms drawn from the Greek rhetorical tradition to leave no doubt that the author is intimately acquainted with that which he is rejecting. The book culminates with the appearance of Peter, whom Clement meets when he finally arrives in Judea. Peter explains to Clement that the philosophers could not resolve his existential dilemma because evil fills the world as smoke fills a house, blinding everyone to the truth, and only outside intervention can bring true knowledge. He then introduces the figure of the "true prophet [*ton alēthē prophētēn*]," who is the only one able to "enlighten people's souls [*phōtisai psychas anthrōpōn*]" (1.19.1).

Along with this introduction of the figure of the true prophet we find a complementary emphasis placed on oral teaching and the master-disciple relationship. Clement is so persuaded by Peter's discourse that he concludes that "the truth of the teaching about the prophet [*tēs <peri> tou prophētou homilias*] is clearer to the ears than things seen with the eyes" (1.20.1). In other words, prophetically inspired discourse, which is heard with the ears, is more persuasive than the performance of miracles and other signs. Books, it should be noted, are explicitly included within the bounds of this oral teaching, provided that they are read or heard under the direction of an authorized teacher.[44] A few sentences later Clement adds, "After I wrote down [*grapsas*] the discourse [*logon*] about the prophet, as [Peter] ordered, he arranged for the volume [*tomon*] to be sent to you from Caesarea Stratonis, saying that he had an order [*entolēn*] from you to send you his teachings and acts [*homilias te kai praxeis*] each year [*kath' hekaston eniauton*]" (1.20.3).

This abrupt switch to second-person address is jarring from a narrative standpoint, since no specific reader has earlier been addressed. Clement must here be referring to James the apostle, who is the addressee of the pseudonymous Epistle of Peter to James, which seems to have circulated as a sort of covering letter to the Homilies.[45] In that letter, Peter makes references to certain "books of my preachings [*tōn emōn kērygmatōn ... biblous*]" that he had sent to James, and in having Clement make this abrupt reference to transcription, the Homilies is clearly trying to present

---

44. As Jaffee, *Torah in the Mouth*, notes, reading "was primarily a social activity in which a declaimer delivered the written text to its audience. In such settings, the oral-performative tradition included not only the recitation of the written text, but also the inflections of voice, gesture, and interpretive amplification.... Oral-performative tradition was a common medium for sharing written texts" (8). The transmission of texts in communal settings continued well into the medieval period; see, for example, the discussion of medieval Islamic public reading sessions in Konrad Hirschler, *The Written Word in the Medieval Arabic Lands: A Social and Cultural History of Reading Practices* (Edinburgh: University of Edinburgh Press, 2011), 32–81.

45. For a compelling argument that the epistle should be taken as an integral part of the novel, see Duncan, *Novel Hermeneutics*, 27–39.

itself as the written record of these preachings. What is significant about this passage of the Homilies for our purposes is that it presents Clement both as disciple and as scribe—as a model student for the reader to emulate and as a guarantor of Peter's (and, hence, the true prophet's) teaching.

The Homilies is thus consciously and deliberately presented as a textualization of oral discourse, and in this self-presentation it reflects the anxieties of Christ followers from a later era who value the primacy of the living voice and yet stand at a distance of centuries from the time of Jesus. Indeed, there may be no better vehicle to convey these anxieties than Clement of Rome. He represents a transitional age in the life of the *ekklēsia*: he personally knows the apostles, but he is not of their era. He has arrived on the scene after the time of the true prophet and can only learn of his teachings secondhand through Peter. Thus, like the Homilies' fourth-century readers, his access to the true prophet is facilitated by an intermediary, although, unlike them, he learns from an intermediary who heard the living voice of the prophet and who conveyed his teachings *viva voce*: Peter does not transcribe his own teaching.

The oral and private character of these writings is made especially clear in the Epistle of Peter to James, in which Peter instructs them to be transmitted in precisely the same way that Moses transmitted his teaching: "I ask and I beg [*axiō kai deomai*] that you do not distribute [*metadounai*] the books [*biblous*] of my preachings that I sent to you to anyone from among the Gentiles [*mēdeni tōn apo tōn ethnōn*] or to a fellow Jew [*homophylōi*] before a trial [*pro peiras*], but if, having been tested [*dokimastheis*], someone should be found worthy [*axios*], then hand down [*paradounai*] to him [my preachings] using the same method [*agōgēn*] as Moses when he handed down [*paredōke*] [his teachings] to the Seventy who succeeded his chair [*kathedran*]" (1.2). What renders this passage somewhat opaque is that the direct object is left unstated for both occurrences of *paradidōmi*; the English translation in the *Ante-Nicene Fathers* library assumes that it must in both instances refer to texts, rendering it as "Moses delivered *his books* to the Seventy." But this is highly problematic, for what else could the "books of Moses" be other than the Pentateuch? Yet, only a few sentences later, the letter refers to what Moses handed down as "the rule [*ton kanona*]" according to which "they endeavored to amend [*metarrythmizein*] the discordant passages of the scriptures [*ta tōn graphōn asymphōna*]" (1.4). Given that the Homilies explicitly denies that Moses wrote *anything* down, it seems likely that what is referred to here is some private oral teaching. It is what ensures that the Jews everywhere maintain the same "rule of monarchy and polity [*tēs monarchias kai politeias ... kanona*]" (1.2).

There is a lengthy description of how Peter's books should be transmitted, along with the text of an oath to be taken by the recipient. We get an excellent sense of how tightly bound up books ought to be with an interpretive community: Peter's books are treated as the functional equivalent of Moses's oral *kanōn*. This appendix, moreover, specifies that those who receive the books must be circumcised (*enperitomos*), that they must not receive them all at once (*tauta mē panta*), and that they should be tested (*dokimazein*) for a period of no fewer than six years (1.1). Here, too, we find the *agōgē* of Moses/Peter described in more detail: the recipient is taken to "living water [*zōn hydōr*]"—a clear allusion to baptism—and must "adjure [*epimartyrasthai*]" the provided words. Specifically, he must witness (*martyreō*) "I will always be subject [*hypēkoos*] to the one who gave [*didonti*] the books of the preachings to me, and these same books [*autas tas biblous*], which he gave to me, I will not transmit [*metadō*] to anyone in any way, neither writing them out [*grapsas*], nor giving a written text [*gegrammenon dous*], nor giving them to a scribe [*graphonti anadidous*]" (2.1). The recipient must also pledge not to be careless in guarding them (*amelōs phylassōn*) and not to allow anyone to look on them, unless this person has gone through a similar six-year period of probation. The books can also never be left unattended, and so they must be traveled with or otherwise entrusted to the "overseer [*episkopos*]" for safekeeping. The consequences of violating these practices are dire. James asserts, "If we should hand over [*paraschōmen*] the books [*biblous*] to anyone, as though at random [*hōs etychen*], and they should be corrupted [*notheuthōsin*] by daring men [*hypo tolmērōn andrōn*] or distorted by interpretations [*tais hermēneiais disatraphōsin*], as you have already heard that some have done, it will be left to those seeking the truth to forever wander astray [*aei planasthai*]" (5.1).

Here we find stated, perhaps more clearly than anywhere else in the Homilies, the premise that books are unreliable—or, rather, that public books, whose circulation has not been regulated with the utmost care, are unreliable. Falsification and misinterpretation are inevitable when books are made available outside the tight boundaries of the communities in which they are produced. The authors of this prefatory material do their best to deny the truism stated by Gamble that texts "quickly slipped beyond the author's reach"; there is the possibility of tightly controlled, private transmission. Yet, even in their fictional and idealized world, corruption *still* happens: "as you have already heard that some have done."

The tension between the unreliability and the necessity of writing is, of course, inevitable. These pseudonymous letters are meant to introduce a *text* and to vouch for its reliability. I follow Patricia Duncan in conceptualizing them as a kind of simulated initiation for the reader/hearer, who is drawn into the oral, communal world of the text.[46] We would, of course, like to know much more about their readers—intended or actual—than we are able to reconstruct. In which context(s) would these texts have been read aloud? Would there have been a wide private ownership of these texts? Would those who read or heard them have undergone any initiation themselves? We do not have the data to answer these questions, but the internal evidence of the letters always connects books to community and to the authority of sanctioned teachers. Books, in this imagined world, are always *physically* connected to people, never being left alone or unguarded, even momentarily, and they can only be received through authorized transmission. Moreover, the Homilies itself, which does not have the same conceptual constraints as the letters, is almost entirely critical of the written word, except in those occasional moments of authorial intervention when its own textualized form is referenced.

This suspicion of the written word is evident from the first book of the Homilies. Scripture is not mentioned at all in the first book; it is only the living, prophetic voice that carries authoritative weight. Clement is inspired to travel to Judea because of the proclamation of an unnamed herald of the Messiah; Barnabas inspires Clement through preaching about the "things that he heard and saw the one who was revealed to be the son of God [*ton tou theou phanenta huion*] do and say" (1.9.2); and Peter convinces him of the immortality of the soul by expounding "who [the true prophet] is and how he is found" (1.20.1). Scripture, moreover, is not mentioned even a single time in the lengthy discourse attributed to Peter with which the second book opens. This book begins with Clement awakening from sleep and finding Peter "discoursing [*dialegomenon*]"[47] with a circle of sixteen companions on the subject of "piety [*theosebeia*]" (2.1.1). Clement takes his seat among the sixteen, allowing the reader to follow him into a space of oral instruction. Peter says that he did not wake him because a tired or weary body will prevent the soul (*psychē*) from properly approaching

---

46. Duncan, *Novel Hermeneutics*, 38.

47. *Dialegomai* is a technical term referring to a philosophical dialogue or lecture (as in Plato, *Resp.* 454a; *Theaet.* 167e; Philostratus, *Vit. soph.* 2.2.1.3; see LSJ, *dialegō* B.2–3).

the "lessons [*mathēmata*]" that are presented, and so he refuses to teach anyone who is distracted, angry, distressed, or suffering from the pangs of love (2.2.1). The reason for this seemingly superfluous aside is that it indirectly instructs the reader of the Homilies as to how she should approach the task of instruction.

The subject of Peter's instruction is prophecy. He says that he need not start from the beginning with Clement, since the latter has already heard "the discourse concerning prophecy [*ton peri prophēteias logon*]" from Barnabas in Alexandria—although it should be noted that the brief description of Barnabas's preaching in the first book does not mention prophecy. For good measure, Peter reiterates that "the greatness of infallible prophecy [*tēs aptaistou prophēteias to megethos*]" is the only way to know the truth of things, and so a "prophet of truth [*prophētēs alētheias*]" is humanity's only hope. In a summative statement, Peter proclaims that "if anyone knows anything [*ei tis epistatai ti*], he has received it either from [the true prophet] or from his disciples [*para toutou ē tōn toutou mathētōn*]" (2.12.1), again situating truth within an oral, magisterial network of dissemination. And the specific teaching of the true prophet is as follows: "There is one God, who is the creator of the world, who, being just, will undoubtedly give to each person their due according to their deeds [*eis theos, hou kosmos ergon, hos dikaios ōn pantos ekastōi pros tas praxeis apodōsei*]" (2.12.2–3).

With this statement, we reach a climactic, or perhaps anticlimactic, moment in the Homilies: the decisive resolution of Clement's philosophical quandary on the immortality of the soul. This problem, it turns out, was but a prologue to the Homilies, and we are now introduced to Simon Magus, the heretic and false prophet, whose conflict with Peter will drive the narrative for the remainder of the text. We also transition from a focus on philosophical dialogue to disputation. Peter informs Clement about the doctrine of the *syzygies* or "opposing pairs"—the order that underlies the whole of creation. While the natural elements (heaven/earth, day/night, sun/moon, life/death) are twinned opposites, this rule holds for human society as well. In particular, there is an orderly succession of true and false prophets (*ho prophētikos kanōn*; 2.15.5), from Cain and Abel (who both were born to the prophet Adam) to Simon Magus and Peter.

It is only with the introduction of the character of Simon Magus that Scripture begins to be discussed, and it appears immediately in a negative light. In prefacing his discussion of Simon's false teachings, Peter makes his bold assertion about the falsification of Scripture, which I quoted at the beginning of this essay, and states that Simon will speak publicly (*eis meson*) on "those passages against God that have been joined to the scriptures for the sake of temptation [*tas kata tou theou en tais graphais peirasmou charin proskeimenas perikopas autas*]" (2.39.1). Scripture, in the worldview of the Homilies, is a profound liability, because it can be used to support Simon's denial of the oneness and goodness of God. Any analysis of the doctrine of the false pericopes must be attentive to this disputational context.[48]

Scripture cannot be authoritative because it falls within the domain of the public: it can at least theoretically be procured by any literate person to read, interpret, and copy. It can thus be corrupted, and it can in turn corrupt others. The Homilies closely connects the public with the written, and so we find clear denials that Moses ever intended his teachings to be written down: "The Law of God was given through Moses to seventy wise men, unwritten, to be handed down [*ho tou theou nomos dia Mōuseōs hebdomēkonta sophois andrasin agraphōs edothē paradidosthai*], so that it might be able to govern by succession; but after Moses was taken up [*analēpsin*], it was written by someone [*egraphē hypo tinos*], but definitely not by Moses [*ou mēn hypo Mōuseōs*]" (3.47.3). This intensifies the claim made in the second book, which only asserted that falsehoods were added soon after its transcription. Here we find an explicit denial that Moses transmitted the Torah in a written form. As evidence for this claim, the Homilies appeals to the rediscovery of Deuteronomy during the reign of the Judahite king Josiah and its removal from the land of Israel during the Babylonian exile to demonstrate Moses's "foreknowledge [*prognōsis*]" in not transcribing it, since it was "often lost [*pollakis apolōlos*]" (3.47.3). In this context, it appears that the problem is not so much the written status of the Torah as it is with the unreliable transmission history of the Torah. Indeed, the logic here is strikingly similar to Augustine's in his discussion of the canonical status of the Enochic books. If we were to sum up the Homilies' position on writing, we could do so as follows: What matters most in ascribing authority to a body of revelation is the reliability of the network in which and by which it was transmitted. Written revelation is

---

48. Christians were particularly eager to textualize their debates, as a way of exerting control over an unpredictable form of engagement. See Richard Lim, *Public Disputation, Power, and Social Order in Late Antiquity* (Berkeley: University of California Press, 1995).

not a priori problematic, as long as it is handed down through an unbroken chain of teachers and disciples. Books, however, unlike oral teaching, can become easily separated from these networks of transmission and made available to the inexpert and the unworthy who are outside them.

The Homilies evinces no clear interest in correcting the false passages of Scripture. Indeed, Peter asserts that God permitted these texts to be added to the true revelation of the law "for a certain just reason [*dikaiōi tini logōi*]," namely, to "expose those who dare to give a friendly hearing to the things written against God [*elegthōsin tines tolmōsin ta kata tou theou graphenta philēkoōs echein*]" (2.38.2). Although the Homilies treats textual corruption as an inevitability, this process still does not fall outside the purview of the one, good God—and thus cannot be taken to demonstrate God's ignorance or feebleness—who permits these false passages to play a role in testing adherents. The errors do not need to be removed from written copies of Scripture, because the one who internalizes the teaching of the true prophet will not be moved by them. This is encapsulated in the *agraphon*, unwritten saying, attributed to Jesus: "Be trustworthy money-changers [*ginesthe trapezitai dokimoi*]" (3.50.2). The disciple of the true prophet will know how to discern the true and false words in Scripture. Peter then furthers this point by appealing to words from Matt 5:17–18, which, for obvious reasons, he does not name as such: "I have not come to destroy the Law [*ouk ēlthon katalusai ton nomon*]" and "Heaven and earth will pass away [*pareleusontai*], [but] neither one letter nor one stroke of a letter [*iota hen ē mia keraia*] will pass from the Law [*ou mē parelthēi apo tou nomou*]" (3.51.2–3). Since Jesus did seem to contravene teachings from the law, Peter asserts that these "were not of the Law [*ouk ēn tou nomou*]" (3.51.2).

The reader is never provided with an exhaustive list of the false pericopes, but a series of rhetorical questions suggests that such a list, were it to be drawn up, would be extensive. Peter does not directly name specific passages but rather obliquely introduces them by asking whether God "tests [*perazei*]," "repents [*metameleitai*]," "envies [*zēloi*]," "hardens hearts [*sklērynei kardias*]," or "makes blind and deaf [*typhloi kai kōphoi*]" (2.43.1–4). These refer to stories in the Pentateuch such as God's testing Abraham by requiring him to sacrifice his son, Isaac (Gen 22:1); his repentance at having destroyed the world in the flood (Gen 6:6); God's forbidding of idol worship in the commandments that he gives to Moses on Sinai (Exod 20:5); God's hardening of Pharaoh's heart when the Israelites were in captivity in Egypt (Exod 4:21); and God's claim to Moses that he takes sight and speech from humans (Exod 4:11). Some of these texts, such as the story of the sacrifice of Isaac or God's remorse at destroying humanity in the flood, proved challenging to early Jewish and Christian interpreters, and were often read in figurative ways. But the final example—the blinding and muting of humans—is more obscure and striking. The passage is in fact about God granting Moses the capacity for eloquent speech—a positive and praiseworthy thing, no doubt—and God is simply declaring God's power over all speech; it is something God can both give and take away. This passage certainly does open up questions about the problem of evil, but these questions would not be resolved by a nonliteral or allegorical reading strategy. Thus even in this short list it is difficult to suggest that the doctrine of the false pericopes is motivated primarily by an aversion to allegory. Peter then goes on to assert that nearly every aspect of the temple cult—from animal sacrifice to the temple vessels to the ark of the covenant itself—was an accretion to the original Mosaic revelation (2.44.1–3). Moreover, the Homilies rejects the ascription of any vice—including multiple marriage—to the patriarchs, even Adam himself (2.52.2–3).

Outsiders, Insiders, and the Problem of Authority in Late Antique Christianity and Judaism

What are we to make of all this? The Homilies clearly presumes that its readers will be familiar—indeed, intimately familiar—with Scripture, since it uses only a single word or phrase to invoke each of the false passages. Its implied readers would thus presumably be engaging in regular study of these books in order to be so familiar with them. But the sheer number of allegedly false passages is so overwhelming, and the logic that is used to identify them so tenuous in some cases, that it is difficult to imagine this serving as a workable hermeneutical guide. If *every* anthropomorphic description of God, *every* aspect of the temple cult, *every* questionable act of the patriarchs is rejected, what left of the Torah is there? The function must, as stated above, be *ideological*. The doctrine of the false pericopes denies all but true Petrine insiders any and all access to divine revelation. Scripture is so fundamentally unreliable that outsiders will inevitably be misled and concoct spurious teachings of their own.

This motif of refusing to engage outsiders in debate over Scripture is not an uncommon phenomenon. Perhaps the most famous early Christian example is drawn from the *Prescription against the Heretics* (*De praescriptione hereticorum*) of Tertullian of Carthage, written at the turn of the third century CE. In this work, Tertullian flatly says that in disputation with heretics there ought to be "no authoritative appeal to the scriptures [*non ad scripturas provocandum*]" and "there ought to be no debating those passages if victory is out of the question, or uncertain, or not very certain [*nec in his constituendum certamen in quibus aut nulla aut incerta victoria est aut parum certa*]" (19.1). The reason he offers for this stark prohibition is that "heresy [*hairesis*]" "does not accept certain scriptures [*non recipit quasdam scripturas*] and even if it accepts certain scriptures [*etsi quas recipit*], it does not accept them untouched [*non recipit integras*], but it perverts [*intervertit*] them with additions and omissions [*adiectionibus et detractionibus*]" (17.1). Those Scriptures, he says, that haven't been corrupted, heresy "distorts [*convertit*]" by "contriving conflicting interpretations [*diversas expositiones commentata*]" (17.1). For Tertullian, these scriptural distortions produce the same effect: "A fraudulent interpreter is as much a hindrance to the truth as a corrupt scribe [*tantum veritati obstrepit adulter sensus quantum et corruptor stilus*]" (17.2). Significantly, Tertullian denies the possibility that there is some objective method by which "orthodox" Christians could definitively demonstrate that their copies of the Scriptures and their interpretations are the correct ones, arguing that regarding heretics, "It is inevitable that they will say that it was actually us who introduced the adulterated passages of scripture and the counterfeit interpretations [*necesse est enim et illos dicere a nobis potius adulteria scripturarum et expositionum mendacia inferri*]" (18.3).

Tertullian's claim about the falsification of Scripture does admittedly differ substantially from the account we find in the Homilies. According to Tertullian, "heretics"—the outsiders—themselves introduce errors into a pristine text, rather than go astray by mistakenly believing the errors in Scripture to be true. When speaking of "additions and omissions [*adiectiones et detractiones*]," he almost certainly has in mind the second-century Christian Marcion, who believed that the letters of Paul and the Gospel of Luke had been interpolated by Judaizers, and who as a consequence produced his own editions of these texts by removing this supposedly false material.[49] But Tertullian does clearly share with the Homilies the belief that publicly circulating books are fundamentally unreliable, liable as they are to falsification and misinterpretation, and

---

49. See now Judith M. Lieu, *Marcion and the Making of a Heretic: God and Scripture in the Second Century* (Cambridge: Cambridge University Press, 2015), esp. 183–269.

he thus denies the legitimacy of Scripture as a *public* archive—that is, as a source that can be relied on to settle disputes between competing sects that hold it as authoritative. Scripture is not a common possession but obtains meaning only within a closed interpretive community; indeed, only in this community can the genuine *text* of Scripture be known.

The operative concept for Tertullian is "instruction [*disciplina*]," which he identifies as the mechanism "by which people are made Christian [*qua fiunt christiani*]" (19.2). Only where this *disciplina* exists can anything be known about Scripture: "For where the truth of Christian *disciplina* and faith is made clear, there will be the truth about the scriptures and the interpretations and all the teachings that Christians have handed down [*ubi enim apparuerit esse veritatem disciplinae et fidei christianae, illic erit veritas scripturarum et expositionum et omnium traditionum christianorum*]" (19.3). This *disciplina* has its origins with Christ, who he "proclaimed in some instances openly to the people and in others separately to the disciples [*pronuntiabat sive populo palam, sive discentibus seorsum*]" (20.2). These disciples he trained to be "teachers [*magistros*]," who, filled with the power of the Holy Spirit, "established churches in every city [*ecclesias apud unamquamque civitatem condiderunt*], from which other churches in succession derived [*mutuatae sunt*] the vine-branch of faith and the seeds of doctrine [*traducem fidei et semina doctrinae*] and are daily deriving [them] so that they might be made churches [*ut ecclesiae fiunt*]" (20.5). Tertullian here uses horticultural metaphors—vine branches and seeds—to demonstrate the living, growing character of Christian *disciplina*, which was planted by the disciples and tended to by subsequent generations of Christians; indeed, he calls these churches the "offshoots of the apostolic churches [*suboles apostolicarum ecclesiarum*]" (20.6).

What matters for Tertullian is this private archive—a living archive, no less—of apostolic teaching, in accordance with which truth is to be judged: "All doctrine that accords [*conspiret*] with these apostolic churches—sources and origins of faith [*matricibus et originalibus fidei*]—ought to be considered truth [*veritati deputandam*]" (21.4). It is passed along orally and guaranteed by the succession of bishops, who can trace their lineage back to the apostles. Tertullian challenges his opponents to "put forth the origins of their churches [*edant ergo origines ecclesiarum suarum*], unroll the record of their bishops [*evolvant ordinem episcoporum suorum*], thus running down the succession from the beginning so that the first bishop has as the one who ordained and preceded him [*habuerit auctorem et antecessorem*] someone from the apostles or from the apostolic men, who although not themselves apostles persevered with them [*qui tamen cum apostolis perseveraverit*]" (32.1).

Tertullian does distill this apostolic teaching in his "rule of faith [*regula fidei*]," which takes the form of a baptismal profession. It runs for approximately fifteen lines in the printed edition, beginning with the confession of "one God [*unum deum*]," and runs through the sending forth of the "word [*verbum*]," the incarnation, the preaching of the "new law [*novam legem*]," the crucifixion and ascension, the sending of the Holy Spirit, and concluding with the final judgment and the resurrection of all flesh (13.1–5). Although most scholarship tends to focus on this *regula fidei* as a kind of hermeneutical key—not unsurprisingly so, since a *regula* is literally a "ruler," a standard for measuring—it only forms a small part of what I am calling Tertullian's "apostolic imagination," and it is, I would argue, better understood as an ideological device, much like the doctrine of the false pericopes, that both legitimates and necessitates the heresiological writings of theologians such as Irenaeus and Tertullian.[50] Indeed, it is immediately after introducing the *regula* that Tertullian dismisses the possibility of arguing with "heretics" and launches into his lengthy genealogy of apostolic churches and practices. Its importance lies less in what it *says* than in the discourses that it *authorizes*.

Tertullian thus shares with the Homilies an ambivalence about the public archive of Scripture, which, to be read correctly (and in its correct form), must be encountered in an interpretive community shaped by the teachings of the apostles, which are ultimately the teachings of Christ/the true prophet. In other words, they each make the public private and foster, in their own unique ways, the proliferation of a complementary,

---

50. Tertullian's notion of the *regula fidei* is clearly dependent on Irenaeus's *kanōn tēs alētheias* ("rule of truth"), which he describes in his *Adversus Haereses*, and most scholarship tends to treat both together, although with a much heavier focus on Irenaeus. See especially Young, *Biblical Exegesis*, "I stressed the importance of the Rule of Faith or the Canon of Truth as providing the extra-canonical framework or 'overarching story' by which the scriptures were to be read and interpreted.... [What] has not been explicitly noted before is that all along creed-like statements and confessions must in practice have provided the hermeneutical key to the public reading of scripture before Irenaeus articulated this" (18). See also Annette Yoshiko Reed, "EUAGGELION: Orality, Textuality, and the Christian Truth in Irenaeus' *Adversus Haereses*," *VC* 56 (2002): 13: "For Irenaeus, the *kanōn* functions as an extra-textual criterion for distinguishing true doctrine from heretical speculations, authentic texts from spurious compositions, and proper Scriptural interpretation from 'evil exegesis.'"

apostolically sanctioned body of teachings. This is perhaps more complex for Tertullian than for the Homilies, since Tertullian's Scripture includes apostolic writings, whereas for the Homilies, Scripture is essentially the Torah. But it seems clear enough that for Tertullian these unwritten traditions, which circulate in the apostolic churches and their offshoots, stand *alongside* Scripture, rather than in subordination to it, as we have with the glossing metaphor.

We also see a reticence to debating outsiders or heretics in rabbinic literature. There is a famous story recorded in Genesis Rabbah of "heretics [*minim*]" who approach Rabbi Simlai with a pointed question about how many gods created the world. It is clearly a loaded question, meant to induce R. Simlai into admitting that there is not only one power in heaven. R. Simlai begins his response with an invocation of Deut 4:32, "For ask the first days [of creation]" (Gen. Rab. 8.9.1).[51] He thus asks the "first day" (i.e., Gen 1:1) for an answer to the question of the *minim* and there finds that "Gods created is not what is written here, but rather, God created." Undeterred, the *minim* counter by asking why Gen 1:1 uses the plural *elohim* to refer to God in the singular, again clearly trying to compel him to admit that God is not one. R. Simlai responds simply by saying that the singular form, rather than the plural form, of the verb "to create" (*bārā'*) is used. The textual unit resolves without any further explanation, other than that the singular form of the verb is determinative in answering the question of how many gods exist.

But a second, closely related textual unit offers a more complicated explanation, one that is particularly illuminating for our purposes. It opens with a teaching from R. Simlai that acts as a sort of hinge between the two units: "In any passage in which you find an answer that heretics [*minim*] may give, you find a remedy right along side" (Hom. 8.9.2). This is the deeper, though unarticulated, hermeneutical principle that guided his interpretation of Gen 1:1 in the preceding textual unit. The potentially heretical force of the plural *elohim* is countered by the singular verb *bārā'*. The logic here is strikingly similar, though not identical, to Peter's claim about Scripture in the Homilies: "Thus the sayings that are slanderous of the God who created the heavens [*hai tou ton ouranon ktisantos theou diaboloi phōnai*] are canceled out [*akyrountai*] by the opposing say-

---

51. I am using the translation of Jacob Neusner, *Genesis Rabbah: The Judaic Commentary to the Book of Genesis*, vol. 1, BJS 104 (Atlanta: Scholars Press, 1985).

ings [*enantiōn phōnōn*] that are with them [*syn autais*]" (Hom. 3.46.1). R. Simlai does not assert that the words on which the *minim* have alighted are false or slanderous of God, as does Peter, but common to both is the idea that obscure or problematic phrases are explained (or explained away) with reference to other nearby passages that cancel out their potentially heretical force. In the disputational context, neither R. Simlai nor Peter attempts to interpret the significance of the problematic phrase; rather, each directs the reader to phrases that blunt its force. Even more interestingly, in the Genesis Rabbah passage R. Simlai's disciples push back on his answer, acknowledging its weakness: "His disciples asked him, after the others had gone out, 'These you have pushed aside with a mere reed, but what are you going to answer us?'" The idea here is that outsiders are not to be debated with but answered as quickly and decisively as possible. Scripture is not theirs, and they are not worthy of participating in its interpretation.

But perhaps the greatest formal similarity between the author(s)/redactor(s) of the Homilies and the rabbis lies with the concept of "Torah in the mouth." As Jaffee has carefully argued, Torah in the mouth is not synonymous with "oral/repeated tradition" and thus developed gradually in rabbinic circles, even as the oral repetition of teachings aurally learned from a master had long been central to their pedagogy. Thus Mishnah Avot, which begins with the claim that Moses "received *torah* from Sinai and passed it on to Yehoshua" (1:1), is not evidence for the talmudic concept of Oral Torah, since it "does not yet speak of the Sinaitic origins of Torah in Script and Torah in the Mouth, but only of *torah*"; instead, it simply "extols the traditionality of rabbinic teachings, linking their authority to the greatest possible source of authority."[52] As noted earlier in this essay, it is essential for Jaffee to distinguish the content and performance of oral teaching from the ideological framing that necessitates and justifies it.

It is, in Jaffee's view, only with the Amoraic sages, in the middle of the third century, that we begin to see such ideological formation, as they "contributed to the Tannaitic tradition not only their interpretation of its laws, but also the interpretation of its significance as an oral-performative tradition."[53] I will focus on two particular passages—one from the Talmud

---

52. Jaffee, *Torah in the Mouth*, 84. Translation from Jaffee.
53. Jaffee, *Torah in the Mouth*, 126.

Yerushalmi and another from a Byzantine compilation—to illustrate, in conversation with Jaffee, some of the key ideological components of Torah in the mouth.

The first comes from y. Pe'ah 2:6, 17a, which consists of a "series of discrete units of tradition" that offer "diverse expositions of how the Amoraic Sages surrounding Rabbi Yohanan understood the origins and significance of the *torah* they transmitted by mouth to their disciples."[54] A verse from Hosea—"Shall I write for him the great portion of my Torah?" (Hos 8:12)—is the locus of a discussion about the revelation to Moses on Sinai. R. Leazar argues that "matters derived from Scripture outnumber those derived from [what is taught by] the mouth" (3), but an unnamed interlocutor counters this by saying that "matters derived from [what is taught] by mouth are more precious than those derived from Scripture" (4). The reason for this special status of oral teaching is given by R. Avin, who asks, "What distinguishes us from the Gentiles? These produce their books and those produce their books" (5). In other words, whereas other nations produce literary traditions, Israel alone produces an oral one.[55] In the following lemma, R. Shmuel b. Nahman uses Exod 34:27—"I have established a covenant with you and with Israel through these things taught orally"—to argue that "those in the mouth are more precious" than those things that are preserved "in script" (6), and both R. Yohanan and R. Udan b. R. Shimon both play on the apposition between "what is in the mouth" and "what is in script" (7). All of these lemmata culminate with the teaching of R. Yehoshua b. Levi, who asserts, "Scripture, Repeated Tradition, Dialectics, and Homiletics ... all were already spoken to Moshe on Sinai" (9). Here, Scripture becomes just one small portion of a massive body of revelation that was taught to Moses on Sinai. Indeed, so expansive is this notion of oral tradition that, in the words of Jaffee, "Whatever insights dawn in the mind of a properly trained disciple are all an unfolding of the original oral disclosure to Moses."[56] It would be difficult to describe this account oral tradition as a kind of hermeneutical supplement; instead, it is an ideological claim that the sum total of all rabbinic activity is an unfolding of the very mind of God.

---

54. Jaffee, *Torah in the Mouth*, 143. Translation of y. Peah 2:6 is taken from Jaffee (142–43). The parenthetical numbers are his labels.
55. See Jaffee, *Torah in the Mouth*, 144.
56. Jaffee, *Torah in the Mouth*, 144.

The second—the Midrash of Rabbi Tanhuma—draws out the ideological dimension, especially as it pertains to writing, even more clearly than the Yerushalmi. This compilation dates to the late Byzantine period, and so is considerably later than the Homilies, but it is still to my mind a useful comparandum, especially given its obvious indebtedness to the Yerushalmi and its logic of Torah in the mouth. The relevant passage begins again with the quotation of Hos 8:12 but turns quickly to a dialogue between Moses and God. After he has "mastered" God's teaching, Moses is told to "Go and teach it to My children" (Tanh. 2).[57] Moses requests that God write it down but is met with the following reply, "I'd like to give it to them in script, but I know that one day the Nations of the World will subdue them and seek to take it from them, so that my sons will become like other Nations. Rather: Let them have the Scriptures in writing. But the Repeated Tradition, Homiletics, and Dialectics shall remain in the mouth" (2). In this passage, writing is coded as a potentially dangerous activity. We see again that having an oral heritage differentiates Israel from the gentiles, but here it is emphasized that this is what protects them from having their divine revelation appropriated and perverted. As Jaffee notes, it is hard not to read this as an instance of anti-Christian polemic: "This passage counters Christian theological supercessionism [sic], grounded in a hermeneutical appropriation of Jewish Scripture, with the bold claim that possession of Scripture alone is no sign of covenantal partnership with God."[58] Revelation transcribed in text can be not only manipulated and falsified but also stolen—it becomes a physical product that can be seized, potentially disinheriting those to whom it was originally given.

It is indeed significant that the author(s)/redactor(s) of the Homilies, like the rabbis, imagine that there exists an oral tradition that can be traced back to the revelation to Moses at Sinai, and that what is oral is in some sense superior to the written. There are, of course, important differences; the Homilies denies that Moses wrote down anything at all, whereas the rabbis are perfectly willing to acknowledge that one portion of the revelation was written down. Moreover, the Homilies preserves apostolic revelations and does not purport to be the Sinaitic revelation given to Moses. Finally, the rabbis never make any claim that Scripture has been falsified, however open to misappropriation, mistranscription,

---

57. Text translated by Jaffee, *Torah in the Mouth*, 145.
58. Jaffe, *Torah in the Mouth*, 145.

and misinterpretation it may be. Still, this similar emphasis on oral revelation at Sinai is at least suggestive of contact and influence between Jewish and Christ-following communities long after the so-called parting(s) of the ways. But to argue that the similarity ends there, as Carlson does, is to miss the most important dimension of Torah in the mouth and the false pericopes. Carlson focuses specifically on the *content* of the oral traditions. Insistent as he is that the doctrine of the false pericopes is an "exegetical criterion," he differentiates rabbinic oral tradition, which he defines as "halakhic/legal," from the Pseudo-Clementine oral tradition, which he defines as "exegetical."[59] But this is to misunderstand their ideological function; Torah in the mouth and the false pericopes are not defined by their substance. Both concepts, in strikingly similar ways, decenter a contested public archive, which can be seized on and misused by outsiders, by positing the existence of a perfect and assiduously transmitted private archive that both engulfs and expands on that public archive. Both Torah in the mouth and the false pericopes authorize a potentially unbounded literary production, straining against the very idea of archival closure.

Conclusion

As Eva Mroczek has persuasively demonstrated in her masterful book *The Literary Imagination in Jewish Antiquity*, scholars of early Christianity and early Judaism are trained to look at the literary productions of those traditions through the lens of "the Bible." Hence, Jewish pseudepigraphal works from the third and second centuries BCE, such as the Book of the Watchers and Jubilees, are classified as examples of rewritten Bible, even though the concept of a Bible would not emerge for centuries.[60] In a similar vein, scholars of early Christianity tend to describe any citation of or comment on an authoritative text as biblical interpretation—as though the apologetic and heresiological works of an Irenaeus or a Tertullian, in which intertexts are piled one on another in compendious fashion, were meant to be read alongside scriptural texts and not perhaps in some sense displace them. This is not to say that there is anything methodologically suspect with examining the use of particular texts—or approaches to sacred writings as

---

59. Carlson, *Jewish-Christian Interpretation*, 124.
60. Mroczek, *Literary Imagination*, 3–18.

a whole—in such works; I offer this observation not as an outsider but as an insider who has written a monograph on the use of the Song of Songs in early Christian writings.[61] But this frame of reference can become overly determinative and lead us to imagine these kinds of texts as early steps on the path to the production of commentaries—the systematic glossing of entire texts—rather than as creative works of an entirely different sort.

My call in this essay is for scholars of early Judaism and early Christianity—and indeed other scripturally based traditions as well—to take seriously the challenge of the Homilies' teaching of the false pericopes. It is natural for many of us (it certainly was for me) to try to situate the false pericopes within the realm of hermeneutics: the Homilies is offering its readers a new way to read and to understand Scripture. Certainly, there are elements of this. The Homilies does, for example, evince a clear suspicion of allegorical reading strategies, and it argues against the possibility of tension between genuine scriptural texts; it even imagines reading as a moral exercise, in which righteous and unrighteous dispositions will be revealed. But the Homilies also destabilizes the ease with which we can assume the centrality of Scripture in late antique Christianity and Judaism. In the opening books of the Homilies, Peter teaches without any reference to Scripture; he does not position himself as an interpreter but as a prophet. As I have argued, the doctrine of the false pericopes functions as an ideological concept that both justifies and necessitates the production of apostolic literature, which connects fourth-century readers and hearers with an ever more distant privileged past.

The Homilies bases its teaching of falsified Scripture on the unreliability of books and written texts. In a world in which texts could only be transmitted by copying them out by hand, writing was a risky business. Even the most careful of scribes could introduce errors; an incautious scribe—or, worse, a devious one—could fundamentally alter the meaning of a text. For scriptural writings, which were held to be authoritative by many Jewish and Christian sects and thus existed in thousands of copies in multiple languages and translations, the potential for serious error increased exponentially. The Homilies resolves this dilemma by claiming for its community alone access to the unvarnished truth, preserved in a private archive of apostolic teachings that were assiduously preserved and

---

61. Karl Shuve, *The Song of Songs and the Fashioning of Identity in Early Latin Christianity* (Oxford: Oxford University Press, 2016).

transmitted. It offers its readers the opportunity to imaginatively participate in this solemn act of transmission through the detailed description of oaths in the Epistle of Peter to James.

While the Homilies' claim that Scripture was falsified was an anomalous one in late antiquity, its suspicion of books and of writing was not. Constraints of space prevent a more thorough listing of examples, but figures as different as North African Latin theologian Tertullian and Palestinian Amoraim seized on textual unreliability to justify the production and proliferation of private archives. Rather than read works such as Irenaeus's *Adversus Haereses* or Tertullian's *De Praescriptione Haereticorum* as offering a hermeneutical key for the interpretation of the Bible, I propose instead treating them as essential, constitutive components of a private archive that is governed by the apostolic imagination and which offers readers the opportunity to imaginatively situate themselves within that archive. Rather than interpret Scripture, they offer new ways of encountering the divine revelation—and countering the heretical teachings of their opponents. I also propose that we should be prepared to read figures such as Irenaeus and Tertullian alongside works such as the Pseudo-Clementine Homilies and other apostolic apocrypha as fellow participants in the crafting of apostolically sanctioned bodies of literature.

Bibliography

Adler, William. "Apion's 'Encomium of Adultery': A Jewish Satire of Greek *Paideia* in the Pseudo-Clementine *Homilies*." *HUCA* 64 (1993): 15–49.
Barclay, John. *Against Apion*. FJTC 10. Leiden: Brill, 2007.
Boyarin, Daniel. *Intertextuality and the Reading of Midrash*. Bloomington: Indiana University Press, 1990.
Carlson, Donald H. *Jewish-Christian Interpretation of the Pentateuch in the Pseudo-Clementine Homilies*. Minneapolis: Fortress, 2013.
Clark, Elizabeth. *The Origenist Controversy: The Cultural Construction of an Early Christian Debate*. Princeton: Princeton University Press, 1992.
———. *Reading Renunciation: Asceticism and Scripture in Early Christianity*. Princeton: Princeton University Press, 1999.
Côté, Dominique. *Le thème de l'opposition entre Pierre et Simon dans les Pseudo-Clémentines*. Paris: Institut d'Études Augustiniennes, 2001.
Dawson, David. *Allegorical Readers and Cultural Revision in Ancient Alexandria*. Berkeley: University of California Press, 1991.

———. *Christian Figural Reading and the Fashioning of Identity*. Berkeley: University of California Press, 2002.
Dibelius, Martin, and Hans Conzelmann. *The Pastoral Epistles*. Translated by Philip Buttolph and Adela Yarbro. Minneapolis: Fortress, 1972.
Duncan, Patricia. *Novel Hermeneutics in the Greek Clementine Romance*. WUNT 395. Tübingen: Mohr Siebeck, 2017.
Edwards, Mark J. "The Clementina: A Christian Response to the Pagan Novel." *CQ* 42 (1992): 459–74.
Ehrman, Bart D. *Forgery and Counterforgery: The Use of Literary Deceit in Early Christian Polemics*. Oxford: Oxford University Press, 2013.
Eusebius. *Ecclesiastical History*. Translated by Kirsopp Lake. Vol. 1. LCL. Cambridge: Harvard University Press, 1926.
Fraade, Steve. *From Tradition to Commentary: Torah and Its Interpretation in the Midrash Sifre to Deuteronomy*. Albany: SUNY Press, 1991.
Gamble, Harry Y. *Books and Readers in the Early Church: A History of Early Christian Texts*. New Haven: Yale University Press, 1995.
Hägg, Tomas. *The Novel in Antiquity*. Berkeley: University of California Press, 1983.
Hirschler, Konrad. *The Written Word in the Medieval Arabic Lands: A Social and Cultural History of Reading Practices*. Edinburgh: University of Edinburgh Press, 2011.
Holzberg, Niklas. *The Ancient Novel: An Introduction*. Translated by Christine Jackson-Holzberg. London: Routledge, 1995.
Jaffee, Martin. *Torah in the Mouth: Writing and Oral Tradition in Palestinian Judaism, 200 BCE–400 CE*. Oxford: Oxford University Press, 2001.
Jones, F. Stanley. "The Pseudo-Clementines: A History of Research." *SecCent* 2 (1982): 1–33, 63–96.
Josephus. *Josephus: The Life, Against Apion*. Translated by H. Thackeray. LCL. Cambridge: Harvard University Press, 1926.
Kamesar, Adam. *Jerome, Greek Scholarhsip, and the Hebrew Bible: A Study of the Quaestiones Hebraicae in Genesim*. Oxford: Clarendon, 1993.
Kelly, Nichole. *Knowledge and Religious Authority in the Pseudo-Clementines*. WUNT 2/213. Tübingen: Mohr Siebeck, 2006.
Lieu, Judith M. *Marcion and the Making of a Heretic: God and Scripture in the Second Century*. Cambridge: Cambridge University Press, 2015.
Lim, Richard. *Public Disputation, Power, and Social Order in Late Antiquity*. Berkeley: University of California Press, 1995.
Mroczek, Eva. *The Literary Imagination in Jewish Antiquity*. New York: Oxford University Press, 2016.

Neusner, Jacob. *Genesis Rabbah: The Judaic Commentary to the Book of Genesis*. Vol. 1. BJS 104. Atlanta: Scholars Press, 1985.
Origen. *Commentary on the Song of Songs*. Translated by Ruth Penelope Lawson. New York: Newman, 1956.
———. *Origène: Traité des principes I*. Edited and translated by Henri Crouzel and Manlio Simonetti. SC 252. Paris: Cerf, 1978.
Quispel, Gilles. *Ptolémée: Lettre à Flora*. SC 24. Paris: Cerf, 1966.
Reed, Annette Yoshiko. "EUAGGELION: Orality, Textuality, and the Christian Truth in Irenaeus' *Adversus Haereses*." *VC* 56 (2002): 11–46.
———. *Fallen Angels and the History of Judaism and Christianity: The Reception of Enochic Literature*. Cambridge: Cambridge University Press, 2006.
———. "Jewish Christianity after the Partings of the Ways." Pages 189–231 in *Ways That Never Parted: Jews and Christians in Late Antiquity and the Early Middle Ages*. Edited by Adam Becker and Annette Yoshiko Reed. Tübingen: Mohr Siebeck, 2004.
———. "'Jewish Christianity' as Counterhistory? The Apostolic Past in Eusebius' *Ecclesiastical History* and the Pseudo-Clementine *Homilies*." Pages 173–216 in *Antiquity in Antiquity: Jewish and Christian Pasts in the Greco-Roman World*. Edited by Greg Gardner and Kevin Osterloh. TSAJ 123. Tübingen: Mohr Siebeck, 2008.
Rehm, Bernard. *Die Pseudoklementinen I: Homilien*. GCS 42. Berlin: Akademie, 1953.
Schoeps, Hans J. *Jewish Christianity: Factional Disputes in the Early Church*. Translated by Douglas Hare. Minneapolis: Fortress, 1969.
Shuve, Karl. "The Doctrine of the False Pericopes and Other Late Antique Approaches to the Problem of Scripture's Unity." Pages 437–45 in *Nouvelles intrigues pseudo-clémentines*. Edited by F. Amsler et al. Prahins: Éditions du Zèbre, 2008.
———. "The Pseudo-Clementine *Homilies* and the Antiochene Polemic against Allegory." MA thesis, McMaster University, 2007.
———. *The Song of Songs and the Fashioning of Identity in Early Latin Christianity*. Oxford: Oxford University Press, 2016.
Smith, Lesley. *The "Glossa Ordinaria": The Making of a Medieval Biblical Commentary*. Leiden: Brill, 2009.
Torjesen, Karen Jo. *Hermeneutical Procedure and Theological Method in Origen's Exegesis*. Berlin: de Gruyter, 1985.
Whitmarsh, Tim, ed. *The Cambridge Companion to the Greek and Roman Novel*. Cambridge: Cambridge University Press, 2008.

Williams, Frank. *The Panarion of Epiphanius of Salamis: Book I (Sects 1-46)*. NHS 35. Leiden: Brill, 1987.

Young, Frances. *Biblical Exegesis and the Formation of Christian Culture*. Cambridge: Cambridge University Press, 1997.

Contributors

Sheila Blair (sheila.blair@bc.edu) is Norma Jean Calderwood University Professor of Islamic and Asian Art at Boston College (emerita) and Hamad bin Khalifa Endowed Chair in Islamic Art at Virginia Commonwealth University. Author or editor of a score of books and hundreds of articles on all aspects of Islamic art, she is particularly interested in the uses of writing and the arts of the Mongol period. She is the author of the monographs *Islamic Inscriptions* and *Islamic Calligraphy* (Edinburgh University Press, 1998, 2006) and the chapters "Inscribing the Qur'an: Qur'anic Texts on Architecture, Coins, and Other Solid Supports" and "Transcribing God's Word: Manuscripts of the Qur'an" in the forthcoming *Oxford Handbook of Qur'anic Studies* (ed. Muhammad Abdel Haleem and Mustafa Shah, Oxford University Press, 2018). Together with her husband and cochair, she has written the chapter on "The Islamic Book" for the forthcoming *The Oxford Illustrated History of the Book* (ed. James Raven, Oxford University Press).

Jonathan M. Bloom (jonathan.bloom@bc.edu) shared the Norma Jean Calderwood University Professorship of Islamic and Asian Art at Boston College with his wife and colleague, Sheila Blair, and still shares with her the Hamad bin Khalifa Endowed Chair of Islamic Art at Virginia Commonwealth University. Author, coauthor, or editor of a score of books and hundreds of articles on virtually all aspects of Islamic art, Bloom is particularly known for his work on the history of paper, the history of the minaret, and the art and architecture of the medieval Islamic Mediterranean region. His book *Paper before Print: The History and Impact of Paper in the Islamic Lands* (Yale University Press, 2001) won the Charles Rufus Morey Book Award from the College Art Association for a notable book in the history of art, and his and Blair's three-volume *Grove Encyclopedia of Islamic Art and Architecture* (Oxford University Press, 2009) won the World Book of the Year Prize from the Islamic Republic of Iran.

C. M. Chin (chin@ucdavis.edu) is Associate Professor of Classics at the University of California at Davis. He is the author of *Grammar and Christianity in the Late Roman World* (University of Pennsylvania Press, 2008) and coeditor of *Late Ancient Knowing: Explorations in Intellectual History* (University of California Press, 2015) and *Melania: Early Christianity through the Life of One Family* (University of California Press, 2016). He is currently finishing a project on late ancient experiences of natural history and beginning a project on theurgy, aesthetics, puppetry, and wonder.

Sidney H. Griffith (griffith@cua.edu) is Ordinary Professor Emeritus in the Department of Semitic and Egyptian Languages and Literatures in the School of Arts and Sciences at the Catholic University of America, where he earned the PhD in 1977. His areas of interest and academic responsibility are Syriac patristics, Christian Arabic literature, the history and culture of the Christian churches in the Middle East, and the history of Christian-Muslim relations, especially within the world of Islam and in the early Islamic period. In addition to numerous conference presentations, public lectures, book reviews, and articles on topics in his areas of interest, his publications include Yaḥyā ibn ʿAdī, *The Reformation of Morals: A Parallel Arabic-English Edition* (Brigham Young Univeristy Press, 2002); *The Church in the Shadow of the Mosque: Christians and Muslims in the World of Islam* (Princeton University Press, 2008); and *The Bible in Arabic: The Scriptures of the 'People of the Book' in the Language of Islam* (Princeton University Press, 2013).

AnneMarie Luijendijk (aluijend@princeton.edu) is Professor of Religion and Chair of the Committee for the Study of Late Antiquity at Princeton University, where she has been on the faculty since 2006. Her expertise is in early Christian papyrology and ancient divination. Her publications include *Greetings in the Lord: Early Christians and the Oxyrhynchus Papyri* (Harvard University Press, 2008) and *Forbidden Oracles: The Gospel of the Lots of Mary* (Mohr Siebeck, 2014). She is currently working on a book called *From Gospels to Garbage*, which traces the life cycle of early Christian manuscripts, with particular focus on the treasure trove of texts found at the ancient Egyptian city of Oxyrhynchus.

Lawrence Nees (nees@udel.edu) is Professor and Chair in the Department of Art History and H. Fletcher Brown Chair of Humanities at the University of Delaware. His special interests focus on art of the early medieval period and include early Insular art, Carolingian art, Byzantine art, and Islamic art. His books include *The Gundohinus Gospels* (Medieval Academy of America, 1987), *A Tainted Mantle: Hercules and the Classical Tradition at the Carolingian Court* (University of Pennsylvania Press, 1991), *Early Medieval Art* (Oxford University Press, 2002), *Perspectives on Early Islamic Art in Jerusalem* (Brill, 2016), and the edited volume *Approaches to Early-Medieval Art* (Medieval Academy of America, 1998).

Karl Shuve (karl.shuve@virginia.edu) is Associate Professor of Religious Studies at the University of Virginia. His first book, *The Song of Songs and the Fashioning of Identity in Early Latin Christianity* (Oxford University Press, 2016), explores the role that the Song of Songs played in shaping attitudes toward the body and sexuality in late antique Christianity. His present book project is a cultural history of the nuptial metaphor—the identification of the church or of the individual Christian as a "bride of Christ"—in early and medieval Christianity.

Primary Sources Index

Hebrew Bible

Genesis
  1:1 — 197
  6:6 — 193
  22:1 — 193

Exodus
  4:11 — 194
  4:21 — 193
  20:5 — 193
  34:27 — 199

Deuteronomy
  4:32 — 197
  4:35 — 157

Esther
  15:5 — 91

Job
  31:26 — 92

Psalms
  17:12 — 93
  37:29 — 139, 145
  78 — 148

Ezekiel
  3:3 — 21

Hosea
  8:12 — 199, 200

Ancient Jewish Writers

Josephus, *Contra Apionem*
  1.8 — 172

New Testament

Matthew
  13:43 — 92

1 Corinthians
  14:25 — 92

2 Timothy
  3:13 — 172
  3:15 — 172
  3:16 — 172

Revelation
  1:8 — 85
  10:9–10 — 21

Rabbinic Works

m. Avot
  1:1 — 198

Genesis Rabbah
  1.1.2 — 173 n.7
  8.9.1 — 197
  8.9.2 — 197

y. Pe'ah
  2:6 — 199

Primary Sources Index

EARLY CHRISTIAN WRITINGS

Augustine, *De civtate Dei*
15.23 183

Clement, *Paedagogus*
2.10.96 121

Columbanus, *Regula monachorum*
2 79

Epiphanius, *Panarion*
30.15.1 176
30.18.7 176
33.4.1 . . . . 175 n. 13

Eusebius, *Historia ecclesiastica*
5.20.2 182

Gerontius, *Vita Melaniae Iunioris*
23 21

Gregory the Great, *Homilies on the Book of the Prophet Ezekiel*
95 93

Isidore of Seville, *Libri sententiarum*
3.14.9 . . . . 79 n.24

Irenaeus, *Adversus Haereses*
1.15.6 183

Jerome, *Adversus Rufinum libri III*
1.6 182
1.9 128

Jerome, *Epistulae*
7.2 27

John Cassian, *Collationes*
14.10 . . . . 79 n.23

John Chrysostom, *Homiliae in Joannem*
11.1 123

John Chrysostom, *In principium Actorum*
3 . . . . 121, 122, 124

Justin, *Apologia ii*
5 183

Letter of Peter to James
1.1 188
1.2 . . . . 187, 188
1.4 187
5.1 188

Origen, *De principiis*
4.2.2 . . . . 173 n.7

Origen, *Contra Celsum*
8.31–2 28

Origen, *Philocalia*
12.1.31–34 28

Pseudo-Clementine Homilies . . . 184
1.3.1 185
1.3.3 185
1.5.1 185
1.7.1–6 185
1.9.2 . . . . 185, 188
1.10.1–2 185
1.11.7 185
1.19.1 186
1.20.1 . . . . 186, 188
1.20.3 186
2.1.1 188
2.2.1 190
2.12.1–3 190
2.15.5 190
2.38 171
2.38.2 192
2.39.1 191
2.43.1 193
2.44.1–3 193
2.52.2–3 193
3.13 . . . . 77 n.22
3.47.3 191
3.50.2 192

Primary Sources Index 213

3.51.2	192
8.12	77 n.22
8.16	183

Pseudo-Clementine Recognitions
4.3	177 n.22

Rufinus, *Origenis Libri Peri archon seu De principiis libri IV*
praef. 4	182

Tertullian, *De cultu feminarum*
1.2	183

Tertullian, *De praescriptione haereticorum*
13.1–5	196
17.1	194
17.2	194
18.3	194
19.1	194
19.2	195
19.3	195
20.2	195
20.5	195
20.6	195
21.4	195
32.1	196

Greco-Roman Literature

Aristotle, *De anima*
2.2	17

Artemidorus, *Onirocritica*
2.45	21

Cicero, *Epistulae ad Atticum*
4.10.1	21
14.19.1	111

Cicero, *Orationes philippicae*
2.7	27

Galen, *De alimentorum facultatibus*
1.1.469	22

1.18.528	22

Livy, *Ab Urbe Condita*
40.29.5–6	24

Ovid, *Tristia*
3.14.37–38	21

Philostratus, *Vitae sophistiarum*
2.2.1.3	189 n. 47

Plato, *Phaedrus*
274c–275a	26–27
276d	27

Plato, *Respublica*
454a	189 n.47

Plato, *Theaetetus*
167e	189 n.47

Pliny, *Naturalis Historia*
13.83	24
13.84–5	24

Plutarch, *De Iside et Osiride*
18.1	28
70.1	28

Theophrastus, *Historia plantarum*
1.1.9	26
1.7.1	26
2.24–26	17
4.8	16
4.8.3	19, 26
4.8.4	19, 20, 26
4.8.9	17
4.8.10–11	25
4.8.15	19
4.12.4	18

Vergilius Maro Grammaticus, *Epitomae*
10.1–13	89

Qur'an

2:61	140
2:75–79	143
2:163	157
2:255	157
3:2	157
3:3	142
3:21	140
3:78	143
4:46	143
4:163	143
4:163–165	145
4:171	159, 160
5:12–19	143
5:44	142
5:46	142
5:48	142
6:89–90	144
6:94	160
7:54	158
7:145	142
7:180	158
10:71	143
10:94	143
16:43–44	143
16:64	160
17:55	143
17:77	139, 146
20:3	144
21:50	144
21:105	139, 143, 145
30:27	158
38:1	144
42:51	160
54:11	160
57:27	142
90:4	159

Modern Authors Index

Abbott, Nabia 37 n. 14, 44
Adams, Christopher S. 18 n. 6, 30
Adler, William 177 n. 22, 203
Albarrán Martínez, María Jesús 127 n. 81, 128, 128 nn. 84–85, 130
Ahtaridis, Evie 114 n. 44, 130
Bacharach, Jere 57 n. 25, 65
Bagnall, Roger S. 106 n. 16, 113, 113 n. 41, 114 nn. 43–45, 124 n. 37, 130
Bamforth, Stuart S. 19 n. 9, 30
Bannister, Andrew B. 145 n. 15, 164
Barclay, John 172 n. 5, 203
Barker, Don C. 103 n. 6, 106 n. 13, 130
Barrett, David P. 119 n. 61, 131
Basil, Lourié 147 n. 18, 148 n. 21, 165, 168
Bauden, Frédéric 43 n. 40, 44
Baumstark, Anton 149 n. 24, 164
Ben-Shammai, Haggai 153 n. 38, 154, 154 n. 40, 155 n. 42, 164
Bergmann, Uwe 61 n. 37, 64 n. 41, 65 n. 42, 67
Bijlefeld, Willem A. 141 n. 10, 164
Blair, Sheila S. v, 8, 38 n. 16, 41 nn. 25–27, 45, 47, 57 n. 25, 62 n. 39, 65, 65 n. 42, 207
Blau, Joshua 151, 151 n. 29, 151 n. 31, 152, 152 nn. 32–33, 154 n. 41, 164, 167
Bloom, Jonathan M. v, 6, 6 n. 14, 8, 10, 33, 33 n. 1, 35 n. 7, 42 n. 30, 42 n. 32, 42 n. 34, 44 n. 42, 45, 62 n. 39, 65, 207
Blumell, Lincoln H. 102 n. 5, 103 n. 6, 108 nn. 20–21, 110 n. 29, 130
Boar, Rosalind R. 18 n. 6, 30
Boyarin, Daniel 173 n. 8, 203

Brakke, David 109 n. 27, 130
Brock, Fiona 64 n. 40, 65
Brody, Robert 153 n. 38, 155 n. 44, 164
Brown, Michelle 59, 59 n. 33, 65, 76 n. 18, 91 n. 38, 94, 97, 149 n. 25, 164
Bruce-Mitford, R. L. S. 59 n. 34, 65
Bulliet, Richard 162 n. 61, 164
Carlson, Donald H. 175, 175 n. 14, 177, 177 nn. 21–22, 201, 201 n. 59, 203
Carruthers, Mary J. 80 n. 25, 90 n. 36, 94
Caspar, Robert 143 n. 12, 165
Cavallo, Guglielmo 70, 70 n. 5, 95, 97, 98
Cecchelli, Carlo 91 n. 38, 95
Chamovitz, Daniel 25 n. 18, 30
Child, S. C. 18 n. 4, 30
Chin, Catherine M. v, 7, 15, 90, 90 n. 35, 92 n. 40, 95, 208
Choat, Malcolm 103 n. 7, 130
Clark, Elizabeth 21 n. 13, 30, 173 n. 8, 174 n. 10, 182 n. 34, 203
Clarysse, Willy 105, 105 n. 10, 116, 116 n. 53, 117 nn. 54–55, 125, 130, 131
Clivaz, Claire 103 n. 7, 118 n. 58, 118 n. 60, 119 n. 61, 131, 134
Cohen, Mordechai 163 n. 64, 164
Comfort, Philip Wesley 119 n. 61, 131
Compton, Michael Bruce 122 nn. 67 and 69–70, 124 n. 72, 131
Connerton, Paul 79 n. 21, 95
Connolly, Richard Hugh 123 n. 71, 131
Conzelmann, Hans 171 n. 2, 172 n. 4, 204
Cook, Michael 64, 64 n. 41, 65

Modern Authors Index

Cragg, Kenneth 163 n. 65, 165
Cribiore, Raffaella 114 n. 44, 130, 131
Cróinín, Dáibhí O. 88 n. 28, 95
Crystal, David 72 n. 10, 95
Curds, Colin R. 19 n. 9, 30
Dawson, David 173 n. 8, 178 n. 23, 203
De Hamel, Christopher 59 n. 34, 66
Deleuze, Gilles 18 n. 5, 30
Derenbourg, Joseph 154 n. 39, 165
Déroche, François 34 nn. 3–4, 38 n. 16, 45, 48, 48 n. 6, 49, 49 nn. 10–11, 51, 51 n. 12, 53, 53 nn. 17–18, 54 nn. 19–20, 56 n. 21, 57 n. 26, 58 nn. 28–29, 59, 60, 61, 61 n. 37, 62, 64, 66
Dibelius, Martin 171 n. 2, 172 n. 4, 204
Dodge, Bayard 39 n. 20, 45, 52 n. 16, 66, 156 n. 46, 165
Donohoue, D. J. 64 n. 40, 66
Dreibholz, Ursula 48 n. 5, 66
Duncan, Patricia 175, 175 n. 14, 186 n. 45, 189, 189 n. 46, 204
Duval, Yves-Marie 91 n. 39, 95
Dye, Guillaume 146 n. 18, 165
Eche, Youssef 41 n. 29, 45
Edwards, Mark J. 184 n. 43, 204
Ehrman, Bart D. 5, 5 n. 7, 24, 182, 182 nn. 36–37, 183 n. 38, 204
Ellery, W. N. 18 n. 4, 31
Emm, Ioannis 149 n. 25, 167
Epp, Eldon Jay 104 n. 9, 110, 131
Everett, Nicholas 23 n. 16, 30
Farge, Arlette 127, 127 n. 80, 131
Finlay, Bland J. 19 n. 9, 30
Finnegan, Ruth 4, 4 n. 4, 10
Fraade, Steve 173 n. 8, 204
Frampton, Stephanie Ann 21, 21 n. 11, 30
Fournet, Jean-Luc 108 n. 20, 113 n. 42, 126 n. 78, 132
Frank, Richard M. 156, 156 nn. 48–49, 165
Fu'ad Sayyid, Ayman 42 n. 33, 46
Furlani, Guiseppe 91 n. 38, 95
Gallo, Maria 158 n. 51, 165
Gamble, Harry Y. vii, 1, 1 n. 1, 4, 5, 5 n. 6, n. 7, nn. 9–10, 6, nn. 11–12, 7, 10, 15, 15 n. 1, 16, 29, 30, 33, 33 n. 2, 45, 48, 48 nn. 7–8, 49, 49 n. 9, 52 n. 15, 66, 67, 70 n. 2, 72 n. 10, 76 n. 19, 95, 101, 101 n. 1, 102, 102 n. 2, 104, 104 n. 9, 110, 110 n. 30, 111 n. 32, 124, 124 n. 73, 124 n. 37, 125, 125 n. 74, 127 n. 82, 129, 129 n. 86, 131, 132, 180, 180 nn. 28–29, 181, 181 nn. 30–33, 188, 204
Gamillscheg, Ernst 56 n. 23, 66
Ganz, David. 73 n. 13, 74 n. 14, 75, 95
Gaudeul, Jean-Marie 143 n. 12, 165
George, Alain Fouad 38 n. 16, 45, 49 n. 10, 53 n. 18, 57 n. 24, 58 nn. 28–31, 66
Ghabbān, 'Alī Ibrāhīm al- 47 n. 4, 66
Gibson, Margaret Dunlop 158 n. 51, 159 nn. 55–56, 160 nn. 57–59, 165
Gilliot, Claude 148 n. 21, 165
Glei, Reinhold F. 88 n. 28, 95
Gonis, Nick 104 n. 9, 131
Graf, Georg 156 n. 45, 156 n. 47, 165
Gribetz, Sarit Kattan 126 n. 78, 131
Grob, Eva Mira 119 n. 62, 132
Gruendler, Beatrice 52 nn. 13–14, 66
Griffith, Sidney H. vi, 9, 137, 138 n. 3, 140 n. 7, 146 n. 17, 157 n. 50, 165, 208
Grohmann, A. 36 n. 8, 45
Goitein, S. D. 36 n. 10, 45, 151 n. 30, 163 n. 63, 165
Goudarzi, Mohsen 61 n. 37, 67
Guattari, Felix 18 n. 5, 30
Gutas, Dimitri. 40, 40 n. 21, 45, 163 n. 66, 166
Haddad, Rachid 149 n. 24, 165
Hägg, Tomas 175 n. 15, 204
Haines-Eitzen, Kim 6, 6 n. 13, 11, 21, 21 nn. 13–14, 30
Halevi, Leor 40 nn. 23–24, 45
Hall, Matthew 17 n. 3, 30
Hamburger, Jeffrey F. 72 n. 11, 96
Harbottle, G. 64 n. 40, 66
Hardie, Philip 27 n. 22, 30
Harnack, Adolf von 121 n. 67, 132
Harper, David M. 18 n. 6, 30

Harrill, James Albert 111 n. 32, 132
Head, Peter M. 111, 111 n. 34, 112 n. 37, 116 n. 52, 132
Healy, John F. 17 n. 2, 30
Herren, Michael 88 n. 28, 96
Hilali, Asma 61 n. 37, 66
Hirschler, Konrad 6, 7 n. 14, 11, 39 n. 19, 42 n. 35, 43 nn. 36–39, 44 n. 41, 45, 186 n. 44, 204
Hodges, Richard 71 n. 6, 96
Hodgson, Marshall G. S. 162, 162 n. 62, 166
Hoernle, A. F. Rudolf 35 n. 6, 45
Holzberg, Niklas 175 n. 15, 204
Horn, Cornelia 146 n. 18, 166
Howlett, David R. 89, 89 n. 32, 96
Hourani, Albert 161, 161 n. 60, 166
Houston, George W. 106, 106 nn. 13–15, 113 n. 41, 114 n. 47, 115 n. 48, 120, 120 n. 65, 126, 126 n. 77, 129 n. 87, 132
Huart, C. L. 36 n. 8, 45
Hudson, P. J. 19 n. 8, 31
Hutchinson, G. O. 27 n. 21, 31
Hurtado, Larry W. 6, 6 n. 13, 11, 103 n. 7, 118 nn. 57–58, 133
Ibn Isḥāq al-Nadim, Muhammad 39, 39 n. 20, 45, 52, 52 n. 16, 66
Jaffee, Martin 178, 179 n. 25, 204
Jeffrey, Arthur 147 n. 20, 166
Jeffery, Peter 78 n. 20, 96
Johnson, William A. 106 n. 13, 112, 112 n. 38, 125, 125 n. 75, 133
Jones, F. Stanley 176 n. 16, 204
Jones, M. B. 18 n. 6, 31
Jördens, Andrea 102 n. 3, 133
Judge, Edwin A. 114, 114 n. 45, 133
Kachouh, H. 150 n. 28, 166
Kamesar, Adam 178 n. 24, 204
Kelber, Werner 4, 4 n. 5, 5, 5 n. 6, 11
Kelly, Nichole 176 n. 16, 204
Kohn, Eduardo 26, 26 n. 19, 31
Kraus, Thomas J. 103 n. 7, 110, 110 n. 28, 128 n. 83, 130, 133

Krawiec, Rebecca 79 n. 21, 96
Lasker, Daniel 151 n. 31, 153 n. 36, 166
Lama, Mariachiara 115 n. 48, 117, 117 n. 54, 118 n. 59, 133
Latour, Bruno 18 n. 5, 31
Law, Vivien 88 n. 28, 89, 96
Lazarus-Yafeh, Hava. 163 n. 64, 167
Leclercq, Jean 79 n. 24, 96
Lehmann, Paul 89, 89 n. 29, 96
Leproni, Ferruccio 72 n. 12, 96
Leslie, Alison J. 19 n. 8, 31
Lévi-Provençal, E. 42 n. 31, 45
Lewis, Naphtali 19 n. 7, 31
Lieu, Judith M. 194 n. 49, 204
Lim, Richard 191 n. 48, 204
Lord, Albert 4, 4 n. 4, 10
Lowden, John 70 n. 4, 91 n. 38, 96
Luijendijk, AnneMarie v, 9, 101, 102 n. 3, 102 n. 5, 103 n. 7, 105 n. 11, 107 n. 17, 107 n. 19, 108 n. 20, 116 n. 51, 118 n. 57, 128 n. 84, 133, 208
MacMullen, Ramsay 112 n. 39, 134
Madigan, Daniel A. 47 n. 2, 66
Mathieson, Erica A. 108 n. 21, 127 n. 79, 127 n. 81, 134
Malter, Henry 153 n. 38, 167
Martin, Henri-Jean 76 n. 19, 96
Massignon, Louis 139, 139 n. 6, 167
Mavroudi, Maria 149 n. 24, 167
Mayer, Wendy 112 n. 39, 134
McAuliffe, Jane Dammen x, 143 n. 12, 167
McCarthy, T. S. 18 n. 4, 31
McCormick, Michael 71 n. 6, 96
McKitterick, Rosamond 74 n. 14, 96
Metzger, Bruce M. 109 n. 25
Meyvaert, Paul 60 n. 35, 66, 91 n. 39
Most, Glenn W. 90 n. 33, 97
Müller, Andreas E. 56 n. 23, 67
Muthuri, F. M. 18 n. 6, 19 n. 8, 31
Mroczek, Eva 173 n. 9, 178 n. 24, 201, 201 n. 60, 204
Nadim, Ibn al- 39, 39 n. 20, 45, 52, 52 n. 16, 66, 156, 156 n. 46, 165

Nees, Lawrence   v, 8, 9, 34 n. 4, 46, 59 n. 32, 59 n. 34, 67, 69, 78 n. 20, 91 n. 39, 97, 208
Neuenkirchen, Paul   147 n. 18, 167
Neusner, Jacob   197 n. 51, 205
Neuwirth, Angelika   147 n. 19, 167
Newton, Francis L.   78 n. 20, 97
Newton, Francis L. Jr.   78 n. 20, 97
Nobilio, Fabien   147 n. 18, 165
Nongbri, Brent   101, 105 n. 11, 106 n. 12, 117 n. 56, 134
Nordenfalk, Carl   72, 72 n. 9, 88 n. 27, 97
Oikonomidès, Nicolas   37 n. 13, 46
Olin, J. S.   64 n. 40, 66
Ong, Walter J.   4, 4 n. 4, 11
Orsini, Pasquale   116, 116 n. 53, 131
Papathomas, Amphilochios   127 n. 79, 134
Parkes, Malcolm   71 n. 8, 76, 76 n. 17, 79 nn. 22–24, 94 n. 45, 97
Parsons, Peter J.   104 n. 9, 106 n. 13, 113 n. 41, 131, 134
Partridge, Robert B.   20 n. 10, 31
Perria, L.   37 n. 12, 46
Pertz, Karl August Friedrich   70 n. 6, 97
Pickering, Stewart R.   114, 114 n. 45, 133
Pingree, David   39 n. 17, 46
Piotrovsky, Mikhail B.   56 n. 22, 60 n. 36, 67
Pirenne, Henri   71 n. 6, 97
Polliack, Meira   153 nn. 36–37, 167
Powell, Owen   22 n. 15, 31
Prowse, K. R.   22 n. 17, 31
Putman, Hans   139 n. 6, 168
Quispel, Gilles   175 n. 13, 176, 176 n. 17, 205
Rabb, Intisar   64 n. 41, 67
Reed, Annette Yoshiko   176 n. 16, 178 n. 24, 179 n. 27, 183 nn. 39–40, 196 n. 50, 205
Rehm, Bernard   171 n. 1, 205
Reinard, Patrick   111, 111 nn. 33–34, 112 n. 35, 134

Reynolds, Gabriel Said   144 n. 14, 146 nn. 17–18, 166, 168, 169
Rice, D. S.   40 n. 22, 41 n. 27, 46
Rice, David Talbot   47 n. 3, 67
Roberts, C. H.   5, 5 n. 8, 11
Rosenkranz, Simone   151 n. 31, 168
Rubenstein, Richard E.   164 n. 67, 168
Saenger, Paul   76, 76 n. 16, 97
Sadeghi, Behnam   61, 61 n. 37, 63, 63 n. 38, 64, 64 n. 41, 65 n. 43, 67
Samir, Samir Khalil   138 n. 4, 158 nn. 51–52, 158 n. 54, 168
Salmi, Mario   91 n. 38, 95
Scarry, Elaine   27, 27 n. 24, 31
Schatzmiller, Maya   37 n. 11, 46
Scheirer, Christopher R. J.   78 n. 20, 97
Schoeler, Gregor   42 n. 35, 46
Schoeps, Hans J.   176, 176 n. 17, 205
Segovia, Carlos A.   147 n. 18, 148 n. 21, 165, 168
Seider, Richard   118 n. 59, 119, 119 n. 63, 134
Shaner, Dr. Katherine A.   112 n. 39, 134
Shaw, P.A.   18 n. 4, 30
Shuve, Karl   v, vi, vii, 1, 101, 171, 177 nn. 18–19, 202 n. 61, 205, 209
Skeat, T. C.   5, 5 n. 8, 11
Staal, H.   149 n. 26, 168
Starr, Raymond J.   118 n. 59, 134
Steiner, Richard C.   154 n. 39, 154 n. 41, 155, 155 n. 44, 168
Stern, David   153 n. 35, 168
Stern, S. M.   36 n. 9, 46
Smith, Lesley   174 n. 11, 205
Subirà, Oriol Valls   40 n. 23, 46
Svenbro, Jesper   76 n. 19, 97
Sutton, S. L.   19 n. 8, 31
Swanson, Mark   158, 158 nn. 52–53, 168
Teeter, Timothy   48 n. 7, 67
Tewes, Babette   72 n. 12, 73 n. 13, 74 n. 14, 75 n. 15, 94 n. 45, 98
Tobi, Yosef   152 n. 34, 168
Torjesen, Karen Jo   173 n. 7, 205
Touwaide, Alain   56 n. 23, 67

Tsien, Tsuen-Hsuin 35 n. 5, 46
Valls i Subirà, Oriol 40 n. 23, 46
Van Bladel, Kevin 146 n. 17, 169
Van Steenberghen, Fernand 164 n. 67, 168
Violet, Bruno 148 n. 23, 149 n. 24, 169
Walker, G. S. M. 79 n. 22, 95
Wachtel, Klaus 115 n. 49, 116 n. 52, 135
Witte, Klaus 115 n. 49, 116 n. 52, 135
Walker, Paul E. 42 n. 33, 46
Wallace, Kevin M. 19 n. 8, 31
Wardwell, Anne E. 62 n. 39, 65
Warren, M. 116 n. 52, 132
Wasserstein, David 42 n. 31, 46
Wayment, Thomas A. 102 nn. 5–6, 108 n. 21, 110 n. 29, 130
Webb, Gisela 47 n. 2, 67
Weitzmann, Kurt 56 n. 23, 67, 69, 69 n. 1, 70 n. 3, 98
Whitehouse, David 71 n. 6, 96
Whitmarsh, Tim 175 n. 15, 205
Willi, Andreas 25 n. 17, 32
Williams, Frank 175 n. 13, 206
Wipszycka, Ewa 128 n. 84, 135
Witkam, Jan Just 37 n. 15, 46
Wright, Wilmer Cave France 128 n. 83, 135
Young, Frances 173 n. 8, 177 n. 20, 178 n. 23, 196 n. 50, 206
Yuen-Collingridge, Rachel 103 n. 7, 130
Zellentin, Holger 147 n. 18, 169
Ziolkowski, Jan M. 80 n. 25, 94

www.ingramcontent.com/pod-product-compliance
Lightning Source LLC
Chambersburg PA
CBHW030825230426
43667CB00008B/1383